Religion in America

ADVISORY EDITOR

Edwin S. Gaustad

RACE AND THE SOUTH

Two Studies
1914-1922

L[ily] H[ardy] Hammond

ARNO PRESS
A NEW YORK TIMES COMPANY
New York • 1972

Reprint Edition 1972 by Arno Press Inc.

Reprinted from copies in
The State Historical Society of Wisconsin Library

RELIGION IN AMERICA - Series II
ISBN for complete set: 0-405-04050-4
See last pages of this volume for titles.

Manufactured in the United States of America

Library of Congress Cataloging in Publication Data

Hammond, Lily Hardy, 1859-1925.
    Race and the South.

    (Religion in America, series II)
    Reprint of the author's In black and white, first
published in 1914; and In the vanguard of a race, first
published in 1922.
    1. Negroes--Southern States. 2. U. S.--Race
question. 3. Negroes--Biography. I. Hammond,
Lily Hardy, 1859-1925. In the vanguard of a race.
1972. II. Title.
E185.61.H22 1972   309.1'75   72-38448
ISBN 0-405-04067-9

Contents

Hammond, L [ily] H [ardy] .

In Black and White: An Interpretation of Southern Life. New York, 1914.

In the Vanguard of a Race. New York, 1922.

IN THE VANGUARD
OF A RACE

BOOKER T. WASHINGTON

IN THE VANGUARD
OF A RACE

By L. H. HAMMOND.

Author of *The Master Word, In Black and White:
An Interpretation of Southern Life,* etc.

Published jointly by
COUNCIL OF WOMEN FOR HOME MISSIONS
and
MISSIONARY EDUCATION MOVEMENT OF THE
UNITED STATES AND CANADA
New York

To that great company of Negro women,
bond and free, unlettered and college-bred,
whose living faith and loving sacrifices
have created and are enriching
the ideals of a race.

CONTENTS

ILLUSTRATIONS

PREFACE

Perhaps the most striking feature of this book is what is not in it. The material for it was sharply limited by reason of the necessity for keeping it within the size and price of the series to which it belongs. Any general survey of Negro literary, artistic, educational, or business achievements was prohibited by its biographical form, in which it adheres to the method adopted for a group of books already issued.

Unless the telling of their stories does them injustice, the men and women whose biographies are included in this book are manifestly worthy of the rank accorded them. But any one acquainted with Negro life can furnish a much longer list of members of the race quite as distinguished as those here given with the exception of a very few preeminent names.

I have felt especially the limitations in regard to the artistic side of Negro life. Mr. Burleigh, the musician chosen, speaks for himself; yet there are so many others of whom the race may well be proud. Among painters there are E. M. Banister, one of whose pictures was awarded a medal at the Centennial Exposition of 1876; W. E. Scott, whose picture, "The Poor Neighbor," was purchased by the Argentine Republic, and who has done mural paintings for many public buildings in Illinois;

and Henry O. Tanner, foremost of them all, who
is a frequent exhibitor in the Paris Salon. Several of the latter's paintings have been purchased
by the French Government and placed in the
Luxembourg.

The honors as sculptors are with the women.
Edmonia Lewis's work was accepted for the Centennial Exposition; Mrs. Meta Warrick Fuller has
exhibited in the Paris Salon and executed a group
for the Jamestown Exposition; and Mrs. May
Howard Jackson has won high praise from art
critics for work exhibited in the Corcoran Art
Gallery, Washington.

Among actors, none who have seen him will forget Charles Gilpin, who drew thousands of white
people to his extraordinary presentation in New
York of "The Emperor Jones," and whose work
was listed by the American Drama League among
the ten outstanding achievements of the American
stage in 1921.

The list of singers is long and notable. It includes Roland Hayes, who has won success in
Europe as well as in America, and who was recently presented with a jeweled pin by King
George of England as a token of appreciation of
his art. Joseph Douglass and Clarence White are
both well-known violinists, the latter having also
won distinction as a composer. One passes Coleridge-Taylor, most distinguished of them all, only
because he belongs to England rather than to

America, yet, like Dumas and Pushkin, he belongs to the Negro race.

So with the other groups; the men and women written of are representative of classes. The consciousness of this large and growing body of leaders should be the mental background against which should be set the individual achievements here related.

One thing which will doubtless strike the reader is the frequency with which, at some vital turning-point in the lives narrated, the mother's character and influence have been deciding factors. These mothers are typical of unnumbered thousands from every level of opportunity, whose standards of faith, conscience, and self-forgetfulness have shaped those of the race and are a light upon the long, hard path which it must climb in the years to come. They show the Negro women bearing their share of the responsibility of womanhood to the Race of Man. The creation of ideals, planting them in the hearts of children, unfolding and enriching them from generation to generation—this, the biggest and finest of all human tasks, is preeminently the work of the women of every race. Like all the big, essential things of life, it may be achieved by common folk because it is primarily of the heart and not of the head. We have perverted the original meaning of the fine old word "common" into something to be regarded as inferior; but the things which are common to the

Race of Man and to the individuals of all races
are the most precious possessions of every race.
However wide and deep the separation of the lowest savage from the most highly developed man,
science and religion alike declare that the things
which they hold in common and which separate
them both from all other creatures are wider and
deeper yet.

The deepest of all our common possessions is
a capacity for God. This the Negro brought with
him from Africa; and it was chiefly the Christian
white women of America, and especially those of
the South, who kindled in the Negro women's souls
that which this capacity awaited—the light of
Christian ideals. Notwithstanding the evils and
wrongs of slavery, in thousands of kitchens,
nurseries, and sewing-rooms the house-servants
of the old days found God through their mis-
tresses' lives and took up their predestined task
of making Him real and lovable to their own people by living in His spirit from day to day.

So the race advanced, in slavery and through
it. To-day the broadening opportunities of its
leading women are quickening its progress; yet
the humbler women still bear their vital part in
the movement. When we think how few generations ago these Negro women had to begin at the
beginning, and of the ages through which our own
women have been lifting our ideals, we must admit that the Negro women are entitled, not only

to our sympathy, but to our respect and cooperation. The advance of both races largely depends
upon the extent to which this respect and cooperation are given henceforth. In a book like this, only
glimpses can be given of the growing recognition
of this fact by both white and colored women; but
it is the biggest and most hopeful of all the hopeful facts in the wide field of interracial relations
to-day.

The authorities for the historical and scientific
statements made in the first chapter of the book
are Green's *Short History of the English People,*
Hallam's *Middle Ages,* Campbell's *The Puritan in
England, Holland and America,* Wells's *Outline
of History,* Kipling's *Short History of England,*
and Scott Elliot's *Prehistoric Man.*

For various statements in regard to the Negroes
and interracial relations before the Civil War, the
writer has referred to Washington's *Story of the
American Negro,* Brawley's *Short History of the
American Negro,* Helper's *The Impending Crisis,*
an anti-slavery book by a white North Carolinian
published four years before the Civil War, and the
Negro Year Book, compiled by Monroe N. Work,
of Tuskegee Institute.

In conclusion, I would thank the following
friends and helpers for information, advice, and
many kindnesses in the preparation of my book:
Miss Ida A. Tourtellot of the Phelps-Stokes Foun-

dation, Miss Flora Mitchell of the Woman's Home Missionary Society of the Methodist Episcopal Church, Mrs. Booker T. Washington of Tuskegee, Mr. Jackson Davis of the General Education Board, Mr. N. C. Newbold of the North Carolina State Department of Education, Mr. W. T. B. Williams of the Jeanes and Slater Boards, Professor G. Lake Imes of Tuskegee, and Dr. A. M. Moore of Durham, North Carolina.

L. H. HAMMOND

February,
1922.

IN THE VANGUARD OF A RACE

I

A LONG ASCENT

Slow moves the pageant of a climbing race.
                                        —*Paul Laurence Dunbar*

BETWEEN fifteen and sixteen hundred years
ago England was a rich and peaceful country with many prosperous cities connected
by splendid roads. Ships from all parts of the
known world came to her harbors bringing rich
cargoes and carrying back grain, wool, furs, and
tin. Churches stood in many towns, and the
homes of the wealthy dotted the country. These
homes were built of stone and marble, with beautiful gardens about them. They were heated by
furnaces and piped for running water which
flowed into splendid marble baths and fountains.
The law of Rome ruled from the Channel to Sol-
way Firth and had ruled, unopposed, for two hundred and fifty years. The island, prosperous and
increasingly Christian, was part of the highest
civilization the world had ever known, for Rome,
after her fashion, had first conquered the wild
heathen Britons mercilessly, and then tamed and
taught them and blessed them with peace and prosperity.

Then came the pirates, swooping down before
the north wind in their queer little ships, each
oarsman bent on plunder and ready for any

cruelty to obtain it. Huge, red-haired, blue-eyed fellows they were, these English ancestors of ours, heathen barbarians every one, bold, cruel, and bloodthirsty. Their gods were like themselves, and they believed in a heaven to which only those who died in battle could go and in which they could drink and boast of their bold deeds forever.

Britain was a fat and fertile land, and these Angles meant to have it; but they wanted no Britons in it, and they left none. The churches and priests they especially hated, burning the former and slaying the latter on their own altars. They destroyed the beautiful country houses and left city after city a heap of ruins "without fire, without light, without songs."

For fifty years they fought and pillaged and butchered and made slaves. By that time all the eastern half of England was theirs. It took them a hundred and fifty more years to root out the last Britons, for the dark little folk fought bravely and long; but at last they were all gone, and with them civilization and Christianity. Britain was England now, a wild heathen country where our forefathers lived in rude huts open to the weather. They ate and drank like gluttons and fought one another like wild beasts.

They lived in little villages made up of kinsfolk, with marshes or forests around them, or perhaps both, as a protection from the men of other villages whose pirate instincts might set them on the war-path against their neighbors. They had very few horses and plowed with oxen. They raised sheep for wool and cattle for plowing. Their usual meat came from their droves of hogs. Each village had a swineherd who took all the pigs to the forest every day, where they could root for acorns and other food.

A stranger was always considered an enemy until he proved himself a friend, and often, to be on the safe side, they killed him anyway, and bothered no more about him. After a while a law was made that when a stranger came to the woods or marsh about a village, he should blow a horn to show that he came honestly and openly, not trying to sneak in to murder or rob. If he failed to blow a horn or if nobody heard him blow, he was to be killed on sight.

A hundred years after these savage men came to Britain, it was written of them that they were "barbarians," "wolves," "dogs," "whelps from the kennels of barbarism," "hateful to God and man." In France and Spain and Italy when barbarians overthrew the power of Rome, they settled down among the cultivated people they had conquered, learned their language, adopted their laws and customs, and took on civilized ways; but the men who came to England made a clean sweep of all these things. They did not even keep many of the Britons alive as slaves, they made slaves of one another. When village fought with village or, long afterward, when one little king whom the growing tribes set up fought another, the captives, nobles and slaves alike, were made slaves by their captors. Sometimes they were taken to their conqueror's home, or, frequently, they were sold to pirate vessels that carried them to the slave-markets of southern Europe.

It was the sight of some of these English slaves put up for sale in Italy that led to missionaries being sent once more to what had been Christian Britain, and which was now heathen for a second time. Missionaries came, too, from Ireland, at this time one of the brightest spots in a dark and troubled world. Roman Britain had furnished many Christian martyrs when the savage Englishmen first came, and now Irish and Roman Christians came to this wild and cruel land, not counting their lives dear to themselves if only they could win the heathen to the gospel.

It took two hundred years to establish Christianity firmly on the island, for now and again there would occur relapses into heathenism when some petty king arose who preferred to worship Odin rather than Christ.

Sometimes we hear people say that foreign missions to-day accomplish very little in China or India or Japan. See how few Christians those countries have, they say, after trying for a hundred years to convert them! That is not quite true, for it is not much over a hundred years since the pioneer of modern missions in China, Robert Morrison, went there. At that time most Christian people who knew about him thought him crazy, or silly, at best, and for long years the Church did almost nothing for missions. It is only in the last fifty years that it has made any great effort as a whole. Fifty years among hundreds of millions of heathen!

In the days when the Roman and Irish missionaries came to Britain, the English could have been counted by only the hundred thousand. Even a thousand years after missionaries came to England, there were only five or six million people in the whole country—about as many as in the city of New York to-day. Yet it took two hundred years to make our ancestors Christian, even in name. We should remember this when we feel like criticizing people of other races whose progress we think is slow. And we should think of it, too, when people ask if missions pay. Has it paid to have a Christian England in the world?

For a long time a tribe was Christian or heathen only as its "king" ordered it out either for baptism or for worship of Odin. However, some of these early Englishmen made noble Christians. But it was not until Elizabeth became queen, a thousand years later, that Christianity had gone deep enough for the people to take such a stand for the open Bible that their rulers did not dare

to forbid it to them or to kill those who disobeyed.
And so, all down the centuries are scattered the
shining names of those who greatly lived or
greatly died for the love of Jesus Christ.

They were splendidly brave, these early Englishmen. They always had been brave, even as
savages, with a rough, cruel, selfish courage, but
now they were brave for finer reasons. It was
not only for personal gain and glory that Drake
sailed unknown and dreaded seas and carried the
flag of England around the world. It was with
no thought of self that Philip Sidney fought freedom's battle in Holland, or that he refused, in
his dying agony, to relieve his own raging thirst
that the water might be given to one suffering
more than he. It was a glorious day when little
England faced the great Spanish Armada to die,
if need be, for God and freedom. Nor can any of
English blood forget Ridley and Latimer and all
that noble army of martyrs who, in Mary's time,
passed through the fire up to God rather than deny
their faith. The barbarians had come far in a
thousand years.

But Christian though they had become in Elizabeth's time, there were still many of their ways
and thoughts which seem neither civilized nor
Christian to us who live over three hundred years
later. A climbing race moves slowly, and behind
the shining banners of those who lead skulk ugly
things and wicked and stupid things which most

of the people do not yet know are ugly or stupid or wicked, and so permit them. Along with all the noble things and the splendid intellectual power of Elizabeth's reign went others, disgusting and barbarous—after a thousand years! Punishments were many and horrible. Mutilation, torture, and death were meted out for petty offenses. The sight of bodies hanging by the roadside and falling into decay was not uncommon. The people lived in filth. Garbage and sewage were habitually emptied into the middle of London's streets, where it rotted and bred disease and smelled to heaven. The people had very little knowledge of washing their bodies. The queen had three thousand dresses; but most people had only one and wore that one day and night till it dropped to rags. Underclothes, if worn, were never washed. Few, even of the rich, had carpets, and those they had were used for table-covers. The floors were of dirt or, in grand houses, of wood or stone covered with rushes into which bones and other refuse of meals were thrown as people sat at table. Forks were just beginning to be known among the wealthy, and it was quite proper to eat with one's fingers and dip them into the dishes as well. Chimneys began to come into use at about this time. Before this, smoke got out as best it could at openings in the walls. These openings, which were without glass, let in both the light and the weather.

Some of the prevailing ideas of justice were much more like those of our pirate ancestors than like our own. The men who first made England famous on the seas were freebooters and traders in human flesh. Many of the great fortunes piled up in the last half of Elizabeth's reign were made by seizing unarmed ships of friendly countries—even those of Protestant Holland—and appropriating their cargoes. Hawkins, one of the sea-heroes of his day, began England's slave-trade with a cargo of Negroes he kidnaped on the African coast and sold in the West Indies. This traffic was legal in England and in America until a little over a hundred years ago. The last serfs of English blood in England were freed by Elizabeth in 1574, but long after that, Englishmen were shipped to the American colonies and sold as slaves as a punishment for crime or for political offenses.

Over three hundred years have passed since these conditions prevailed, and the higher a nation climbs, the faster it can go. We have come further, as a people, in the last three hundred years than in the previous thousand years. Who can say what heights are ahead? Would any of those Christian Britons have believed when Roman civilization was being blotted out by the English barbarians that that same race would one day stand as one of the world's great bulwarks of justice among men, creators of wonders beyond the dreams of magic, with ideals that reached the stars? Yet all this we have seen come to pass in England and in America in these last few years.

We are yet far from where we would be. There are wrongs and injustices still to give way before God's laws of justice and kindness rule us all. How soon this comes to pass depends largely on the young people now coming into power. If we assume that our own race is already on the heights, it will never attain its highest possible plane through help of ours. If we forget our own slow and incomplete progress as a race or despise others who are climbing the same hard and painful path, we shall be, not lifters of mankind, but a stumbling block in the path of the human race.

The part of Africa best known to us is the little strip around the Mediterranean Sea. But this, so far as we can tell, was not settled by Negroes, but by peoples who came out of Asia in widely-separated times. South of these lands lived the Negroes, of whose life at that time little is known. Few explorations have been made south of Egypt, though at one point, Zimbabwe, the ruins of a vanished civilization have been found.

For hundreds of years the upper western coast of Africa was raided by white pirates, most of them English, and the people were kidnaped and sold as slaves. Probably for thousands of years the east coast was raided in the same way by

Arabs and other Asiatics, but except along the coast, the continent was almost unknown to white men until within the memory of men now living. Between 1850 and 1900 the land was explored, and European nations seized it for themselves as though the people who had lived there for thousands of years had no rights in it at all. The only parts of Africa still belonging to Negroes are Abyssinia and the little country of Liberia. These fifty years and the twenty following have seen thousands of white men from Europe and America flocking in—missionaries, explorers, traders, men bent on service and men bent on ruthless gain —until Africa's geography and races are fairly well known.

The oldest races are the pygmies of the Congo and of South Africa. They are a queer little folk who, Professor Elliot says in his *Prehistoric Man,* "seem to have been the very first race to understand and realize the importance of botany." Their knowledge of plants is quite wonderful. They are also "clever artists and musicians, and may be the inventors of the first violin." But they are a very savage little people for all that and very deadly to their enemies by reason of their cunningly-poisoned weapons. Between them and the Zulus and people of Uganda, the most highly developed of the many African races, are peoples as varied as those of eastern Europe or Asia and of many grades of intelligence. Many of them are clever iron-workers. In fact iron is believed to have been made into tools and weapons in Africa long before Europe learned its uses and even while our own forefathers still had no tools but flints.

But except for its sea-coasts, Africa has been cut off for ages from the rest of the world. In Europe and Asia men passed back and forth so that what was learned in one place, sooner or later became known in others. Isolated people cannot learn very fast, and Africa, in some respects ahead of Europe when we were all savages together, seems to have stood still while other countries have forged far ahead of her.

Among Americans the first knowledge of Africans came through the Negroes who had been stolen from their homes by Dutch and English pirates and sold in the colonies as slaves. Later, Americans joined in this trade. It must be remembered that Christian nations had no idea, in those days, that they should behave like Christians to savages. Wicked things went on because good people did not understand it was their duty to stop them. When some of the unjust things still allowed by Christian people are put a stop to, it will be by the same steps that ended first the slave-trade and then slavery.

First a few people who best understood God's thoughts of justice began to talk and write and work against the slave-trade. They were misunderstood, laughed at, and abused just as are the people who nowadays fight social abuses. But they kept right on until more and more people understood what was right, and then, in 1807, laws were passed forbidding slave-trading in England and America. Since that time England, where only two hundred years before Christian Englishmen had sold their own countrymen into slavery in the colonies, has led the world in trying to end slavery everywhere.

In our country some people, North and South, defended slavery by saying that the Negroes had not sense enough to rise much above the animals, and that God meant them to be ruled as such. But the Negroes themselves proved this to be untrue. From the very beginning, among the slaves brought here from Africa were some gifted men and women who showed unusual mental ability. Phillis Wheatley, born in Africa, wrote a book of poems which ran through three editions and won her recognition in England and America. Ira Aldridge, whose father came from Africa, became an actor and was decorated by the Emperors of Austria and Russia and by the King of Prussia. Edmund Kean, the great English actor, played *Iago* to his *Othello*. Sojourner Truth, born in Africa, and Frederick Douglass, born a slave in Maryland, both became famous as speakers against slavery. Douglass was well known in England, and in his later life he not only saw his great hope for his people realized, but found himself their trusted leader. Harriet Tubman, born a slave in Maryland, ran away when about twenty years old; but instead of enjoying a peaceful freedom, she spent her life, until the Civil War, in helping others of her people to freedom, often at the cost of great risk and hardship to herself. She showed an ability, courage, and resourcefulness which would have been remarkable anywhere. In the Revolutionary War, Negroes fought bravely, as they have in every subsequent war of ours.

Many of the old slaves were noted for their eloquence as preachers. John Chavis, of North Carolina, was the first home missionary of the Presbyterian Church; and John Stewart, who went as a missionary to the Indians, is said to have been the first missionary of the Methodist Church. Cæsar Blackwell, an Alabama slave, was bought by the Alabama Baptist Convention for $1,000. As he could not be set free, a white man was made his guardian, and he was given practical freedom, traveling with the white preachers and helping them in their work. Amanda Smith, another slave, became a great evangelist, preaching not only in America, but in England, India, and Africa. John Jasper, of Richmond, a slave for fifty-two years and a preacher for sixty, had the respect of all Richmond, white and black; and Jack, another Virginia slave, born in Africa, was considered by men of both races the best preacher in his county. Many white people were converted under him, and plantation owners, instead of punishing their slaves who did wrong, sent them to Jack to be disciplined. The white people of his county bought his freedom and gave him a house and land, that he might give his whole time to his work. Alexander Crummell, whose father was a native African, graduated from Cambridge, England, and went to Africa as a missionary. Afterward he came back to America and was long the rector of an Episcopal church in Washington. A number of these old-time Negroes gained distinction as composers of music and as singers, some of them being recognized in Europe.

These and many others stand out from the great mass of Negroes who were slaves in America. But back of the more gifted folk is that great throng whom the white people of the South learned to love and trust: the men who gave their masters honest service; the women who kept the house, cared for the children, were faithful in all things, and whose lives and teaching made Christianity real to their little white charges. A race that can keep faith in slavery, can keep faith in freedom. There is proof enough from the days of the early slave ships that among the captives were men of business ability, of intelligence, and of various and worthy gifts. But after all, the possibilities of a people cannot be measured wholly or chiefly by their brains. Character is worth far more, and where we find so much of it among a people, we may be sure that as a race they may yet go far. They need time and opportunity. We ourselves, the scientists tell us, have been learning some hundreds of thousands of years; yet as a people, we are only beginning to learn that first great law of justice—to love our neighbors as ourselves.

We like to believe that the men and women of loving hearts, noble minds, and heroic lives who through the centuries stand out from the mass of our own race, foreshadow the destiny of the race itself when it has had full time for growth and training. This book, in giving the life-stories of a very few of our fellow-citizens of African blood, would lead you to think of their race in the same way. May you not only respect the achievements of to-day and yesterday, but see them as foreshadowings of the possibilities of a people. How fast they climb will depend in large part on us, on our faithfulness to our common Lord, and on our obedience to His big, simple laws of justice and kindness to all.

II

A STORY OF SERVICE

DOWN in Alabama is a big school called Tuskegee Institute, covering 2,300 acres of land. There are on the ground one hundred and twenty buildings built mostly of brick, with stone trimmings. The bricks were made and the buildings were put up by the students, hundreds of whom have in this way been able to pay their way through school. Without this opportunity, they could have had no education worth the name.

There are big brick dormitories and a great dining-hall with windows on all sides and a gallery where, on state occasions, the Tuskegee band plays beautiful music. And the food in the big, spotless kitchens! The mere sight of it makes the visitor's mouth water. There is a beautiful chapel seating over two thousand people, with a place for a choir of five hundred, whose singing, once heard, is never forgotten—there is not anything quite like it anywhere else. There is a handsome library, a fine hospital, buildings for classes and industries of all kinds, a wonderful power-house which supplies light and heat for the whole place, from the lamps that twinkle at dusk over the campus to the necessities of the biggest of all the big buildings.

There is a large farm, with barns for cattle, horses, sheep, pigs, poultry, and farm machinery. Why, there isn't room in this book to tell about all there is at Tuskegee, much less about all that is done there. One must go and see for oneself. The value of the whole plant is nearly two million dollars, and the endowment nearly two million and a quarter more; and every penny is wisely invested and yields wonderful returns.

These are the things at Tuskegee. There is also that which things are made to serve—life in the making. Sitting on the chapel platform, looking into two thousand faces dark of skin yet alight with eager, intelligent interest, watching the students march out, trim and spotless, with heads erect and steady step, one sees beyond question that, like our own, the Negro is "a climbing race."

The students at Tuskegee come from most of our states, from the West Indies, and from the countries of far-off Africa, and they go back to all these places to show in their daily lives that skilled hands should go with skilled brains and that character and the spirit of service are the finest things in the world. Tuskegee has transformed thousands of homes and of lives. It has changed the people in whole stretches of country. It has brought hope, knowledge, self-respect, thrift, independence, and happiness to thousands all over the South. It has promoted friendship and understanding between the races in every Southern state. It is known and honored all over the world, and educators and statesmen of many races and countries travel thousands of miles to see the Institute and learn its ways.

Now a great institution like this does not spring up overnight like a mushroom. Where did Tuskegee begin?

It began with a little black slave baby. His mother, a slave in Virginia, could not read or write and knew little of anything except cooking. She never could tell her little boy just when he was born, but she thought it was in 1858 or 1859.

There were three children, and they and their mother lived in a one-roomed cabin that had a dirt floor, a rickety door with cracks all round it, and holes in the walls instead of windows. There was no furniture, and only rags on the floor to sleep on. It was frightfully cold in winter—almost like outdoors, and in summer it was frightfully hot, for the mother had to cook for all the slaves by a roaring log fire in the big fireplace. The children ate around a skillet, fishing the food out with their fingers. They each wore one little cotton garment. In short, their way of living was quite like that of the red-haired, blue-eyed pirates who came to Britain long ago.

The little boy had only one name—Booker. The Civil War ended when he was six or seven years old. Already he had been at work for some time. He helped clean the yard, carried water to the men in the fields, fanned the flies off the white folks' table at meal-times, and carried corn to the mill to be ground. He was so little that he and his bag of corn had to be lifted on to the horse. Often they would both slip off to the road. Then Booker would have to wait, sometimes for hours, till some one came along who would take pity on the crying, frightened child and put him and his bag on the horse again. Often when he reached home, it was far into the cold, black night, and he would still be terrified from coming through the dark woods along the road.

After freedom came, the family moved to West Virginia, the little boy walking most of the long mountainous way, and all of them sleeping by the road at night. They went to Malden, near Charleston, where Booker's step-father, his older brother John, and even Booker himself went to work in the salt mines, beginning work as early as four o'clock in the morning.

The boy had always been determined to learn to read, and when his mother somehow got him an old blue-backed speller, he learned the alphabet without a teacher. He was only eight or nine years old when he persuaded some one to teach him a little at night, when the long day's work in the mines was over. Sometime later, a school for Negroes was opened, and for a little while Booker was allowed to attend it by getting up extra early for work in the mine before school and by working again when school was out. The first day he went to school, the teacher asked all the children their names. Booker noticed that the others had two or three names. When his turn came, he made up a last name for himself, saying, "Booker Washington." Afterward he found that when he was a tiny baby he had been called Booker Taliaferro, so he took Taliaferro for his middle name.

As the years went on, the boy worked in a coal mine and later as a house-servant, but always with the thirst for an education in his heart. At last he heard of Hampton, where boys might earn enough to pay for their education by working part of the time on the farm and in the shops. He went to Hampton, walking most of the distance, sleeping out of doors, working along the way for money to buy food, but hungry much of the time. He reached Hampton tired out and so dirty and shabby, having had no chance for so long a time to wash or change his clothes, that he looked like a tramp. The teacher who first saw him did not like to admit him. Finally, however, she told him to go and sweep one of the rooms. He wanted to study books, not sweep floors; but instead of crying or getting angry, he saw his chance and took advantage of it. This spirit explains much of the secret of his wonderful life. So instead of a book, Booker took a broom and, without knowing it, showed the teacher the kind of boy he was. He swept that room three times, —closets, corners, and all. Then he dusted it four times, furniture and woodwork too. When he called her, how that teacher hunted for dirt! When she couldn't see any, she took out her pocket-handkerchief and rubbed suspicious places, but not a speck could she get on it. "Well, boy," said she, "I guess you will do."

There followed many years of hard work and privations, but when Booker Washington graduated, he carried away the trust and friendship of every one at Hampton, white and black. He had in his heart a passion for truth, for knowledge, and for service. His power was won.by doing every least thing within his reach, however hard or disagreeable, as perfectly as he could and as cheerfully as if it were the deepest desire of his heart.

After graduation, Booker taught school, denying himself severely that he might help his brother John and an adopted brother also through Hampton. He was then called back to the Institute and given charge of the dormitory for Indian boys. His power to understand, control, and inspire these boys of a race so widely different from his own showed once more his unusual quality.

Then came the call to his life-work. Some white citizens of Tuskegee, Alabama, wrote to General Armstrong, Hampton's founder, asking him to send them a teacher to take charge of a school to be opened there for Negroes. General Armstrong sent Booker Washington. It was the American Missionary Association that, backing General Armstrong, made Hampton possible, and it was Hampton that had made possible Booker Washington as America and the world came to know him and through him, Tuskegee. Thus Hampton and Tuskegee, two of the greatest forces in the world for Negro betterment, both owe their existence to the Christian Church.

Arrived at Tuskegee, Mr. Washington found no school building and only a small sum to provide one, pay the teacher's salary, and meet other expenses. A dilapidated church and a near-by shanty were secured, neither of them weather-proof. When it rained, the teacher had to stand under an umbrella. But here, with thirty pupils and one teacher, there began on July 4th, 1881, a school which has become one of the famous institutions of the world.

Soon after, an abandoned plantation, the "big house" of which had burned down, was offered for sale for five hundred dollars. To the man who afterward raised millions, this seemed an almost staggering sum, but he was able to borrow the money, penniless as he was—a fact which shows not only his own courage, but the kind of faith he inspired in white people. The four old buildings on the farm—a cabin, a kitchen, a stable, and a hen-house—were cleaned and repaired after school hours, teacher and students working together. Soon these new class-rooms were ready for use, and Mr. Washington sent to Hampton for an assistant teacher. Together they got up suppers and festivals to pay for the new place. White and colored people helped raise the money, though both races were poor. Often the Negroes could give only a nickel or a dime. One old colored woman, too poor even for this, brought six eggs "to put into de eddication ob dese boys an' girls."

Most Negroes at this time thought of an education as some magic good that would help them to live without working. But Mr. Washington had learned at Hampton that every one who earns the right to live must work in some way, and that the great majority of people of every race must work with their hands. He wanted to teach his people to honor work and to put brains and character into it. He believed in everybody, white and black, having all the education possible; but he knew that the first thing for his people, poor and ignorant as they were, was to learn to work intelligently and happily at whatever they could get to do, such as farming and the simpler industries.

He knew they could learn a kind of farming that would bring them money enough to build comfortable homes instead of such cabins as the one in which he had been born. He wanted them to learn how to be clean and healthy, to have plenty of fruit, vegetables, chickens, eggs, and milk for their children, instead of their everlasting diet of fat pork and cornbread. He undertook to revolutionize the habits of a people, their thoughts, and their standards. And he did it. And in so doing, he, more than any other one man, taught the world the kind of education that the masses of every race need. All over the world "the Hampton idea" is being adopted by governments, mission boards, and experts in education for those masses of people whose development has been retarded. It is the Hampton idea—General Armstrong's idea—which he worked out at Hampton; but Booker Washington, even more than its great originator, made it famous.

At first the Negroes did not like this idea of work. They came to school in order that they might not have to work. When the land of the new farm was to be cleared and planted, the students balked. But when their teacher took an ax and went to the woods, inviting them to come with him, they went. If he would chop trees and plow and hoe, they were willing to do it also. They were very proud of a teacher who was a real graduate, and if he was willing to work like that, possibly it was not so bad, after all.

The white people, watching, were well pleased, more and more so as they saw the Negro hovels changing into thrifty homes, and intelligent farming bringing larger crops for themselves as well as for the Negroes. The white stores began to prosper, also. The Negroes were putting money in the bank and buying land. But they were buying building material, too, and better clothes and comforts and conveniences such as they had never had. They did better work for the white people and were to be trusted more. The white people saw that Negro prosperity was good for everybody, and they began to believe in that kind of education for all races. They saw that honest work means the building of character, and that intelligent work means mental growth and independence and happy homes. These things are good for everybody. The Negro needs them not because he is a Negro, but because he is a human being.

The whole wonderful story of Tuskegee cannot be told here. It can be found in a book which should be read by every American, black and white; a book to interest young people and old people and to make even a coward brave—*Up from Slavery* by Booker T. Washington. The North Carolina State Board of Education has included it in its list of books for high school libraries of both races. It will broaden the mind and cheer the heart of any who will read it.

Mr. Washington began to speak in public to his own people first, then to white people of the North, where he went to raise money, then to Southern white people. If the test of oratory is the speaker's power to make people who do not sympathize with him or believe as he does feel sympathy, see as he sees, accept his doctrine, and believe in him, then Booker Washington was one of the greatest orators America has produced. In New Orleans he spoke before a great audience of Southern white people most of whom, in those early days before Mr. Washington was known, were hostile to any Negro set forward as a leader. In five minutes he had gripped their interest, and soon he held them in the hollow of his hand. They laughed and cried as he moved them—men and women, thousands of them; they rocked the walls with their applause; they flocked about him afterward, eager to grasp his hand. Over and over he aroused the same enthusiasm. Presidents, governors, bishops, heads of great universities publicly honored him. At Charleston, five miles from the old salt mines, the governor of West Virginia and his staff gave him a public reception to which both races flocked. In Atlanta he swept the crowds off their feet, including the governor of Georgia who sat beside him on the stage. It was the same way in staid Boston and in England, where the greatest came to hear him. But it was not just emotion that he stirred. He made people see and love the real things, the big, simple, Christ-like things that never change. He made right look wise and beautiful, as it is, and he showed two different races the way to live side by side in justice and friendship, "in things purely social as separate as the fingers, yet one as the hand in all things essential to mutual progress."

Booker Washington did the work of a dozen men. He stimulated Negro business throughout the country by his organization of the Negro Business League and his inspiration and direction of it. His health work has influenced the whole South and has won cooperation, not only from local white organizations, but from state officers, boards of health, federations of women's clubs, chambers of commerce, and the like. He never spared himself, and, as men see things, he died before his time. Broken down in body, Mr. Washington was taken to St. Luke's Hospital in New York. When he found the end was near, he asked to be taken home to die. They put him in a special car with doctors and nurses and his devoted wife. The country watched that journey, and the great newspapers told everywhere how he was standing the trip—this man born a slave on the earthen floor of a windowless cabin. He reached Tuskegee just alive, and there, in his own beautiful home, amid hearts that loved him and the folk he had lifted up, Booker Washington passed out to meet his Master and to get his praise from God.

What made him great? He had a strong, broad mind, but not a preeminent one. Some of his own race, many of ours, were his mental equals or superiors, yet they were not in the same class with him at all. He was a highly gifted administrator, a remarkable speaker, but so are many lesser persons. Where was the secret of his power? I puzzled over it until I heard him talk to his own people one day, and then I knew.

Speaking to white people, he appealed to their common sense, their love of justice, their spirit of sympathy and fair play, their business interests. To his own people that day, he spoke of Jesus Christ and of how He would help them meet difficult conditions in the right way. He spoke of injustices the Negro often suffers and of the danger of bitterness and hatred against a people because of the wrongdoing of some. "I have felt these things," he said. "I suffered much. I grew to hate white men as some of you do to-day. I hated them until my soul began to dry up. My power to love and help my own people was shriveling. I found that hate in my heart to any man would kill my usefulness to all men. Then I carried my hate to Jesus Christ, and He delivered me from it. He took it out of my heart. He keeps me free. He showed me how to love white men, and now I can serve them and my own people together and alike.''

That was the secret. God had given him, in answer to his prayer, a wonderful largeness of heart—the greatest greatness that there is. It magnified every natural gift, and set him in the class of those who are great by eternal standards.

Riding down Fifth Avenue some months after his death, a crowd of people was seen blocking the sidewalk. Coming nearer one noticed a different look on their faces—not the alert Fifth Avenue look, keen for new fashions and costly trifles, but one that seemed to go beyond the great buildings and splendid shops. They were gazing at a bronze bust in the window of a great silversmith. Its face was furrowed and tired and black—the face of this same Negro and one-time slave. Yet there stood before it rich and poor, glimpsing something of the beauty of a life of unselfish service and its splendid eternal unshakableness; and one Southern woman thanked God death makes so plain the things really worth living and dying for, and looked at the black face through a mist of tears.

But what of Tuskegee when the heart and brain from which it grew were gone? The spirit of service which had filled its founder's life was still there, a flame kindled in hundreds of hearts; and God, who carries on His work even when He calls His workmen home, had a man ready for the task now grown so great.

This man, too, is from Virginia, born soon after the Civil War. One unusual thing about him is that he knows all about his ancestors for generations back. Not very many white people, and few Negroes, know as much about their great-great-great-grandfather as does this black man.

When this grandfather was young, in 1735, his father, an African chief, fought a battle in which he took many captives. Some of them he sent in chains down to the sea-coast, to be sold as slaves. His son had charge of the convoy. The young man sold his slaves and then accepted the invitation of the traders to go on board their wonderful ship and inspect it. Afterwards he took dinner with them. His food must have been drugged, for when he came to himself, he was far out at sea, chained in the hold with the very slaves he had himself so recently sold.

This young man, the son of an African chief, was brought to Richmond, Virginia, and sold. He lived to a very great age, trusted and kindly treated by his master. He told the story of his capture to his great-granddaughter, who, in turn, told it to her grandson, Dr. Robert Moton, now president of Tuskegee Institute.

Dr. Moton's father's mother also came from Africa, and all his people afterwards, on both sides, were slaves. He himself was born free and grew up happily on the plantation where his father was foreman and his mother the cook for "the big house."

His mother had learned to read, and she taught her little son at night by the light of a pineknot fire. When at length the white folks in the big house found this out, one of the young ladies taught Robert herself. Afterwards, he went to the country school when it was open, working the rest of the time, first as house-boy and then in the fields. For years he attended the colored Sunday-school, which was taught by the best white people of the neighborhood, among whom he had many friends.

But for his mother, Robert Moton might have missed the great opportunity which came to him at Booker Washington's death. When he was only eighteen, he was superintendent of the Baptist Sunday-school, leader of the church choir, and a notable speaker at religious and political gatherings of his people. This was in "reconstruction" times, and some white and colored politicians wanted him to go to the legislature. It was against the law for a minor to fill such an office, but he was six feet tall and could pass for twenty-one. The politicians said that the only thing necessary was for his mother to swear that he was of age. It was a dazzling offer to a poor colored boy, and he was finally talked into a half-hearted consent. But he reckoned without his mother.

Not even for her beloved and only child would she swear to a lie, and instead of going to the legislature, Robert went to Hampton—the beginning, little as he dreamed it, of a far more distinguished career.

The next years were filled with hard study and harder work in the school lumber mill and at all sorts of jobs in summer. One whole year he took off, teaching a country school. On graduation, young Moton made so fine a record that he was offered the position of assistant to the commandant, the white officer in charge of the students' discipline. When the commandant resigned, Major Moton, as he was then called, took his place. There were many Indians in the school, a sprinkling of Chinese, Japanese, African Negroes, Armenians, and Hawaiians. The faculty was made up of Northern and Southern white people, with Major Moton the only Negro on it. To maintain both discipline and good-will among those students of many races and to grow in the confidence and esteem of the white faculty was no small accomplishment. But for twenty-seven years it was done.

North and South, Major Moton made friends for the school, speaking before audiences of white and of black people. In Virginia he drew into the Negro Organization Society all the scattered colored societies—educational, economic, secret, and open—to work together for "better schools, bet-

TUSKEGEE NORMAL AND INDUSTRIAL INSTITUTE
Exhibition of the Girls' Physical Culture Class

ter health, better homes, better farms." They began with clean-ups and health work, securing hearty cooperation from the state and from local organizations of white people. They bought a farm on which the state put up a sanitarium for Negro consumptives. Many leading men and women of both races have been brought into contact with one another through the work of the Society, and interracial good-will has been promoted to a noteworthy extent.

When Dr. Washington died, in 1915, Major Moton was elected president of Tuskegee Institute. He was perhaps the one man who could take the position without being dwarfed by his great predecessor. The influence of the school goes on as before, broadening and deepening with the years.

During the war, Dr. Moton was frequently called to Washington by the Government for consultation about matters concerning the Negroes within and without the army. Tuskegee did fine work in training colored officers and technical experts, and the school's great service flag is a wonderful record of loyal Americanism. In stimulating production among colored workers, in the thrift, Liberty Loan, and Red Cross campaigns, and in all other war work, Dr. Moton was a force felt, not only throughout the state of Alabama, but among his people throughout the country. In this work he was brought into contact as never before with the leading white men of the South, whose confidence and respect he won. He is, therefore, a great force for interracial understanding and friendship. When colored men were added to the Interracial Commission, composed of leading white people from every Southern state, Dr. Moton was the first Negro chosen to represent his race in that body.

In 1918 President Wilson and the Secretary of War sent Dr. Moton to France to look into and report upon conditions affecting the Negro soldiers and to suggest whatever changes he thought would add to their usefulness and well-being. This mission called for tact and insight of a high order and was of great benefit to both races, clearing up misunderstandings, removing friction, and promoting justice and good-will.

His work still broadens out. "Speaking the truth in love" to both races, never dodging an issue, but meeting men of both races in the spirit of Christ, Dr. Moton is one of the constructive forces in America to-day.

III

A DOCTOR OF MEDICINE

TWENTY years or so before the Civil War, a Maryland slave ran away from his master and went to Canada by the "underground railway." That was the name for the chain of homes and stopping-places where Negroes fleeing from slavery were hidden and cared for by those who sympathized with them. If slaves were discovered before they got out of the United States, the law required sheriffs and policemen, even in the free states, to arrest them and return them to their masters; but if they once got across the line into Canada, they could not be brought back. Quakers and others who thought, even then, that slavery was wrong arranged stopping-places from many points along the borders of the slave states and all the way up to Canada, and many colored people made their way along these routes to freedom. So this Maryland slave, named Roman, when once he had found friends, was passed on from hiding-place to hiding-place until at last he reached Ontario, in Canada, and there he lived and worked for over twenty years. He married the daughter of a Negro farmer who had, himself, run away from Virginia long years before.

When Lincoln's proclamation freeing the slaves made it safe to return to the United States, Roman took his family to Williamsport, Pennsylvania, and there, on the 4th of July, 1864, his son Charles was born.

There was a large family, and they knew what it was to be poor and without many of the comforts of life. Sometimes, however, people who do without comfort get something bigger and better in its place; they learn to be brave and cheerful no matter what their surroundings are. This little colored boy was one of these fortunate people. The hard lessons he mastered helped him during the struggle of his early years. Now that he has won comfort and independence for himself and his family, these lessons still help him by giving him a quick sympathy for those who struggle. Much of his happiness comes from giving to others the help he himself used to need so much.

Charles was a chap who liked to discover things for himself. A little brook ran near his home, and he wanted to find out where it came from. He was a tiny child, only three or four years old, but he set out to find the beginning of that brook. He walked a great distance, resting by the way, no doubt, but he was gone so long that his mother roused the neighborhood to help her find him. They searched the fields and the woods, and at last they found the boy at the place where the brook began—a little pool with a bubbling spring at the bottom of it. He was watching it as hard as he could, more puzzled than ever as to where the water came from and still determined to find out. But his mother carried him off home, and if he had intended trying to get down the hole at the bottom of the pool, his plans were nipped in the bud.

When he was six years old, Charles's father, a broom-maker by trade, went back to Canada, and until he was twelve, the boy spent much of his time on his grandfather's farm. He had all sorts of adventures here, trying to ride the steers like the big boys and being tossed over the fence, walking a mile to the pasture gate to open it for his grandfather, that he might ride back with him as a reward, climbing the fruit trees to eat all one boy could possibly hold, trotting after the sheep, and often getting into mischief which tried his grandmother's patience more than he found comfortable. His grandfather was his refuge at such times and usually arranged a peace for him. The old man liked the boy's fearlessness, his honesty, his eagerness to find out things, his readiness to take a hand in whatever came along. Like most men, he did not take the messes the child made or his mischief as seriously as his wife, who had to set things in order.

But play-days were soon over. When Charles was twelve years old, his parents moved to Dundas, and the boy went to work in a cotton mill.

The machinery started at six o'clock, and any one who was not at the mill ten minutes beforehand had to go to the office for discipline. This was such an unpleasant experience that most of the boys arrived far ahead of time. Charlie Roman put himself on the safe side by being on hand every morning at half-past five.

With work lasting for ten and a half hours, there was little time left for other things. But the boy's heart was so set on having an education,—there were so many things he wanted to find out,—that he spent two hours every evening at night-school, studying afterwards at home until far into the night. He read every book he could lay his hands on, borrowing them wherever he could. On Sundays he went regularly to Sunday-school and studied his Bible as far as his opportunities made possible. Charlie belonged to a little band of teetotalers, who were much less numerous then in Canada, or anywhere else, than they afterward became. And behind everything he did, this boy had one settled purpose in life.

One day at the noon hour the boys at the mill were telling each other what they meant to be when they grew up. Charles, the one colored boy in the group, and a white boy named Arthur were the only two who had nothing to say. The colored boy, kindly treated by many of his mill associates, was made by others to feel very sharply that they looked down upon him, not because of what he was, but because of the color of his skin; so when the others talked, he often listened and said nothing. Arthur said nothing because he was a shy boy with different thoughts from most of the others. After a while, one of the bigger boys turned to him in a bullying, sneering way and asked, "Well, Arthur, what are you going to be?"

"I'm going to be a musician," replied the boy, quietly.

A howl of derision went up at this. They looked at him, poorly clad, without money or friends, tied to a factory ten hours a day for barely enough to keep him alive, and they laughed until they nearly lost their breath.

When the delightful edge of the joke was dulled a little, the big boy, in an effort to repeat his success with Arthur, turned to the silent colored boy, sneering more than ever. "And what are you going to be, if you please?" he inquired.

"A doctor of medicine," came the answer, quick as a flash.

How they roared at that! They laughed until they almost cried, and went back to work at last still chuckling and thinking the big boy who had asked the questions a very master of humor.

But both those boys told the truth. The white boy has gone home already, carrying back to God the gift which had been given him and which he did his best to develop and use. When he died, he was the leader of an orchestra. And the colored boy—but you shall hear what the colored boy did.

He worked in the mill for five years—until he was seventeen years old. All this time he studied and read at night, and all this time his thirst for knowledge grew. Then came an accident at the mill which sent him to the hospital badly hurt. He was there a long time. One operation after another was performed, and for months the boy fought for his life through suffering and almost despair. When at last he came out of the hospital, he was on crutches, lame for life. To such a big, strong, active young fellow, this must have been a great trial. It was well that he had developed a strong Christian faith, for he needed all the comfort it could give him.

But often, through the very troubles which seem to block our way, God opens a door through which we pass to something even better than our dreams. Now that Charles was hopelessly disqualified as a mill worker, it was decided that he must have a chance at the brain work he so wanted. On crutches, therefore, he went to the Collegiate Institute in Hamilton. Here he worked as hard as though lameness did not exist, finishing the six years' course in three. Before school and after, Charles found time to help pay his way through school. He sold "notions" wherever he could find a buyer and did all the odd jobs possible to one in his condition. Despite his drawbacks, the young

DR. ROMAN'S CLINIC

First operation performed in the George W. Hubbard Hospital connected with Meharry Medical College. Dr. Roman is second from the left.

man kept such brave good cheer that he made friends for himself everywhere he went, among both white and black people. Whatever could help him, his friends put in his way, and above all, the mother whom he so devotedly loved stood by him as brave and cheerful as he himself, helping him in every possible manner. His teachers were especially kind to him, not because he was black, but because he was an eager student and learned so quickly and even brilliantly.

"I have taught hundreds of boys," said one, years afterward, "but among them all this boy had the brightest mind I ever touched."

After graduation Charles went South, feeling that there he could best serve his people. He taught school in Kentucky, then in Tennessee, and at length in Nashville, the capital.

Meharry College, the best medical school for Negroes in the South, is in Nashville. The school has been, and is, a blessing to both races all over the South, for with Negroes in every white home and business house, sickness for either race means sickness for both. Meharry raised health-standards for Negroes first in Nashville, then in every state to which its graduates have gone. Young Roman was anxious to enter the college at once, but could not for lack of money. However, while teaching in the public schools, he began to study the books in the medical course. As soon as he had saved enough money, he entered Meharry as a regular student. He worked during vacations in a colored physician's office and finished his course with honor.

After practising briefly in Tennessee, Dr. Roman went to Dallas, Texas, where he built up a successful practice. He was still a student by nature, and from time to time took post-graduate courses in Chicago and Philadelphia. Then he went to London and Paris, specializing in diseases of the eye, ear, nose, and throat. On his return from Europe, he was offered a professorship at Meharry along the lines of his special preparation. He has been there ever since, except during the World War when the Government appointed him special lecturer to the colored troops, on social hygiene. He traveled all over the country in the war-years, reaching many thousands of young men of his own race with sound teaching and powerful appeal founded both on his knowledge of medicine and his living faith in Jesus Christ.

While teaching at Meharry and attending to his large and growing practice in the city, he still found time to study, not alone to keep up in his profession, but to broaden his life in other fields. He had been offered the degree of M.A. from several colored colleges of excellent standing as an honorable recognition both of his scholarship and of his services as a citizen, but he would have nothing he had not earned. Professor though he was, he studied at Fisk University, winning his

M.A. in 1913. He was nearly fifty years old at this time, but he never expects to be too old to learn. He is now director of physiology and hygiene at Fisk as well as a professor at Meharry.

Dr. Roman is an active worker in the A. M. E. Church, of which he is a member. Into his Bible class of two hundred young men and women, he puts his whole heart. Sunday after Sunday and year after year as the students crowd his class, the hold he has upon them is evident.

It is the same with his medical classes. Because of a real love for teaching and for his students, he quickens both their minds and their hearts. They love him and trust him, and he has helped so many in difficulty and trouble, both outward and inward, that he cannot remember the half of it himself. He has never forgotten his own struggles with poverty, with misunderstanding, with pain, and with discouragement, and he knows how to help and comfort others who are themselves struggling in like manner.

For years Dr. Roman has been known to Southern white people as a man of unusual character and gifts. He has stood for full justice to his own people, but he has always taught and lived his belief that full respect is possible between the races without intermingling and without antagonism. This was the burden of his message to the white people at the annual meeting of the Southern Sociological Congress in Atlanta a few years ago.

This address, published afterward in "The Human Way," a pamphlet issued by the Congress, is, like all of Dr. Roman's addresses, full of epigrammatic thought. For example:

"Misunderstanding, rather than meanness, makes men unjust to each other."

"Ignorance and prejudice feed upon each other."

"As a man thinks, not as he looks, finally fixes his status."

"Thoughts, not bites, win the battles of life."

"Man's attitude toward new or unpleasant truth is the greatest tragedy of human life."

"No man is secure in his rights so long as any man is deprived of his."

"Let us accept it as a fact, that the Negro and the white man must survive or perish together in the South, and that there can be no mutual fair play without mutual respect."

To bring this respect about, Dr. Roman pleaded for fairer dealing in the newspapers. They report crimes committed by Negroes as if they were especially Negro crimes, not as a crime committed by a criminal, as white crimes are reported. No one thinks of blaming a whole race for one bad white man's deeds, but a Negro's crime is reported as something different—something any member of that race might be expected to do.

He asked three other things which would do much in promoting fair play and mutual respect:

The first was to clear white speech of such contemptuous terms as "nigger," "coon," and the like. Courtesy, one might say, never belittles either its user or its recipient. The second was never to report the speeches of race agitators who try, especially on certain political levels, to stir prejudice for personal gain. The third was to publish the creditable things the Negroes do and to try to learn more about those members of the race whose lives and achievements are worthy of respect.

These are sensible suggestions. Hundreds of Southern white people are now at work trying to get them and others like them adopted throughout the South. In every Southern state and in over eight hundred counties in the South there have been formed in the last three or four years interracial committees composed of leading white and leading colored men and women. Sometimes they all belong to the same committee, sometimes there is a white committee and a colored one. In the latter case, the two committees meet frequently together. All over the South the best members of both races are coming to know one another. Dr. Roman is an influential member of the Tennessee state committee, and the white men who serve with him believe in him. One of these men, Dr. Kirkland, the chancellor of Vanderbilt University, said of him that he had the respect and esteem of the thoughtful men of both races, and that his life and work had done much for the uplift of his race.

Dr. Roman's own people have honored him in many ways. Layman though he is, his Church sent him as fraternal messenger to the Canadian Methodist Church and also as a delegate to the Ecumenical Methodist Conference which met in Toronto in 1911. His fraternal address was widely commented on in the Canadian papers as of remarkable eloquence without regard to the speaker's race. He has served as president of the National Negro Medical Association and has done much to raise the standards of health and sanitation among his people. Dr. Roman is much sought after as a speaker at Negro colleges, North and South. His addresses make, not only for better living and higher standards within his own race, but also for helpful relations of the two races one with another. He has written much for the best class of Negro publications. A book written by him on American civilization and the Negro has won high praise.

Dr. Roman does not propose to grow old if he lives to be a hundred. He thinks hard work, hard study, and helping others, if wisely mixed and regularly taken, is a better elixir of youth than Ponce de Leon's fabled fountain. He is still in full vigor, still studying, still growing, still broadening his service to his fellow man.

IV

SAVING AN IDEA

SOME people seem born to get those things done which nobody else would even attempt. Some driving force within sends them out on a new, untried, hard way, on what seems to all their friends to be a wild-goose chase. To them, however, it is a veritable quest of the Holy Grail. They go from one difficulty to another, with no better sense, the onlookers think, than to tackle the impossible; and then, all at once, when the wild project is thought to be dead and as good as buried, the thing, in some amazing way, is done —a success beyond dispute. Then people begin to praise it and the doer of it, and forget that they said it couldn't be done. That is what happened to Nannie Burroughs and her big idea. She says the Lord worked it out, and that it couldn't possibly have been done without prayer and faith.

Nannie was born in Orange, Virginia. Her mother's people and her father's belonged to that small and fortunate class of ex-slaves whose energy and ability enabled them to start towards prosperity almost as soon as the war which freed them was over. When she was still a very little girl, one of her grandfathers owned a good farm, and the other made a comfortable living as a skilled carpenter. Her mother, left with her little girl to provide for, could have been supported by either of these men, but she was unwilling to be dependent on relatives; and besides, she wanted her child to have a better education than the country town could afford. When Nannie was five years old, her mother went to Washington. Here she worked and kept her child in school until Nannie graduated with honor from high school.

The young girl took a thorough business course, and special work in domestic science. She wanted to teach the latter branches, and as she had led her class in all her work, she was given to understand that if she would take this special preparation, she would be made assistant teacher of domestic science in the high school. The position was given, however, to some one else, who, it was rumored, had "pull" with the authorities.

"I can't tell you how it broke me up," she said. "I had my life all planned out—to settle down in Washington with my mother, do that easy, pleasant work, draw a good salary, and be comfortable the rest of my life, with no responsibilities to weigh me down. I never would have done the thing I have done; I would not even have thought of it.

"But somehow, an idea was struck out of the suffering of that disappointment—that I would

Miss Nannie H. Burroughs

some day have a school here in Washington that politics had nothing to do with, and that would give all sorts of girls a fair chance and help them overcome whatever handicaps they might have. It came to me like a flash of light, and I knew I was to do that thing when the time came. But I couldn't do it yet, so I just put the idea away in the back of my head and left it there.''

She went to Philadelphia and worked in an office for a year. Then she went to Louisville, Kentucky, where, at the headquarters of the National Baptist Convention of the Colored Church, she became bookkeeper and editorial secretary. Like her mother, she had been a devoted church member from childhood, and she put her energy, her training, and her great gifts into the service of her church.

But even the heavy official work for both the men's and the women's conventions could not consume the energy of this human dynamo.

Because she had had such good opportunities at school and knew so much about right ways of living, Miss Burroughs felt a responsibility toward helping those who had had no chance to learn. She was teaching in Sunday-school and was being asked to talk at all kinds of church meetings. ''But what's the sense of talk,'' she said, ''if you don't do something? You talk, and people get stirred up and think they'd like to do something, and that makes them feel good, and they go off happy and satisfied, feeling as though they're some account in the world because they've felt like doing something—and they haven't done one thing to help one soul alive. If you're going to be a Christian, you've got to do something week-days as well as talk and feel about it Sundays.''

So she organized a Woman's Industrial Club. They rented a house and served cheap, wholesome lunches for colored working-folk. In the evenings she taught domestic science there. She started a class in millinery and a class in what she called, ''every-day things needed in the home.'' This included sanitation, hygiene, suitable dress, care of children, cooking, sewing, and laundry work. The women of the Industrial Club, her helpers and backers, each paid ten cents a week toward the work, and she managed the rest of it herself. She carried on this work during the nine years she lived in Louisville.

One day one of the leading white women of the city came into her office and asked if she was running the cooking-school at the colored women's club. When Miss Burroughs said yes, the woman asked how she got the money for it.

''Why, we club women pay ten cents a week, and we make pies and cakes and sell them.''

''Well,'' said the white woman, ''don't give your lessons for nothing any longer. People value more highly that which they pay for. If they can afford only a penny, let them pay that. I will pay you regularly for every pupil you have, so that you can get whatever you need for the school.''

After this, the club grew until Miss Burroughs was forced to put others in charge of the classes, merely supervising the work herself.

In 1900 she went to the annual meeting of the Colored Baptist Convention and gave a talk which seems to have electrified the assembly. As one result, she was made secretary of the Woman's Auxiliary, a small and feeble missionary organization of this great Church which had raised the year before just $15 for the general mission work of the denomination. She has been its secretary ever since. In her first year as secretary, the women raised over $1,000. In 1920 they raised over $50,000, and in the twenty years of her leadership they have put $366,000 into the missionary treasury of their Church.

But while Miss Burroughs worked with enthusiasm and energy for her denomination, she wanted to enlist her churchwomen in something which would draw together and help all the women of her race.

That idea of a school for girls who needed help had been tucked away for some time in the back of her head; now she took it out and considered it.

There were schools for colored girls, of course; but they were, for the most part, founded and all were largely supported by white people. While Miss Burroughs knew how invaluable this help to her race had been, and is, yet she felt that the Negroes were far enough along now to begin to do more for themselves.

The year after she became secretary of the Woman's Auxiliary, she tried to get her Baptist women together as a starting point for this broader work.

"We will work harder than ever for the foreign fields of our Church," she said; "but let us start a national school for girls here at home—not a Baptist school, but one that all Negro women, of every creed, can come together on. We don't know what we can do until we all get together."

But the women would not listen. They would have none of Miss Burroughs' school. They were Baptists, working for the great Baptist Church. Again she put her idea away in the back of her head for safe-keeping and returned to her work in Louisville and to the building up of her Baptist organization in the one direction it was as yet willing to take—that of Baptist good works.

Five years later the Auxiliary was raising $13,000 a year. The women had just put up a brick building for some of their mission work in Africa. Miss Burroughs told them that they needed to help girls here in America as well as in Africa, and that if they had the school she proposed, they could bring girls here from Africa and prepare them to go back as missionaries. They liked that idea and proposed to rent a little cottage somewhere and put some African girls in it to be trained as Baptist missionaries.

"That's not my idea," said the secretary. "It must be national, not Baptist,—something all colored women can do for all colored girls."

They appointed a committee. "You know," she said, with a flash of the laughter that is always ready to bubble up, "when we women just must dodge an issue, we put it over on a committee. But when the committee met in Louisville, in January, 1907, they endorsed the plan I suggested." When Miss Burroughs had her vacation that summer, she went to Washington to look for a site. With a horse and buggy she drove all over that part of the District, and found a hill site.

"Somehow I felt the school had to be set on a hill. It was all red gullies up here and a sight to see, with a dilapidated eight-room house atop of it all; but there were six acres of land and this beautiful view. It was for sale for $6,500, $500 to be paid in ten days and $500 more twenty days later; the remainder could wait at interest. I took it."

"Had the women given you the money?"

"Why, no, not a cent."

"Had you saved all that yourself?"

Again that look of flashing laughter.

"Why, no; I hadn't saved any money. I'd had too many things to do with my money. I had saved an idea."

"I see. But what about the $500?"

"I went to Louisville and raised it. From my own people—yes. You see"—soberly—"I'd prayed about this thing for a long time. I felt God wanted me to go ahead, and I knew if I did what I could and trusted Him, He would see it through. And He did."

She stayed on in Louisville for two years until the whole $6,500 was raised and the place paid for. Then she went to Washington and opened her school in October, 1909, with eight pupils. The property is vested in a self-perpetuating board of trust, the majority of the members being women. If the board is ever dissolved, it goes to the Baptist Convention and the Women's Auxiliary jointly, to be used for educational purposes.

Both races bewailed Miss Burroughs' leaving Louisville. She was offered a site for her school as a gift if she would stay, but she felt that as a national institution, it should be in the nation's capital. The Louisville *Courier-Journal,* one of the most distinguished papers of the South, paid her a remarkable tribute: "Probably no woman's organization in Louisville or, for that matter, elsewhere is doing as much practical, far-reaching good" as the organization founded by "this remarkable young colored woman, Miss Nannie Burroughs."

Of course the school grew. And its young principal, still secretary of the Women's Auxiliary and having to raise money for her teachers' salaries, must provide means for enlargement. She decided to turn an old stable back of the house into class-rooms and a dormitory.

But for once it looked as though she must fail. The women who had wanted the school to be a Baptist training-school did not call it the National Training School, as Miss Burroughs did. Most of them just called it, "Nannie Burroughs' school" and washed their hands of it. But one Baptist woman stood by her. When things looked most hopeless, Mrs. Maggie L. Walker, the woman banker of Richmond, gave her $500 on condition that she would not tell any one who gave it to her. That started the fund, and soon all the money needed was in hand.

"I had to keep my promise, of course," said Miss Burroughs, "and not say a word. But you see what I did."

My eyes followed hers to a substantial, well-painted building which bore above its white columns the legend, "Maggie L. Walker Hall"—a monument to a woman's faith in a woman and in her idea of service.

The briers and weeds were gone by this time; the girls were cultivating a three-acre garden and canning the surplus yield; they had filled the gullies themselves, students and teachers; they had set out trees; and soft green slopes covered the once-bare hill. Concrete walks came next, and then Pioneer Hall, built new from the ground up, three stories and a basement. A white man lent the money for this building, but colored people paid for it. During the war two additional acres were purchased, with a dwelling which was remodeled for sleeping-rooms, industries, and a clubroom. The Northern Baptist white women then offered $3,500 for a model cottage to be used in the domestic science work. Negroes added $500 for the building and furnished the cottage tastefully. The senior class in domestic science runs the Home on a practical and profitable basis. Conventions meeting in Washington and all sorts of local organizations, clubs, and groups come out for luncheons and dinners. The girls serve them, and the money goes to the school.

One day a Washington bank called up Miss Burroughs and told her they had $1,000 for her.

"For me?" she gasped. "Where'd you get it? Are you sure it's for me?"

"It's for Nannie H. Burroughs of the National Training School. Come down here and we'll tell you what we know about it."

She lost no time. The money, she learned, came from the estate of a white Californian who had left a certain sum for work begun and developed by Negroes who showed initiative and vision. A colored man had told the executors about Miss Burroughs' school, and after due investigation they had sent her $1,000 for her work.

"I couldn't put a big gift like that into something already started," she said. "There's always a place for money—our water-works cost us $7,000 up on this hill, and we've put in steam heat and electric lights. But this money had to give us something we never would have had without it. I got $3,000 more from my own people and we built the community house down there at the foot of the hill, across the road. Then we put four thousand books into it, upstairs. The public schools and our school and the whole community use those books."

They showed use when we went to look at them —use, not abuse. They are undoubtedly appreciated. They are in a big room used for community gatherings and entertainments. Downstairs is a store. Formerly there was not a place within a mile where a spool of thread could be bought. Here the neighbors can get notions, staple groceries and canned goods, and almost anything that a housekeeper is likely to need in a hurry. The girls of the domestic science department have a cake and pie department that is very popular.

The community house quickens the mental and spiritual life of the whole neighborhood, ties the school and the community together, gives the girls training both in business and in service to the community, and yields the school an annual cash income of nine per cent on the investment. Doesn't a thousand dollars have to be energized with vision, business ability, and human sympathy before it can bring in returns like that?

With the war came a severe testing of the quality of the work the school was doing for the souls of the students. The bitter cold of the war-winter put the school pump quite out of commission—this was before the $7,000 water-works went in. All winter long—and how long that winter lasted!—teachers and girls carried in buckets every drop of water used on the place from the neighborhood springs and wells up that steep, icy hill to the tank in the third story of Pioneer Hall: water for cooking, bathing, laundry, dish-washing, cleaning for a hundred and fifty people. "And we all kept clean, and we all kept sweet," said Miss Burroughs, who did her full share of water-carrying.

They carried coal, too,—all of them, Miss Burroughs included,—for the coal companies, hard pressed for labor, refused to carry coal up the difficult hill. They would dump it at the bottom, at the entrance to the grounds, or they would not deliver it at all.

"I just explained it to the girls," said the principal. "I showed them it was really a part of our service to our country,—and a mighty small part compared to what our boys were doing without a word of complaint,—and they caught the spirit and the coal-scuttles too. We all did. We brought every piece of coal the school used that winter all the way up this hill. Not a man on the place, you understand. We carried coal and water, tended to our pigs and chickens, cooked, cleaned, and did our school work in a cheerful, happy spirit. You know,'' she went on thoughtfully, ''I think the 'hard' years were the best ones we had. We built more character. Souls grow under pressure.''

So do ideas—the kind Miss Burroughs saved in the back of her head so long. That special idea took a fresh start once the water-works were in, and assumed the shape of a laundry. The girls had done their personal laundry with the primitive equipment of wooden tubs, but the school had been paying $500 a year for laundering its household linen, and its principal has that rarest of business gifts which can turn liabilities into assets. Since sheets must be laundered, they should bring money in by the process instead of taking it out. If they had a big, modern laundry, the girls who desired to do so could learn the work as a trade, and by taking in outside work, those who needed to earn their school expenses could do so, at least in part, and the school could earn a profit on its investment—all instead of paying out $500 a year to somebody else for washing sheets. Miss Burroughs worked it all out after due investigation and so convinced her board of trustees that they told her to go ahead. If she could

raise $10,000, the remainder could remain on mort-
gage for a while. One of her trustees told her
if she would get $9,000 by a certain date, he
would give her a thousand himself. So she did
an amazing thing.

She went to white contractors, told them she
hadn't a cent as yet, and asked them to begin
on the building at once; and they did. When the
building was almost finished,—a fine, big, modern
plant,—she was asked, "Have you got the
money?"

"I haven't tried yet," she answered. "I've just
been preparing for my campaign. I'll get it, because God will give it to me. I look to Him, and
He never fails me. It's His work. I began it
for Him, I take it to Him day by day. When we
need anything, I look to Him for it, then I think
and pray and work over my part of it the very
best I can, and what we need is given."

A $15,000 building almost finished on pure faith
—faith of white contractors in a Negro woman,
faith of the woman in God! The school has been
run like that throughout its twelve years of life.
In the first eleven years $232,000 in cash has gone
into it. Of this, the Women's Auxiliary has given
$4,300, the white Baptist women, $3,500, a white
Californian, $1,000, and a few thousand dollars
have come from the students in board. All the
remainder has been raised by the principal from
people of her own race, and secured while she has

been raising the income of the Baptist Women's Auxiliary from $15 a year to $50,000.

Yet the test of a school is not the money put into it, but the character that comes out of it. By this standard the National Training School is an asset to the nation. No one can see the girls without being impressed with their efficiency and their spirit of service. It is hard to estimate the loss to both races from lack of room at the school for those who apply for admission.

"But I believe," says the woman who has built all this out of the idea she saved so carefully, "that some day God will move some white person to give the school something big—endowment and equipment to do the best work it is capable of. I've felt all along that if we colored people could start it and prove that it is worth while and would do our very best for it, that before I am clean worn out and can't do any more, He would put it into the heart of some one of His rich white children to do what we can't—endow it and make it a permanent help to my people and my country after I'm dead and gone. I pray for that, and I'm trusting for it, too. But I'm not asking anybody but God for it. It must come from Him."

Miss Burroughs is at present working to unite the women of her race for mutual service. She is organizing them as workers—including artists, teachers, business and professional women, domestics, and home women in one big group, without regard to class distinctions. She wants them to stand together as women with common ideals of work, of standards of living, of service, and of self-respect. She wants the most favored women of her race to stand beside the poorest and, in doing so, to give the latter a new respect for themselves and their work, new hope, and new ambition, that, through a better service, they may win a better reward.

Miss Burroughs' influence over her people can hardly be estimated. She has dynamic power. Measured, not as a Negro woman, but as a woman, she has extraordinary ability; and her living faith in God and in all His children, of whatever race, her spirit of service and sacrifice have energized her gifts as only faith and love can do.

V

A CITY PASTOR

THERE was once a colored boy who thought he would some day be a preacher, but as he grew older, he decided that being a preacher was too poor an occupation for a young man with brains and an education. He wanted to make money and of course that cut preaching out. Yet to-day in a Massachusetts city, William DeBerry is the pastor of one of the largest Congregational churches for colored people in America. Far from being as rich as he once hoped to be, he is, however, as happy as the day is long, and he is bringing happiness to hundreds of others every year.

William DeBerry was born in Nashville, Tennessee, where for thirty years his father worked in the railroad shops on week-days and preached to his people on Sundays. The boy's idea of preaching came from his father's example and also from his mother, who taught him that to be a preacher was to have the noblest of opportunities.

The boy had a well-developed bump of persistence. This characteristic was evident even when William was a little chap, for one bitterly cold day he nearly turned himself into an icicle finishing up something that was almost too much for him—almost, but not quite. On this day he was outdoors, not too warmly clad, when an old Negro came by leading a horse and asking the way to the mill, which was on the edge of town. The old man could not understand the child's directions, and William, not having been out long enough to realize how cold it was, became suddenly fired with a great ambition. He offered to go with the man to the mill if he could ride the horse. In a moment he was lifted to the horse's back, and rode off gloriously, the envy of all his playmates. But it was two or three miles to the mill. The weather was making a new low record, and a high wind cut like ice. The little boy ached with cold and nearly cried with it. His hands could scarcely hold the reins. He wished he had stayed at home. He longed to get down on his poor frozen toes and dance to warm them. But he had said he would ride to the mill, so he tried to set his chattering teeth and went on. When they reached the mill, the boy was just a little frozen lump, too stiff to stand, at first. "But I managed to limber up a little walking home," he said, laughing. "I was glad I hadn't said I'd ride both ways."

A few years after this, when he was about ten years old, the city was repairing its streets with macadam, and many small boys of both races broke the stone for the roadways. They called

DR. DeBERRY AND HIS STAFF OF PAID WORKERS

These include (seated) assistant executive and boys' club worker; Mrs. DeBerry, matron of the parish house; Dr. DeBerry; social worker among women and girls; treasurer and head of housing department; (standing) caretaker; matron of boys' club and domestic science teacher; director of music; head of employment bureau; assistant matron of parish house; farm manager.

it "pecking" stone. The boy who persisted till he "pecked a perch"—a pile of rock a foot high and five and a half feet each way—was rewarded with the munificent sum of fifty cents. So William decided to peck a perch. He worked after school every day and at last received a slip of paper giving an order on the paving company for half a dollar. To get it cashed, the boy had to go two or three miles, from away out in North Nashville nearly to the river, but that was a small matter. He trotted off gaily, got his money, and turned back home, when a wonderful thing happened! A man asked him to hold his horse for him. When he came back, he gave the boy a whole silver dime—just for holding a horse!

William never knew quite how he got home; he thinks maybe he flew. But in any case, he rushed in to his mother, almost bursting with excitement, and thrust all his wealth into her hands.

"I earned it myself!" he shouted joyfully. "It's to buy you a dress with. I earned it! Go get a dress!"

And so she did. All the way to town she walked and bought with fifty cents calico enough to make a dress. The ten cents she would not take; William must spend that for himself. But the dress! How they both loved and admired it, and how proudly the mother wore it, with her boy who had given it to her walking beside her!

William attended public school until he was

about fourteen, when his father thought he should go to work. He "hired out" in the country that summer, tending to the horse, doing the chores, helping in the garden. He was very proud of having money of his own, and he meant to get a place in one of the hotels in the fall. He had quite sufficient education, he thought, to preach when he was old enough.

But in the fall a friend who was entering the preparatory school at Fisk University persuaded him to go to school again. His mother was very much pleased that her boy should want more of an education. But his father, who lived usefully with very little book-learning, was doubtful about so much schooling doing William any good. However, he did not oppose his wife's wishes, and the boy entered Fisk. Once started, he stuck to his work.

The same quality of persistence helped the boy to win in the preparatory school a scholarship which aided him year after year. He worked hard during vacation, spending two summers in a saw-mill. In the fall he did odd jobs in the hotels. After entering college at Fisk, he taught school in the summer except for one year when he was a porter on a Pullman car—a year that tested him as no year had done yet.

He went to Cincinnati for this job, and a friend lent him his carfare and ten dollars over. He carried letters of recommendation from Dr. Cravath, the president of Fisk, from the school superintendents where he had taught, and from several white people for whom he had worked. But in Cincinnati he was met by other Nashville boys who told him no more porters were being engaged, they had all applied in vain. Yet he went to see for himself. The man who employed the porters was out, he was told, not to return until morning. He spent the afternoon looking for other work, but without success. The next morning he returned to the Pullman office.

"There's the boss," said the office boy. "He won't give you a job, but there he is."

The "boss" was talking with friends, among whom was a lady. Young DeBerry knew that if he interrupted the man to ask for a job, he would be told, as his friends had been, that there were no vacancies. So he walked up to the great man's desk, without a word laid before him his sheaf of recommendations, and stepped back, waiting in silence.

The "boss," not knowing what the papers contained, read them. Then he turned. "Are you William DeBerry?" he demanded.

"Yes, sir."

"What do you want?"

"A porter's job on a Pullman."

"Can you fill out an application blank?"

"Yes, sir."

"Then go fill out this one and bring it here to me."

He could scarcely believe his good fortune. He filled out that blank with the greatest care.

"Did you write this yourself?" inquired the man.

"Yes, sir."

"Well, I'll take you—if you can buy your uniform. You must pay twenty-five dollars for it, cash down. Can you get it?"

"Yes, sir," came the instant reply. ("I knew I could get it some way," he said afterwards, "because I just had to, and I had ten dollars toward it in my pocket.")

"Very well," said the boss. "Here's the address of the tailor. You can report for duty tomorrow."

The tailor was an old Jew. William told him his story and showed his recommendations. He offered ten dollars cash and a draft for fifteen dollars on his first month's wages. The old man shook his head.

"I never give credit," he said. Then he paused, read over the letters again, and looked at De-Berry with sharp eyes. "I believe you're honest," he said, "and I'll take a chance on you, since you want an education. Here's the suit."

So began the young man's best summer for money-making. He was sent first to help an old porter who taught him his duties. This man, offering him a cigarette one day, was astonished to learn that DeBerry neither smoked nor drank.

"Well, you'll do both pretty soon," he said. "If you aren't smoking and taking a drink in two months, I'll give you a new uniform myself." He failed to do this, however, even though two months later he had to admit that his prophecy had not come true.

When DeBerry finished his first run as a full-fledged porter, the conductor handed him a roll of bills, saying it was his half of the "cutting." He knew already that the conductor was keeping back some of the company's money, because he had not given him the checks to certain berths for which passengers had paid on the train rather than in the station. The conductor was required to give the porter checks for all berths occupied, and these checks, turned in by the porter at the end of the run, must tally with the cash given in by the conductor. But if porter and conductor agreed to steal—or "cut," as they called it—the money of those passengers who paid on the train, the checks were destroyed, and there was no way for the company to find them out. Many conductors kept the money for such fares, dividing it with the porter at the end of the run. This insured the porter's silence and made the conductor safe.

When the conductor gave him the money, De-

Berry was frightened. If he refused it, he was sure the conductor would suspect him of wanting to better himself with the company by reporting the conductor, and that official would probably protect himself against this imaginary danger by making up some complaint against him and so have him dismissed. He couldn't afford to lose his job, it would mean dropping out of college. Anyway, it was the conductor's stealing, not his, he tried to think. So he took the money for that and for several trips afterward.

But the young man kept getting more and more miserable. His mother had taught him from his babyhood that he must be honest no matter what happened, and he knew he wasn't honest now. At last he felt that he would rather lose his job and drop out of his class than to take the money again. When he refused it, the conductor could hardly believe his ears.

"Why, you're a fool," he said. "Everybody does it. Here, take it as a present from me; you've got nothing to do with where it came from."

When he still refused, the conductor was angry, thinking DeBerry meant to report him. He assured him he would not, but the conductor did not trust him. He warned all the other conductors not to "cut" when they had DeBerry along, he was queer and wouldn't go halves, and he might tell. So nobody offered him any more money. Soon afterward, William was assigned to an old conductor who had been with the company thirty years and had never "cut" a dollar. He stayed with this man, who turned in some report on the young porter which brought him an unusual trust. At the ends of the run the conductor changed to another car, and DeBerry, in sole charge, collected the money paid for these short-distance rides, sending in his own reports. He was very happy over being trusted—a young Negro, only four months on the road.

William had decided by this time that preaching was out of the question for him; he would be a doctor. He knew a good many preachers, and few of them were educated men. Most of those he met were ignorant leaders of ignorant folk. The Church, he thought, was given over to emotionalism and superstition or to blind ignorance, which was almost as bad. He did not respect the institution as he had when he himself was ignorant. Besides, ministers never made any money, and money he meant to have—money and the comforts and power money brings.

While he was in his senior year at Fisk, DeBerry went to Dr. Hubbard, the dean of Meharry Medical College, also at Nashville. Dr. Hubbard knew the young man's record as a student and was glad to have him enter Meharry. He knew nothing of William's ·old determination to be a preacher. He offered him a position as tutor in

Latin at the college, the income from which would help him through his course. He should be happy now, William thought, with most of his struggles behind him and the way to a profession clear. But instead, he was very unhappy. The inward struggle was acute.

One of his teachers at Fisk sensed his difficulty. She would not urge him, but she asked him what he thought was the need of his people for educated ministers as leaders. He found it a hard question to put out of his mind. Then she lent him Drummond's *Natural Law in the Spiritual World,* and the book left him with a new sense of the world's need of God's love and of ministers to interpret it. Not long afterward, Mr. Moore, field agent of the American Missionary Association, came to Fisk as a lecturer. He talked at chapel about the Negro Church.

"Some of you young people," he said, "think you've outgrown the Church, you think you're too educated for it. You look down on it because you think its ministers are ignorant. I want to know which of you who criticize the Church in this way is willing to give your life to make conditions better?"

"That question," says Dr. DeBerry, "was meant for me. God meant it for me. I couldn't get away from it, day or night. I went to Dr. Hubbard at last and told him I couldn't come to Meharry. I had to preach."

DeBerry went to Oberlin for his theological course and won a scholarship. He was assigned to a little church where he preached on Sundays and during vacation. In this way, together with the scholarship, he worked his way through to graduation.

He wanted to work among his people in the South, where he felt the need was greatest, but when he graduated, there was no opening in a Southern Congregational church. The home mission board advised his going temporarily to a small church in Springfield, Massachusetts, whose pastor had just died. He went, expecting to stay only until he could find an opening in the South. He has remained in Springfield twenty-two years.

St. John's Church had about a hundred members when William DeBerry became its pastor. There was no parsonage, but they wanted a married preacher. This suited the young man beautifully. He went back to Tennessee and married the girl who was waiting for him, another Fisk graduate, and brought her to Springfield. Of course a parsonage had to be built then. With his wife to help him, the new pastor began to build up his work in earnest.

While he was still hoping for the Southern opening, the missionary authorities of his church began to send him to large white gatherings and to churches to speak of church work among the Negroes and to tell what the church schools were accomplishing. He knew the need as only a Negro could; he knew what the work of the Church meant in his own life and in that of his friends; and his heart was burdened for his race. He spoke with such force and effect that wherever he went, he made friends for his people and for the effort to help them. At last the Missionary Association urged him to stay in the North. They felt he could do more for his people in this way than in any other.

For years Mr. DeBerry's church grew steadily in members, in liberality, and in the regard of the white churches of the city. But he himself was not satisfied. He had received calls to several large churches, and now one came from his home city of Nashville. He told his people he could not stay with them unless they would undertake a broader service to the colored community of Springfield. He wanted a church that would be open seven days in the week, helping people on work days and rest days alike. It seemed an almost impossible undertaking, but the elders were willing to follow their leader. The church raised the first thousand dollars in cash toward a new church and then went to work to raise more. With this backing, Dr. DeBerry went to the white church and to white friends. The result is a big, modern church on a large corner lot. It has a beautiful organ and fine institutional equipment. There are large, well-furnished parlors, with a piano and a victrola, magazines and books, a sub-station of the public library. Prayer-meetings are held here on Thursday nights, but on all other week nights the rooms are open to various clubs for women and girls under the care of a trained worker. Three hundred are enrolled in these clubs. Downstairs is a big room with movable seats for Sunday-school and for entertainments. Here also are kindergarten rooms, the church kitchen, and rooms for classes in cooking and in arts and crafts.

The clubs for boys and young men, which have a hundred members enrolled, are in a building around the corner, where are billiard tables, games, books, and magazines. A brass band flourishes here also. A printing-press has just been bought, and printing and other trades are to be taught. There is an employment bureau for men in this building, and one for women in the parish house.

Next door to the church is the parish home for working girls, which cost $15,000. It contains an apartment for the pastor's family and rooms for fourteen girls. It is tastefully furnished and beautifully kept. Mrs. DeBerry acts as matron. The rooms are always full, with a waiting list for vacancies. Parlors and an office are on the first floor. In the basement there is a well-equipped laundry and a kitchen for the girls' use, with small individual lockers in which each girl may keep her stock of groceries.

During the war the munition factories of Springfield attracted numbers of colored workers, and the housing situation became acute. A white friend of St. John's bought a large apartment house and let it to colored people under the church's management. Later, the property was deeded to the church. Other friends who believe in the pastor and in the kind of spiritual and social upbuilding he is doing, followed this example. St. John's now owns a number of small houses in addition to the apartment house and provides shelter for twenty-eight families. The net rent from these properties goes to the support of the institutional work. Recently a farm of fifty-four acres was given to the church. This is being used for vacation groups of boys and men. A Hampton graduate in agriculture has charge of the place. The vacation guests this summer have given their mornings to work on the farm and their afternoons to fishing, games, and various sports. This part of the work is as yet in its earliest stages of development.

The church members are no exception to their race in point of liberality. Like most colored Christians, they put white people to shame when it comes to ''giving as the Lord hath prospered.'' The membership is divided into circles, each unit of which does his or her part in a cheerful spirit of teamwork. But the expenses are heavy, and the church could not meet them all, even with the help of the rents. Including the pastor, eleven paid workers are necessary, eight of them giving full time to the work. In the lean days since the war, there is the same unemployment and suffering among the Negroes as among the white poor. Some help has been given by the white Congregational church, but for the social work the principal aid comes from the Springfield Community Chest. This fund receives the gifts of all citizens for all forms of community service. The trustees apportion it among carefully-selected agencies. To St. John's is entrusted the amount set aside for social work among the colored people of the city.

Dr. DeBerry, in addition to his work in Springfield and his wider work for his people in the Congregational Church, has been made a trustee of Fisk University, his *alma mater*—an honor which any college graduate appreciates. The Interchurch World Movement, after its recent survey of American churches, reported this church of a colored Tennesseean as having "the most efficient system of organization and work of any church in the group surveyed, regardless of race or denomination." The man who is called to be a physician has a noble calling; but the man who is called to preach and answers with his whole life need not fear that he will be shut up to a service less than the best.

VI

A BELIEVER IN HAPPINESS

NOT so very many years ago there lived in Georgia a little colored girl who needed no fairy godmother for she had some of the most beautiful gifts in the world. One of them was a mother of remarkable character and insight; one was an inborn spirit of happiness which nothing could dampen and which those around her found contagious; and one was an opportunity for development such as few children of her race and generation dreamed of.

Janie's mother, a widow, was housemaid and seamstress in the home of a Northern woman of wealth and education who lived in the South for a number of years. The little colored girl came to the white home with her mother. The children in the family were about her own age, and they all played together, as would have been the case in any household while they were little. The white children found something oddly attractive about Janie. It wasn't just that she was pretty or that she had loose, wavy hair and a skin no darker than an Italian's or that wherever she was, a good time was sure to be going on; it was something that belonged to her soul—a kind of delight in living and a love of living things that radiated all about her. The white children and their mother really loved her.

When her mother married again and went back and forth to work between her own home and her employer's, Janie was kept at the "big house" and became almost a member of the family. The children were read to a great deal, and Janie was always an interested listener. As the years went on, she gained a knowledge and love of good literature such as only favored folk can have. She was very prettily dressed, her room was daintily furnished, and all her surroundings were those of refinement and ease. She knew little of school, but her education from reading and from her associations was superior to that of most of her race.

Life went on pleasantly for the children until they grew old enough for their continued companionship to seem strange to the neighbors. The mistress of the house loved Janie and was unwilling to send her away to live among untaught Negroes. The life of the average colored woman seemed terribly hard to the Northern white woman, and she offered to send Janie North, to give her as good an education as could be had there, and to establish her afterward in some community where her race would not be known and where life would be easy and pleasant.

"But of course," she said to the child's mother, "you must give her up. You must make me her legal guardian and agree never to see her again. You will do this because it is for her good and because you love her.''

But the mother would not hear of it. She was wise enough to know that no good can come to those who run away from the obligations into which they are born. Janie was colored, she said; she had had a wonderful chance in life, so far; she must share it with her people. She might go North for her education,—her mother would be most grateful,—but she must come back South to live and work. Furthermore, her mother would never give her up.

They argued for days. The white woman, firm in what she thought was right, refused to do anything more for the child unless she were given to her outright. The mother, equally determined, took Janie home and prepared to give her such an education as she could afford.

Janie's step-father was a prosperous Negro, a worker in the railroad shops. He had been taught, as a slave, the trade of a mechanic and had been allowed to ''hire his time'' before the Civil War; that is, he had worked where he pleased, paying his master a yearly sum to offset what he might have been worth as a slave, and keeping the rest himself. When the War ended, he had money enough to buy some land and build himself a home. He had worked and saved ever since. He meant to do as well by his step-daughter as by her half-

MRS. JANIE PORTER BARRETT

sisters, his own children. Janie's mother, too, had worked and saved; and if Northern colleges were beyond their means, Hampton wasn't; they would send her there.

The white woman was aghast. "Oh, Janie," she wept, "I've ruined your life! It's a work school! They require rough work such as you have never done, and there are rough students there, such as I never meant you to know. Child, you'll have to scrub floors there—I've seen them do it. Think of your having to scrub floors!"

Janie had no wild desire to scrub, and she felt a bit dashed for a minute; but her belief in the happy possibilities of life was not to be daunted. Something rose up within her and answered almost without her knowledge.

"I don't believe you've ruined my life," she said stoutly; "I don't see why I can't do something for my people yet that will be worth all you've done for me—and worth the floor-scrubbing too."

Years afterward she said she hadn't an idea of doing anything for her people when she spoke; she didn't know where the words came from. She wanted to make her weeping friend happy; and in the crisis, the deepest thing in her, unknown to her as yet, stirred to life and spoke.

So she went to Hampton and scrubbed floors, and incidentally scrubbed the skin off her knees.

"I hated scrubbing floors," she said, laughing

as she told of it. "I'd never learned how. But I had learned that I must obey, so whatever they told me to do, I did the best I could, whether I liked it or not; and I learned."

But helping her people! She didn't want to. Everybody thought it so great and solemn an obligation. Janie hated solemn things—she wanted fun. She was homesick for the old home, the old friends, the old, beautiful refinements of life. Why should she scrub floors or help ignorant folk?

Then one day she read a book—Walter Besant's *All Sorts and Conditions of Men*. All young people should read it. "The Palace of Delight" would intrigue their hearts as it did hers; and perhaps it would change their lives as it did hers.

"Why, that's helping folks—to make them happy!" she exclaimed. "It needn't be solemn at all. I'd love to help that way; and I will."

Her head was full of the idea after that, and her heart too. When she graduated, Janie chose, out of several places offered her, to teach a school in a little community in the "wire-grass country," one of the most backward places in Georgia at that time. The salary could hardly be discovered without a microscope.

"Why, child," gasped her mother, "are you crazy? That's no place for you to go to!"

"I don't believe they ever have much fun down there," Janie answered. "I'm going to give them

a good time. Of course I can't live on the 'salary';
but you can help me out.''

Janie's mother always had stood by her, and
she did now.

They had a good time in that community that
year. Janie visited the children's homes week-
ends to find out what they needed most. Such
places! Poor souls, no outlook on life at all—
just a grind of work and poverty and deprivation.
She taught the children calisthenics and games.
They played. They bought some croquet sets and
learned the game. They had picnics and trips in
the woods. They learned in school, too. And the
white people were all kind. Janie was told they
wouldn't be, but they were.

Then she was offered a position at Hampton,
and in the fall went to Virginia for life.

In 1889 she married Harris Barrett, a Hampton graduate who, from his graduation until his
death in 1915, was cashier and bookkeeper at
Hampton. He took her to the home he had bought
for her, and for years they worked over it together until it became a beautiful place. One
rule they made and never broke: nothing was
ever to go into the home that was not theirs,
paid cash for to the last cent before it entered
the house. The furniture came piece by piece,
and was the better loved for that reason. But
Janie had to have some lovely things to start with.
She called her home the ''Palace of Delight,'' be-

cause she meant it to be that to everybody around her; and though a palace might be short on furniture, what there was of it must be dainty and beautiful. She asked her mother to give her only the plainest and most necessary clothes for her wedding outfit, but to buy her some household linen and solid silver.

"Silver!" gasped her mother. "I can't fit you out with solid silver, child."

"Oh, no," agreed Janie; "I don't want to be 'fitted out'; but I want a table like the one I was brought up to see every day—with flowers and the whitest cloth and enough silver spoons and forks for us two to eat with. I can't have tin spoons on my palace table!"

So she had silver things from her mother and from her many friends at the Institute, and added to them, piece by piece, through the years. When her home was furnished, with a good many gaps where pretty things were going to be some day, yet dainty and attractive as far as it went, she hunted up people to give a good time in it.

She found them literally at her gate—the little black children turned out in the streets to shift for themselves while their mothers cooked or washed all day. Mrs. Barrett scrubbed them clean and told them stories and played games with them. In no time she had a whole kindergarten on her hands. Evenings she coaxed in the mothers and the young folks, who had so little chance for clean, happy fun in their lives, and some of the men. She formed clubs for all of them. While they were having a good time, she showed them all sorts of ways of better and healthier and happier living. By and by the "Palace of Delight" wasn't big enough to hold the people who flocked to it.

All this time Mrs. Barrett and her husband were saving money for a bathroom. She wouldn't have one until she could have the kind she wanted,— white-tiled, with a set-in tub, and a beautiful big bowl,—a bathroom to enjoy for a lifetime. It would cost several hundred dollars; and at last the money was ready. There was nothing to do but select the fixtures and engage the workmen, when in came, quite uninvited, the most disconcerting thought!

For a long time Mrs. Barrett had tried tremendously hard to get the mothers in her clubs to love cleanliness. You have to love it very much to keep your home and children clean when you wash or cook for other people all day and are tired out when you get home. Mrs. Barrett never had to work out, the mothers said; she had time to be clean, and they didn't. Now if she had a bathroom—a lovely, shining, white place with hot and cold water on tap instead of stone-cold in a well down the street, and a big porcelain tub instead of an old wash-tub to bathe in—oh, she could never do anything with them again! They would say,

"You don't know anything about our hard times —you with your comforts and conveniences. Let us alone!"

She thought about it a long time. She did so want that bathroom! She had dreamed about it so long! But at last she decided she wanted happiness more—everybody's happiness, which is the only real kind, though everybody doesn't know it yet. She talked it over with her husband, who always understood things, and they decided to spend the bathroom money on a community house to be built in their own yard. When the clubs gave entertainments, as they constantly did, the house wouldn't hold the people any more. They needed a great big room. And so, by love's magic, the bathroom became a house that was all one big room and could be used by turns for a kindergarten, a bad-weather play-ground, a club house, a gymnasium, a reading, assembly, concert, and lecture room—surely the most Protean bathroom ever known.

The work Mrs. Barrett was doing broadened until it touched the whole colored community. Teachers and students at Hampton helped, and many an Institute boy and girl found there inspiration for community service in their own far-off homes. Love is always like that—a seed that grows, bearing other seeds that fly on the winds of life to all sorts of unsuspected spots. The

"Palace of Delight" came true, too big for the walls of any one building to hold.

Mrs. Barrett's work did more than leaven the Negro community: it built a bridge between the races. Long before the women's federated clubs generally adopted "Clean-up Week," a civic-minded white woman of Hampton, a leader in social circles, planned a "Clean-up" for her town. She knew it would never be clean without the Negroes' help, and having heard of Mrs. Barrett's work, she asked her help with the colored people. Thus brought together, the two women became friends, with large consequences, as the sequel will show.

During these happy years, the colored club women of Virginia made Mrs. Barrett their state president. They had a small, struggling organization with a very few hundred members.

"And it will never be any bigger," thought the president, "until it does something together—something for somebody else and together."

Who needed happiness most? Girls needed it, surely; girls who grew up without care, either because their mothers were dead or because they had to work away from home all day so that their children grew up in the streets and never had any chance. Her heart had often ached over such girls. Sometimes they stole something—a trifle, usually, or they got into some other trouble the police had to notice. Then they were sent to jail and shut up with hardened criminals; not taught anything useful or good, but shut up where there was nothing to learn but sin. And yet they were just children who had had no chance. Couldn't the fortunate colored women of the clubs do something to help these girls? Perhaps the thought of her own two protected daughters helped her to see the need of these unfortunate girls who were neglected.

So she and all the club women went to work.

"We must show Virginia that colored women can be useful as citizens," said the president; "that we can and will serve our state in a worthwhile way. We will take this poor human wreckage that is such a dead loss and waste and turn it into an asset for the state."

They worked three years, that handful of women, and they raised $5,300. They bought a farm of a hundred and forty acres at Peake, eighteen miles from Richmond. Mrs. Barrett wrote Dr. Hart, head of the Child Welfare Department of the Russell Sage Foundation, for advice about plans for an industrial training school, and he gave her the best the Foundation had. The school was to be built on the cottage plan, that the girls might have the home life they had missed. The first cottage, built of concrete and brick, was for thirty girls and cost $8,000.

The women wanted the state to help. It did

nothing now for delinquent colored girls, and they wanted an appropriation for the building. To get it, they knew they must have white people on their board of trustees. So Mrs. Barrett went to the civic-minded white woman who believed in "clean-up week." She was interested at once. Soon she had secured the white half of the board —herself, and two Richmond women distinguished in club and social life, the rector of General Lee's old church in Richmond, a prominent business man, and one or two others. Mrs. Barrett secured Negroes equally well-known among their people for her half of the board; and then the white and colored women went together to the legislature. The committee agreed to recommend an appropriation of $3,000, and two white women promised $2,000 more.

It was about this time that Mrs. Barrett's great sorrow came. Her husband died. For twenty-five years they had lived in understanding love. One can only state the loss and leave it.

Dr. Hart wrote her that when the house at Peake was built, she ought to take charge of it herself. "You had the vision," he said; "you must go there and make it come true."

She showed the letter to a white friend in some indignation. "I go to Peake!" she exclaimed; "and leave my lovely home and my friends and all my pretty things—to eat in an institution dining-room off thick plates with tin forks! Of

course I'm going to work for it harder than ever;
but to live there!"

Her friend looked at her a minute and then said
quietly, "Of course, if you don't feel you ought
to go, that settles it."

Somehow she could not get away from these
words. Then came a telegram from Richmond.
The legislature, about to pass the appropriation,
had received a protest from the white people of
the Peake community; they didn't want the school
there. "The legislature won't give the money
in the face of this protest," telegraphed one of
the white women trustees. "What shall I do?"

Mrs. Barrett answered, "Beg them to give us
one chance—to try us. If the school proves ob-
jectionable, I promise to move it."

"That settled me," she said, laughing a little
as she told the story. "I had promised to move it,
and I wasn't going to move it, so it was up to
me to make it succeed. I went there to live, and
I've been there ever since."

"You must miss your home," it was suggested.

She looked sober for a minute and then laughed.

"Oh, well, I carried my silver spoons—and
sometimes, on grand occasions, I use them. My
two girls have been so sweet about it. And the
other girls—did you notice when you went over
the place any difference between the girls in the
new cottage—the fifty-nine new-comers—and the
honor girls in the first cottage?"

"I certainly did," was the reply. "The honor girls had a look—it was as though something inside of them had waked up."

"That's it," she cried. "That's it exactly! Their souls wake up. There is scarcely a girl there who isn't a Christian, and their lives and their work show it. We fail sometimes; but when our girls go out on parole they nearly all make good. Most of them go out to service—until they marry. They all know how to make a good home when they leave us. Some of them win scholarships in good schools and become teachers. Some of our old girls teach here now."

During the World War Mrs. Barrett had a surprise. One afternoon when she was out, a party of white people came from Washington, inspected everything on the place, and went off. Soon after, there came from the federal government an offer of $20,000 to enlarge the place for work among the colored girls around the Virginia camps, if the state would give $20,000 to match it. The state did, promptly, and two buildings were erected which were crowded all during the war.

The first cottage is the "honor cottage" to which the best girls are promoted with privileges after proving their trustworthiness. The girls in this honor cottage are those whose faces showed so plainly the spirit which had been kindled within them. In the white uniforms which they are allowed to wear on Sundays and special occasions, they are a happy, promising looking group.

The third building is a big one, midway between the other two, and still little more than a shell. It was a crowded dormitory in war days, a real emergency building, where many a neglected girl obtained shelter and care and a start toward better things. It is used now for class-rooms, for entertainments, and for industries. Eventually it will be finished and equipped in a manner worthy of the great commonwealth to which it belongs. This faith which Virginia has in the work the school is doing was strikingly shown two or three years ago when the state legislature passed the following resolution:

Whereas, it has come to the knowledge of the General Assembly that most valuable and important services have been rendered by the colored women of the State of Virginia, known and organized as the "Virginia State Federation of Colored Women's Clubs," and

Whereas, this organization originated, raised funds for, and established an institution for the reform of wayward colored girls in the establishment of the Industrial Home School at Peake, Hanover County, Virginia, which has met with signal success and performed services of reform and conservation at this vital time, when all the services of all the people are so sorely needed,

Therefore, be it resolved, by the House of Delegates, the Senate concurring, that the services and sacrifices on the part of these citizens be recognized, and that this resolution express our appreciation of this work looking to the betterment of the morals of the State of Virginia.

Certainly Mrs. Barrett has made good. Of the white neighbors who feared to have such an institution come among them, not one can be found to-day who is not a warm friend of the school. In the state, appreciation of the work has so grown that support of it, at first entirely borne by the colored women, and then shared by them and the state, has been entirely taken over by the state.

But that isn't the whole story. Loving-kindness is a very contagious thing. Down in South Carolina the State Commissioner of Charities and Correction heard of Peake, and so did the colored women's clubs. They decided that the colored women should begin a similar work in their state, the Commissioner to help them in every way he could. Accordingly, the South Carolina colored women started a school. They have run it now for two years, and they have done so well with it that if it had not been for the after-the-war money troubles of the country and the farmers' losses in cotton, the state would probably have taken it over before this. But even though that step must wait, the white people are helping in other ways.

So good work spreads. As time goes on, there will be more schools and fewer prisons everywhere because people will see more and more clearly that the just and sensible thing to do is to take care of the children who have had no chance, and more people will understand the responsibility their own opportunities have placed upon them.

VII

A BUILDER OF PROSPERITY

IN Nottoway County, Virginia, in a little country village lives John Pierce, a man who serves his country in eight states. He is a Negro, and his service is primarily to his own people; yet it is of scarcely less importance to white people than to his own race.

The reasons for this fact are plain. All merchants are helped when ill-housed, poorly-clad, underfed people become able to buy lumber and plumbing and electric lights and screens and rugs and furniture, to build and furnish comfortable homes. The grocers and butchers and dry-goods men make more money when those who have been poor become able to buy plenty of good food and comfortable clothes. They will soon want farm machinery, too, and automobiles and fertilizers and books and musical instruments and life and fire insurance—everything, in fact, that anybody in America makes a living by selling.

People who are prospering also have money to put in banks. If the government needs to borrow money, these people can lend it. The Negroes in the South were once an almost beggared folk, but during the World War, a single business company of Negroes, the Mutual Life Insurance Company of Durham, North Carolina, bought $300,000 worth of Liberty Bonds, a Negro in Louisiana bought $100,000 worth, a Negro farmer near Tuskegee, Alabama, who has made every cent of his money out of his land, gave his check for $20,000 worth of bonds at one time, and the Negroes altogether put $225,000,000 into Liberty Bonds and War Savings Stamps, besides giving great sums to the Red Cross. Was it not better for our government and our cause and for every kind of business in America, that these people were no longer the penniless slaves they had been sixty years before?

John Pierce was born in Greensboro, Alabama. His father, a devout Christian, was a brick-layer and a hard worker. His mother was a hard worker, too, and a Christian whose daily living impressed all who knew her. But despite hard work, the family was very poor. Not only were wages low, but there were ten children to feed and clothe, all healthy and hungry and as busy as only children can be in wearing out and outgrowing their clothes. It was a hard test, such poverty as theirs, yet they met it cheerfully and with much love for one another.

Their main trouble lay in how to get an education. In those days few colored people were prepared to teach, and in the long years of poverty in the South after the Civil War, there was very little money for schools for either white or black people. The colored schools would have been even poorer than they were, had the Negroes themselves not made sacrifices, sometimes little less than heroic, to eke out the school-money given by the county. John's mother, hard as she struggled, took the teacher to board at half what she was asked for board anywhere else, because she felt that the mere presence of a better-educated woman in the home would help her children to better ways of speech and a better outlook on life.

As soon as he was old enough, John followed the family tradition and went to work. By the time he was ten, he was helping his father lay bricks. Of course he had done other things before then. He had been "totin' chips" from the woodpile to the kitchen ever since he could walk, and "chopping cotton" in the little family patch, and picking it, too, from the time he was five or six. From the white folks' house to his mother's tubs and big iron pot in the back yard, he could carry on his head an amazing bundle of "washin'" all tied up in a sheet; and he could take it back again, snowy white, still on his head, but folded carefully in a big basket of "splits." John didn't mind the load, for he was proud to be trusted and to help.

Even when he was a little chap, he had friends among the white people and earned many a welcome nickel by running errands. His mother

JOHN B. PIERCE

taught her children to be honest and to work honestly, and for this reason people trusted them. They were thrifty, too. When they would earn a nickel or a dime, their mother taught them to save it. As a result, when John Pierce went to Tuskegee, he had money saved, and it helped him to get a start.

The same ambition that led his mother to take the school-teacher to board, was largely responsible for John's going to Tuskegee. Booker Washington came to Greensboro once when John was just a boy. His mother had heard something about the man who was helping so many Negro boys and girls, and she had him come and stay at her house that she might find out more about means of securing an education for her children. Mr. Washington told her all about Tuskegee, how boys and girls could work their way there even if they had no money. That settled things. John went to Tuskegee, and so did his sister and several of his brothers. The first year he was at school, his father died. He wanted to go home at once and take charge of things, but his mother would not hear of it. She told him to stay where he was and to make the most of his opportunity, that that was the best way to help her, and that she and the younger children would manage alone.

When John graduated, Mr. Washington recommended him as a teacher of brick-laying and other work at the Quaker school at High Point, North Carolina, where he taught for two years. One day he found on the ground some clay that would make brick. He and his pupils dug it out, used the excavation for a cellar, made the bricks, and built a dormitory with student labor.

At that time—it was while Cleveland was president—there was great business depression in the country. It was a very hard time for the Negroes. Grown men worked all day for fifty cents or even less; tenants could not make anything out of their cotton. They lived the year round on corn-pone and bacon, and the farmers they worked for had to advance them that. The cotton hardly paid in the fall for their poor food. They were sunk in a hopeless grind of drudgery, with not one comfort in life. John Pierce was greatly troubled. He knew there was a better way; he had seen it at Tuskegee. All those tenants could have raised vegetables for the year round if they had only known how, and they could have had chickens and ducks and eggs and could have lived well. And if they would learn how to do better farming, they could raise bigger crops and have enough even to sell some. Gradually they could live in real homes instead of huts, and they could educate their children and have money in the bank. He wanted to show them how.

But he knew he had to learn more himself before he could teach others. He had seen the farming at Tuskegee and knew what could be done; but he had not learned farming, his work having been in the trades. He had to know about analyzing the soil and building it up and rotating crops and a lot of things an agriculturist should know.

He took what money he had saved and went to Hampton. He partly worked his way there and worked in summer on the school farm. For three years he studied and finished all the post-graduate work in agriculture. Part of the time he was assistant instructor in the Whittier School gardens at Hampton, and after he graduated, he was instructor in the normal agricultural work, both in class and in the gardens for three years more. The head of the States Relations Service in Washington said his work was the best in school gardens in the United States.

In the spring of 1906 Mr. Pierce began to do the work he had been looking forward to. He went out from Hampton on extension work to near-by places—school gardens and farm demonstrations. The government had no farm demonstration work among Negroes then, but in the fall the General Education Board offered to pay the salaries of some Negro demonstration agents if the Department would select the men and take charge of their work. Mr. Pierce was made county agent and later state agent for colored work.

When he goes to a meeting which the county

agent has worked up, the district agent goes with him, and they have meetings for one or two or three days. They talk over the school situation and make plans to better it. They spray fruit trees and potatoes, make the proper kind of sweet-potato beds, test seeds and soils, and plant cotton and corn and tobacco in demonstration fields, explaining everything as they go. They test cattle for tuberculosis and immunize hogs from cholera. The farmers learn much better if they see the things actually done as well as hear that they should be done. They pull down a poor poultry house or an insanitary toilet and build it back again right. They show the people how to screen their houses, how to keep their water-supply pure, how to grow and store vegetables, how to grow flowers and make things attractive. They do not do all these things every time at every place, but as many as they can each time. Sometimes the people come from adjoining counties, and they all bring their problems and ask questions. The wives and children come too—especially the boys. Pig and corn clubs are started, in which the boys and girls make their own money and save it for schooling or to buy a little land. Often at these demonstrations the boys put on a ball game in the afternoon, and the girls of the canning clubs put on contests and games.

In telling of these things, Mr. Pierce said: "Yesterday I was over in a county where we've put on a special poultry campaign. We had about a hundred people—men, women, and children. We pulled down and reconstructed a chicken house, freed it of mites and the hens of lice, taught how to breed for better stock, how to feed for eggs, and how to keep eggs for winter. When the meeting was over, the women made lemonade, the boys and girls put on games, and we all had a social time. There'll be a new poultry record in that county after this, better fare on the tables, and more money for little comforts and conveniences in the homes.''

When America entered the War, and it was vital to speed up food production, Mr. Pierce was put in charge of the colored work in eight states —Maryland, Virginia, the Carolinas, West Virginia, Tennessee, Kentucky, and Arkansas. The extension work the Government had been doing for ten or twelve years was largely responsible for the intelligence, loyalty, and efficiency with which the Negroes responded to the country's call. It was largely responsible, too, for the good relations existing between the races. The white people see how much better it is in every way and for every one for the colored people to prosper, and they aid the work wherever it is established. In speaking of his work, Mr. Pierce said, ''I am just back from a meeting in Henderson, Tennessee, promoted by the cashier of the white bank. We had five hundred people out, a number of them white.

We often have white people, especially the county superintendent of education, and people of both races talk. It cultivates a friendly feeling; and the white people take an interest. Over in Henderson they're planning new buildings for our schools. Out in Arkansas, in Elaine, where the riots were, white people are employing colored farm demonstration agents. There was a meeting in Little Rock, too, and the governor and the secretary of state recognized the need of better state colleges of agriculture. They said the Negroes could count on having better provision made for them.''

The record of crop yields is an interesting commentary on John Pierce's life-work. Fifteen years ago the average yield of corn in Virginia was fifteen bushels per acre. Now it is forty bushels, and in the last five years men have often raised as high as seventy-five bushels per acre. Cooperation is growing, too. The white farmers are forming associations to market their crops better, and they admit the colored farmers on exactly the same terms as the white. That means more money for all the people and more friendliness, too. In Charlotte County the county association has put a colored farmer on the executive committee. The interracial committees also cooperate with the farmers.

The story of Wellville and Nottoway County, John Pierce's home territory, is another example of this man's ability and helpfulness to his country. Wellville is just a village, with Blackstone the nearest town. When Mr. Pierce went there in 1908 the schoolhouses were one-roomed log cabins; school ran five months; there were only "emergency" teachers in the whole county—those who have not even the lowest certificate. They each received twenty-five dollars a month the five months they taught.

The colored people bought some land and deeded it to the school board. The white people gave lumber, and the Negroes gave labor. They built a good one-roomed school, painted it, and fitted it out with patent desks. Such a school is now in every colored community in the county, with teachers holding first or second grade certificates. They run seven months of the year, and the teachers get fifty dollars a month.

Agricultural teaching and farm demonstration work have gone on all over the county. Corn production has risen from fifteen to seventy-five bushels an acre, and other crops have increased in the same way. The people put in "cover crops" to build up and preserve the soil; and they have vegetables the year round.

The houses used to be built of logs. Over seventy-five per cent of them have been rebuilt or remodeled, and painted or whitewashed. They all have sanitary outbuildings. Musical instruments are now in the homes, the people have better clothes, and they have money in the bank. The church at Wellville was poor and there was no way to baptize the people in it. It was remodeled, a baptistery was put in, and church finances were put on a business basis. The church is now used as a community center. At first the pastors of country churches thought it was not religious to use a church to talk about community health or to give community pleasure; but all that has changed in Nottoway—and in many other counties, also.

Mr. Pierce's extension work was the beginning of the County Training School at Blackstone. "We can't claim credit for all of it," he said, when asked about it. "We had co-operation from colored and white people too." The colored people raised a certain amount, and the county board promised so much more. The colored people agreed to employ at least five teachers, to have eight grades and an eight months' school, to have instruction in agriculture and home industries, and an elementary course in the art of teaching. As soon as possible, they were to add at least two years of high school work. That is the standard for a county training school; and where it is met, the Slater Fund and the General Education Board both cooperate with the county board and bear part of the expense. There is a fine school at Blackstone now, with seven or eight teachers, and they will never lack for good teachers in the county again. There are dormitories for those who live too far away to go back and forth, and land for school gardens and for pig and poultry and farm demonstration work.

By this time Dr. Knapp, of the Department of Agriculture at Washington, thought Mr. Pierce had done enough for the people in Virginia and wanted to get him down in the Gulf States. But the white people rose up and refused to let him go.

"The white people are good friends to us here in Virginia," said Mr. Pierce. "It is good for the colored people to feel safe. In Blackstone a colored man committed a horrible crime. The city officials feared a lynching and telegraphed the governor for troops, but the leading white men of the town got together, telegraphed the governor their pledge that the man should have a fair trial and asked him to let them guard Blackstone's good name. No troops were sent, and those white men guarded the jail and the courtroom until the trial was over and the prisoner lawfully executed. It made the colored people feel they could get justice there and a fair trial. They are buying homes and putting their money in the banks.

"My own boys are getting a start already. They go seven miles and back every day to school at Blackstone. In addition they each cultivate a piece of land and bank their money. This summer they cut fifteen tons of hay from their land and sold it for thirty dollars a ton."

Looking at the quiet, kindly face, peaceful with years of service, despite the many outward struggles, one wondered if there have been any very sharp inward struggles—temptations and difficulties that threatened to wreck his life.

"Why, of course," he said slowly in response to such a question. "Every one has temptations enough to prove his mettle. There have been those who would exploit the farmers, one way or another, and I could have made a good deal of money if I had agreed to help them in their schemes. But I—things like that never really mattered. You see, for all our family our mother has been—well, just a clear light before us. It was always so, and even the white people knew it. When I was a little fellow at Greensboro, another colored boy set on me one day in the street. I fought him off the best I could—he was bigger than I—and a policeman came along and took us both up to the city court. The judge sent the other boy to jail and told me to run along home. He said he knew my mother, and he knew how she raised her children. She was just like that."

"Did she live long enough to know anything about this work you are doing now?" he was asked.

His whole face lighted up. "Why, she's living now, down in Greensboro! I see her every now and then. All her children want her to live with them—we can all take good care of her; but she likes to stay on in the old home. So we all take care of her there and see her when we can. She knows all about my work.''

Thinking of one's own home and of those who grew to manhood and womanhood in it, one knows that the highest honor which can come to any woman is that she should be ''a clear light before'' her children. Ignorant she may have been, struggling on in grinding poverty through years of hardest work, but measured by God's standards, which are the only real ones, this colored mother had attained.

VIII

A WOMAN BANKER

ON a corner just a block from Broad Street, in Richmond, Virginia, stands a handsome three-story building of brick and stone which bears a tablet with the legend, "St. Luke's Penny Savings Bank. Established 1902." This is said to be the first bank in the country founded by a woman, and it is still one of the very few that have a woman president—the only bank founded or run by a colored woman.

St. Luke's Bank started with $25,000 of paid-up capital. This was afterwards increased to $50,000; and it has a surplus of $25,000 more. It has paid its stockholders a five per cent dividend steadily, regardless of panics and hard times; and once, during a severe money stringency, when the white banks of Richmond were unable to extend further loans to the city, this colored woman banker lent the city $100,000 in cash to carry on the public schools for both the white and black races.

How did the daughter of a colored laundress and one-time slave come to start a bank and guide it to success through twenty-one years filled with other important work? Something went before it, of course; not merely unusual ability, which she plainly has, but long, hard, faithful work in helping the poorer members of her race to win through in times of adversity and to get on their feet.

Mrs. Maggie L. Walker was born in Richmond. Her mother was Elizabeth Mitchell—a woman born a slave and unable to make a living for herself and her little girl except at the washtub. But what she could do, she did well, and her own lack of opportunity fixed in her the determination that her child should have a chance. What this determination cost the mother in toil and sacrifice one may not know,—washing was not a lucrative profession in those days in the South. But mother and daughter took their hardships cheerfully, and the girl did her best to lighten her mother's load so far as she could. When she was eighteen, she graduated from high school, and that fall became a teacher in one of the public schools. From that time to the present, one of her main purposes in life has been to make life easier for the mother to whose sacrifices she owes her first start toward better things.

Mrs. Walker was married when she was twenty and went into the business of home-making with the same joyful and energetic efficiency which had marked her work as a teacher. Her husband, a skilled workman, prospered, and with his wife's good management, they and their two little sons lived in comfort and began to prosper.

As the boys grew older and went to school, the mother found herself growing restless. She was well and strong, her home work was thoroughly organized and went like clock-work, her husband and the boys were away most of the day, and although her church work had grown considerably, she still had time on her hands for more work. "I felt like a spendthrift," she said, in speaking of this time. "I knew I had the energy to do a lot of things for my people that needed doing, and I felt I ought to be about it some way. Yet I didn't know what I could do or where to begin. I was restless and wanted work that was of some account."

Then her opportunity came—such a tiny one, apparently, that one could hardly have blamed her, had she refused it. But she had made it the rule of her life to do what she could with whatever came to her hand. That was one of the valuable lessons she learned from her mother, the laundress.

There was a little benefit society in Richmond—one of probably a dozen or two such. They are pathetically popular among Negroes, to whom sickness is a catastrophe such as only the poorest people can fully comprehend. This particular society was the Independent Order of St. Luke. It collected small weekly dues from its members, of whom at that time it had a thousand. If they fell ill, it paid them a certain sum weekly. If they died, a death benefit was paid which provided for the funeral expenses, thus saving the family from what is often, among the very poor, a crushing burden of debt.

Mrs. Walker was offered the secretaryship of this society at the munificent salary of eight dollars a month. She was to collect dues, verify cases of illness and of death, keep the books, and pay out all sums due.

She accepted the opportunity at once. The Order might be a small one—for an Order, but looking after a thousand members did seem a job to keep one busy, and it certainly helped the people it reached. As soon as she had the work at her fingers' ends, however, she began reaching out. If the Order helped a thousand, why shouldn't it help twenty thousand—fifty—a hundred thousand? Why should it confine itself to giving help in trouble? Why couldn't it train people to help themselves in time of health to save, to invest, to win their way to economic independence? Why couldn't it get hold of the children and teach them thrift, build up self-control and forethought in their careless little souls, and start them on the path to success before they should form habits of self-indulgence and waste? Why, it could do all that! And it should, and it would. So it has done and still does to-day.

There are now a hundred thousand members of the Order in twenty-one states, seventy-five thousand of whom have held their membership long enough to be entitled to benefits if they become ill or die. Five dollars a week is paid in case of sickness; and from one hundred to five hundred dollars, according to the amount of dues paid, in case of death. There is over $70,000 cash in the emergency fund—a fund that didn't exist when Mrs. Walker took charge. A hundred and forty field workers are employed, and forty-five clerks are in the home office. The assets of the Order amount to $360,000. A handsome office building has been put up at 900-904 St. James Street, Richmond, costing $100,000. It provides ample office space for the work of the Order, a large auditorium, a number of rooms for club and lodge meetings, a large supply department where the badges, regalia, account books, and so forth, of the Order are manufactured and sent out, and a complete printing establishment with two linotype machines. Here the *St. Luke's Herald,* another of Mrs. Walker's enterprises, is printed and goes out to its big constituency. It gives full reports of the Order's business, stories of members, both children and adults, who are getting ahead financially or doing anything else worth while, suggestions for meetings, and sound teaching in regard to health, thrift, morals, and education. It goes to city and country, to educated and ignorant. To scores of thousands of unprivileged Negroes it is giving inspiration and a horizon.

Office force of the Independent Order of St. Luke, of which Mrs. Walker is the head

It was because of all this rapidly extending work that Mrs. Walker felt the need of a bank. In 1902 she started one and built a home for it a few blocks away from the headquarters building. In 1920 this bank had nearly six thousand depositors and resources of over half a million dollars.

This does not, however, nearly represent the thrift work of St. Luke's. Over fifteen thousand children who are members, scattered through many states, meet weekly with a regular program which includes Bible instruction and lessons in thrift and in hygiene. Each child is given a cardboard "rainy-day bank"; as soon as he has a dollar, the leader encourages him to put it in a regular savings bank just as is done with adult members. These savings, for the most part, find their way to local white banks, the Richmond institution serving only adjacent territory.

"When any of our girls is advanced to making as much as fifty dollars a month," said Mrs. Walker, "we begin to persuade them to buy a home. As soon as they save enough for the first payment, the bank will help them out. There is a woman in the office here who came to us eighteen years ago. She did odd jobs of cleaning, and we paid her a dollar a week, which she was glad to get. But we encouraged her to fit herself for better things. She studied, took a business course at night-school, and has worked her way up until now she is our head bookkeeper, with a salary of one hundred and fifty dollars a month. She owns a nice home, well furnished and fully paid for, and has money in the bank.

"Then there was that one-legged little bootblack at Second and Clay streets. He joined our Order. He had a rented chair out on the sidewalk in the weather. We helped him save, and when he had fifty dollars, we helped him rent a little place with three chairs. That was seven years ago. Now he has a place of his own with twelve chairs. He has bought a home for his mother—paid $1,900 for it—and has it furnished and free of debt. And his bank account never falls below five hundred dollars.

"Numbers of our children have bank accounts of from one hundred to four hundred dollars. They sell papers, cut grass, do chores, run errands, work in stores Saturdays. We teach them to save with the definite purpose of wise use of the money. We try to give them a sense of moral responsibility for its wise use. Of course we can't do that without religious teaching. We teach them the Lord's Prayer and the Ten Commandments, the words of Christ, and some of the Psalms. We try to connect these things with every-day living and to show them that part of their duty in becoming independent is getting where they can help others.

"We do a good deal of the same kind of work with the grown people. Our bank lends money for home-building at six per cent, and we tide the deserving ones over times of trouble. Six hundred and forty-five homes have been entirely paid for through our bank's help.''

All this really does look like work enough for one woman, with the travel it involves through nearly half the states of the Union, the constant speaking, writing, and oversight of so many activities.

Besides these business interests there is Mrs. Walker's church work, which includes her local church and Sunday-school, and her position as one of the trustees of the Woman's Auxiliary of the National Baptist Convention.

But Mrs. Walker's social service work is enough for a story in itself. Through her club affiliations, she became deeply interested in Mrs. Barrett's school at Peake. She organized in Richmond a Council of Women with fourteen hundred members, which did yeoman service in raising the first five thousand dollars to buy the farm at Peake and has ever since given liberally to all the needs of the school. Mrs. Walker is one of the colored members of the school's bi-racial board of trust. As a result of this work for Peake came the community work in Richmond.

''The white women of Richmond began it,'' she said. ''You know what some of them have done here—women who stand at the top socially and who are leaders in the church and the club life of the city and state. They had done fine community work for white people, and at length they went to our preachers and asked them to invite their leading women to a conference. As a result, we began some forms of community work. Then a white philanthropist who gave the white women a house for a working girls' home said that if we colored women would show our interest in social work among our people by raising a thousand dollars for it, he would give us the use of a large house, and if we made good, he would deed it to a board of white and colored women for colored work.

"You know we had to make good after that. We raised the thousand dollars, and we have kept right on. The house has been deeded now to our bi-racial board. The white women don't work for us,—they work with us; and they've helped us to connect up with every charitable organization in the city. We have four paid workers, and the Community House is just such a center of influence as we have needed all these years."

Of Mrs. Walker's interest in this work, her grasp of the problems it touches, and her willingness to spend and be spent in it, the white women of the joint board speak with high praise. Here, as at Peake, and as a trustee of Miss Burroughs' school at Washington, she shows her concern especially for the young womanhood of her race.

When Mrs. Walker, who is a literal believer in

the injunction to keep one hand in ignorance of what the other does, told Miss Burroughs that she ought not to have put her name over the building she gave to the National Training School, Miss Burroughs replied,

"You ought not to feel that way. It helps those girls there struggling for an education to know that a successful woman like you cares about them; and the thought of your success is an inspiration to them to try harder to succeed, themselves. And better than all, it's an object-lesson to teach them that the finest use of success is to serve others."

When asked about the new laundry at the Washington school and the ten thousand dollars Miss Burroughs so urgently needed for it soon, the banker trustee said placidly:

"She'll get it. She always does. Nannie Burroughs sits down there in her office when she wants some money and writes off a letter. Then she mimeographs it and sends it to our people all over the country. If you read the first line, you finish it; and by the time you finish it, your money is as good as out of your pocket into hers. There's nothing to do but to send her what she asks for. Don't you worry about that laundry; it's all right, and she is too."

One can but be impressed with the way Mrs. Walker, Mrs. Barrett, and Miss Burroughs work together. Their personalities are markedly different, their gifts differ, their calls to service lead them along divergent lines. Yet each is among the most notable present-day women of their race; and their friendship and cooperation, their hearty faith in one another's work, the absence of petty self-consciousness and the rivalry which springs from it are beautiful to see.

Mrs. Walker's two sons, grown men now, are closely associated with her in her business. They talk things over together; and sometimes, when a decision in some matter is hard to come by, the boys discuss it between themselves. Such talks are liable to end with:

"Has Mother been praying over this thing?"

"Why, of course she has."

"Well, there's no need to worry then. I notice when Mother prays things do straighten out."

That is really the secret of all these women's power. They are all women of unusual endowment; but they are also women of faith and prayer.

IX

"A COMPOSER BY DIVINE RIGHT"

IF Harry Burleigh's musical gift had been less genuine, it might have been smothered out by the difficulties of his life, for this composer-to-be was born and reared in deep poverty, with the added handicap of Negro blood.

In that blood, however, there was a strain of courage and determination the boy might well be proud of. His grandfather, Hamilton Waters, was an escaped slave who became blind as a result of the hardships which he endured. Yet blind, he worked on down to a ripe old age, supporting himself and aiding as far as he could his children.

His daughter Elizabeth, Harry's mother, was born near Lansing, Mich., in a wagon in which her parents were trying to make their way into Canada. Perhaps it was her baby needs which changed their plans for they did not cross the border, but turned aside and settled in Erie, Pennsylvania. Here the blind father set himself to provide for his family.

Whether through independence or through friendlessness—perhaps through both—the father set up in business for himself as a presser of men's clothing. For this, he needed only an iron and a board and the wise touch of fingers which serve the blind for eyes. He brought character to his work and the will to succeed.

For many years Harry's grandfather was also the town crier, a position not to be obtained nowadays when an extra paper is printed at any hour of the day that anything unusual happens. In those days, newspapers, even the biggest of them, were printed but once a day, and those issued in small places, but once a week. If anybody died, the town crier went through the streets ringing his bell and telling the hour of the funeral. If an important meeting was to be held, he told that. He carried the news of any outside happening that was of importance to the community or to the world at large. But it was hard work tramping the streets in all weathers, and did not bring in very much money. Yet by the time the baby born in the wagon had grown up and finished high school, her father was able, by what sharp self-denial one can guess, to send her to college. She graduated, only to find that no place was open to her to do the work for which she had fitted herself. The Civil War was not yet over, and neither North nor South had any place for educated colored people. She married later and had five children. One, born in 1866, was christened Henry Thacker and grew up to become known as Harry T. Burleigh, singer and composer.

While he was still a little fellow, Harry's father

died, and his mother had to go out from her home to win bread for her children. She took the only kind of work open to her and became janitress of a public school. It was poorly paid work, and it was all she and her father could do to keep the wolf from the door. As soon as they could, the children worked too. From the time he was big enough to do anything at all, Harry sold papers and ran errands and did any odd chores he could find to do. Later he was employed as a lamplighter. Boys and girls of to-day are used to the flashing on of electricity in a moment, but not so very many years ago oil lamps lighted the smaller cities, and even New York and London were lighted at night by dim gaslights. As each lamp had to be lighted by hand, quite an army of boys and men found employment in lighting them at dusk and turning them out at dawn.

During these years, the boy was going to public school. Children, then as now, were taught singing in school, and here it was discovered that Harry had quite a wonderful voice. His teachers took great pains with him. The gift which God had given him began to grow and blossom until a passionate love for music filled his soul.

His mother, like her son, was eager to do any extra work which would bring more money to the family purse; and being both intelligent and highly trained, she was in demand to help in serving at large entertainments in the homes of wealthy people of Erie. In this capacity she was frequently employed by a lady who brought to her home for the entertainment of her friends many distinguished musical artists. Harry's mother would tell the boy when a recital was to be given, and he would stand outside, often in bitter cold weather, in the hope of hearing some of the masters of the art he so loved. One day his mother told him that the great Joseffy was coming. That night he stood outside the windows of Mrs. Russell's home, the snow up to his knees, drinking in the great artist's magic. He barely escaped pneumonia as a result of this experience. To prevent the repetition of such an illness, his mother told her employer the story; and after that, when Mrs. Russell gave a concert for her friends, Harry was inside, opening the door to guests.

Mme. Carreño was one of the artists whom he heard in this way, and with her at Mrs. Russell's home was Mrs. MacDowell, the mother of the American composer. Harry saw and remembered Mrs. MacDowell, and years afterward she played an important part in his life.

Through his school singing the boy's voice became known to a number of people. From the time he was sixteen, he sang in church choirs in Erie on Sunday and in the Jewish synagogue on Saturday. He went to school until he was twenty, always working hard outside of school hours and in vacation. In summer, as he grew older, he worked on the big lake steamers. But all the money he could earn was far from enough for what he wanted, and the desire of his heart seemed destined to remain a dream. He studied stenography and worked at that until he was twenty-six years old.

Then he heard that the National Conservatory of Music in New York City had, through its president, Mrs. Jeannette M. Thurber, offered some scholarships, and he decided to try for one of them. He came to New York and sang before a committee of judges, Joseffy himself being one. There was some question of his winning a scholarship, but when he sought out the registrar of the conservatory, he recognized her as Mrs. Mac-Dowell and gave her a letter of recommendation which Mrs. Russell had written for him. She turned the scale in his favor and during his four years of study was his unfailing friend. She gave him clerical work in her office and helped him in every way she could.

Dvorák, greatest of Bohemian composers, was the director of the conservatory, the faculty of which was composed of famous men. Dvorák was interested in the eager student and gave him much of his time outside of class hours. Burleigh copied many of his orchestral compositions for him. He also played and sang for Dvorák the old Negro "spirituals." These weird and beautiful melodies made a deep impression on the great composer, who wove one of them into one of his greatest compositions, the "New World Symphony."

Burleigh studied hard during these four years, developing his splendid voice and learning harmony and counterpoint under men who were real masters. But always there was the struggle for daily bread. His scholarship covered only his tuition. Odd jobs and chores were still necessities to supply food and clothes. His mother, firm in her belief in her boy's great gifts, found ways to help him out, as mothers will. What he could not have, he did without, and there was no complaint or self-pity. The first summer after he came to New York, he went to Saratoga and worked in a hotel; but by the next summer his voice was becoming known, and he went again to Saratoga for the vacation months, this time as baritone soloist in an Episcopal church. The worst was now behind him. Since that time, while he has worked hard, he has been doing work he loves and is fitted for. Later years have brought him the rewards of work well done. His early struggles and privations have left not the slightest touch of bitterness on his spirit. He went through them all and conquered them with that best of all courage which carries good cheer high, like a guidon.

In 1894, when the position of baritone soloist became vacant in St. George's Episcopal Church in New York, one of the largest churches in the city, Mr. Burleigh applied for the position. He was the only Negro among the sixty applicants, but he had the voice wanted, and Dr. Rainsford, the rector, and the vestrymen did not think the color of his skin should rule him out of serving with it in God's house. For twenty-eight years he has remained a member of this choir. For twenty-two years he has sung also in Temple Emanu-El, one of the largest synagogues of the city.

Burleigh's voice became known far and wide, and work crowded in upon him. He undertook the training of choirs in a number of churches in New York and its vicinity, doing the work with such modest courtesy and yet with such ability and success that each effort added to his reputation. His voice was beautiful, rich, full, and musical to the last vibration, and it had been splendidly trained. He was soon in demand at concerts and at private musicales. Several European tours were arranged for him, and for years his annual vacations were spent abroad, where he sang in England and on the continent with great and increasing success. He sang for King Edward VII, who greatly admired his voice, and for many of the other crowned heads of Europe. But the real test of his ability was the power of his voice to move all kinds of people in the mixed audiences of great cities. Measured by that standard, he sang greatly.

It is as a singer that he classifies himself. "A composer?" he says, when his musical works are spoken of. "Oh, no. Just a few songs I've done, and practically no orchestration. My life has been spent as a singer—is spent that way now. I cannot lay claim to the name of composer."

But many musicians of rank disagree with him. He has composed the music for about a hundred songs and several festival anthems for choruses, and he has written the scores for a volume of Negro "spirituals" which are not the least of his achievements.

These old Negro melodies were sung, as all Southern people know, by groups of slaves and were without any instrumental accompaniment. So sung, by hundreds of voices, their beauty fills the heart and makes words difficult. One feels them, and in them the faith and aspiration of a race. They may be heard in perfection at Hampton, Tuskegee, and Fisk University, and at many of the Negro schools of the South. But except for the occasional tours of some small group of Negro singers in the North, until recently they were seldom heard outside the Southern states. Yet some of the world's leading musicians and composers agree that these melodies are America's most distinctive gift to the music of the world. For a long time Southern people thought lightly of this treasure. Many of them regarded Negro songs as a joke, and laughed

over them until the Negroes themselves grew half
ashamed of their wonderful melodies and tried
above everything to "sing like white folks."

But with time came a broader view of the unique
place of Negro music in the world of art. Among
white people, those who laughed were silenced by
those whose hearts had always been moved by the
weird and haunting melody of Negro songs. Before they dropped into oblivion, white and Negro
scholars and musicians began to collect them and
teach them to the rising generation. Mr. Burleigh's contribution to this movement, of such
value to America and the world, has been the setting of the old melodies to a musical accompaniment so that they may be sung anywhere, by any
singer, just as other songs are sung.

It was, owing to the very nature of the music,
a most difficult thing to do, and perhaps no man
not a Negro, however gifted, would have dared to
attempt it. But Mr. Burleigh has done it su-
premely well. "Each composition," says a musical authority, "is a classic in itself." Their success is attested by the famous singers who to-day
use Burleigh's settings of the "spirituals."
Perhaps the most famous of this well-known
group of songs is "Deep River"; but it is hard to
select where all are of merit.

One of Burleigh's finest pieces of work, according to musical critics, is "Ethiopia Saluting the
Colors," a setting of Walt Whitman's poem. An-

other noted song is his setting of Rupert Brooke's sonnet, "The Soldier." "Jean" has been sung by thousands of people here and abroad, and also "The Young Warrior," a wonderful setting of the war song of a Negro poet, James Weldon Johnson. The words themselves are noble:

> Mother, shed no mournful tears,
>   But gird me on my sword;
> And give no utterance to thy fears,
>   But bless me with thy word.
>
> Now let thine eyes my way pursue
>   Where'er my footsteps fare;
> And when they lead beyond thy view
>   Send after me a prayer.
>
> Still, pray not to defend from harm,
>   Nor danger to dispel;
> But rather, that with steadfast arm
>   I fight the battle well.
>
> Pray that I keep, through all the days,
>   My heart and purpose strong,
> My sword unsullied, and always
>   Unsheathed against the wrong.
>
> The lines are drawn, the fight is on,
>   A cause is to be won;
> Mother, look not so white and wan:
>   Give Godspeed to thy son.

The music stirs the blood. There is in it a very passion of patriotic fervor and sacrifice. That it was sung all over America and France by our Negro troops is no wonder. It swept Italy like a flame; the soldiers of the Italian army sang

Photo by Mishkin, New York

HARRY T. BURLEIGH

it on the battlefield, and their people sang it at home. Zandonai, a notable Italian composer, wrote an orchestration for it, that the song might pour from thousands of throats with the full power of the instruments behind it. One musical critic has said that it is "one of the few really admirable songs America has produced in recent years."

One of Mr. Burleigh's greatest successes has been his music for a song by Walter Brown, "Little Mother of Mine." John McCormack sang this with tremendous effect in the New York Hippodrome before "the largest audience ever seen in America's largest playhouse." A thousand people sat on the stage behind the singer for want of room in the house. At the close of the song the audience rose in an ovation, and McCormack insisted that Burleigh, who sat near him, should go forward with him to acknowledge the applause.

"You went, of course," he was asked.

He shook his head. "I couldn't. I couldn't. But he sang it wonderfully."

The songs are not all. There are "Southland Sketches," four compositions for the violin which have won high praise; and orchestrations for some of the songs arranged as choruses. The "Five Songs of Laurence Hope" are counted among his best work.

Harry Burleigh is still a singer with a voice which is a joy to hear. But he is a composer, too;

those who know his work agree with Kramer, who calls him "a composer by divine right." Concerning this, his publisher has also a word to say.

"He has done remarkable things," said he; "things which would have been remarkable in a man who began with everything in his favor and had no such fight to make as Burleigh had. But he has so much more in him. If only some one had had the vision, in Burleigh's youth, to set him free from that long struggle for mere existence and make it possible for him to spend his strength in the work he was made for, he would rank with MacDowell himself. One must have time for symphonies, months and years; and they bring in no ready money. America, and the whole world of art, is the poorer because Burleigh had to fight for his daily bread so long."

But Burleigh himself only smiles at this. "I had my living to make," he says. "I am like other people, I must do the best I can with what I have and not cry for what I can't get."

He is the musical editor for the American branch of the Ricordi house. No piece of music is submitted to them which does not pass through his hands and rest its fate on his judgment. But with all his success as a singer, composer, and judge of music, Harry Burleigh is as modest, as simple, as unspoiled as the boy who stood knee-deep in snow to catch a strain of the music he so loved.

X

A LIGHT IN A DARK PLACE

MARTHA DRUMMER was born in a little Georgia town. Her people were very poor, and her father's death left the family an added burden of poverty. She had two sisters, and while they were still small, their mother moved to Griffin, a larger town, where there was a better school. For poor and ignorant though she was, this colored mother planned the best her love could compass for her girls, love and the spirit of sacrifice being God's common gifts to the mothers of all the world. She worked and pinched to keep her girls in the public school, and of course they helped by working in vacation, even when they were little.

Martha finished the sixth grade—no small achievement under the circumstances. Then, she "hired out," as is said in the South, to white folks, and began at the age of twelve or thirteen to support herself.

But two things had happened to her: meager though it was, her schooling had awakened a bright mind, and she was athirst for an education; and her soul had wakened too, so that she wanted the education as a means of better service to God and her fellows. It seemed like wanting the rainbow, but she wanted it, and the Lord knew how great her desire was.

There were schools in the South for just such girls as Martha. The Southern white people hardly realize yet what the schools for Negroes opened in the South by the Northern churches after the war have done for the development both of the Negroes and the South. There were bitter years in which both races lost their old trust in one another; and a time of such poverty that adequate schools for white children were impossible, and little was done for Negroes. If the Northern Christians had not stood in the breach, bringing opportunity to gifted Negroes and a chance to many more of fair ability, the race would have been leaderless during most critical times, a prey to every evil influence. What would be the relations of the races to-day without the lives and influence of men like Booker Washington, Dr. Moton, Isaac Fisher, George Haynes, Bishop Clinton, John Hope, Bishop Jones, Archdeacon Russell, John Gandy, and scores and scores more —ministers, teachers, doctors, business men, who have taught their people higher ways of living for mind and body and soul!

The South is spending thousands of dollars now where it scarcely spent hundreds in the lean years for Negro education. But for many years there were no Negro teachers worthy the name except those trained by the Northern churches. They sent out such women as Miss Lucy Laney, Miss Georgia Washington, Mrs. Julia Harris, Mrs. Charlotte Brown, Mrs. Washington—one is perplexed about naming any of so great a company because of the many who must be omitted. All over the South these women have built character and industry and Christian service, a blessing to white and black alike.

There was a school, therefore, for Martha Drummer. Dr. Thirkield, who is now Bishop Thirkield, was at that time in charge of the theological department of Clark University. At one time when he visited Griffin to preach to the Negroes, Martha's pastor told him about her. Dr. Thirkield went to see her and was impressed, as the pastor had been, by her unusual promise. Maybe the twinkle in her eyes helped, for, as good judges of human nature know, a keen sense of kindly fun and humor is a pretty good indication of brains and force, and Martha's eyes have twinkled all her life. Dr. Thirkield secured a tuition scholarship for her, and she went to Atlanta to enter the preparatory school at Clark.

The first year, she worked for a family who gave her time during school hours to attend her classes; but she needed more time for study. She so clearly showed her worth that the second year a way was made for her to live at the girls' dormitory. She worked on Saturdays and taught school in vacation. By hard economy, she eventually graduated from Clark.

One of her teachers relates that when she first entered the dormitory, she would cause outbreaks of laughter during study hour by her comical "asides" on the lessons. But her teacher soon found that what she said was not only funny, but that it set the girls to thinking, so that she always had better lessons from them the days after Martha had bubbled over.

Her sense of humor sometimes helped her to shrewd decisions in a tight place. One summer she had in her vacation school seven or eight children from one family. In those days the county schools had very short terms, which the colored parents lengthened by paying the teacher themselves by the week or month after the public term was over. When Martha called on the mother of this numerous brood for her first payment, she was told that in that family school bills were always paid in a lump at the end of the term, and knowing the woman to be prosperous, well able to pay the money all at once, she waited. But at the end of the term she was calmly told that her patron had no money at all and could not pay a cent. Martha knew this was not true. She also knew that she had earned her money, and that she had to have it. So she borrowed a horse and wagon and a rope and drove out to the woman's home. Her eyes must have danced on the way, though she looked as solemn as possible when she arrived. The woman was more than solemn, she "was plumb worried to death," she said, "but she didn't have nary a cent to pay—not one."

"Never mind," said Martha kindly, "some of your farm products will do. I would just as soon have a couple of pigs. I'm sure I can sell them, and don't you worry another minute."

The pigs were all over the yard, so the woman could not possibly say she didn't have "nary a pig." Martha caught two, got them into the wagon and tied them, the woman looking on, petrified. Martha bade her a cheerful good-evening and started off; but before she got to the big road, the woman came to life. She couldn't lose all that bacon and sausage, to say nothing of hams and "chitlin's"! She found a purse or an old stocking in no time and ran after the teacher hotfoot. They had a pleasant chat down by the gate. The pigs went home with their mistress, while Martha went home, her eyes dancing more than ever, with her hard-earned money in her pocket.

She wanted to be a foreign missionary. There was need at home, she knew, but out in Africa were millions who had never heard of a God of love; millions who knew no comfort of body or mind or soul. Whoever helped them must give up home and friends and comfort. When one really sees the need, things which to most people seem essential do not matter; and Martha Drummer saw.

She took the two years' deaconess course at the Methodist women's training school in Boston, and then the three years' course for a nurse. In February, 1906, she was ready to go. She was sent to Quessua, Angola, West Africa, where there was only one colored missionary in the province—Miss Susan Collins, at the Quessua orphanage and to her village and school Miss Drummer was assigned.

Being a missionary in Africa is a pretty sharp test of one's desire to serve, and Quessua is no exception to this rule. It is in Angola, down on the West Coast, in the temperate zone, 3,500 feet above sea-level. If the swamps could be drained, it would be a pleasant country. The village takes its name from a little stream which springs from the foot of Mount Bango near by. Several native villages are close around, but the nearest post-office and telegraph and railroad stations are at Melange, six miles away. When Miss Drummer first went out, the railroad stopped eighty-five miles away, and that distance had to be traveled in a hammock slung on poles carried by native bearers. This seemed to Miss Drummer a selfish way of traveling, so she tried to walk; but she found it a dangerous thing for one unaccustomed to the climate to attempt. She couldn't afford to waste the years and the money her preparation had cost by killing herself with dengue fever as soon as she reached Africa. The porters, trained for generations in such work, and quite at home in the African sun, had no trouble at all in carrying her.

At length she was set down in the Quessua orphanage of the Methodist Women's Foreign Mission Society. It was a low, small, crowded building, with none of the conveniences or comforts to which she had grown accustomed in her years of training; but neither she nor Miss Collins, her fellow-worker, ever mentioned these facts. They were working among savage folk, all of whom lived in poverty and need. Even to-day many of the villagers have no clothing except the skins of wild animals; and many more wear loin cloths or a few yards of cheap cotton wound about their bodies. Those who manage to get something more like our clothes are without any of the comforts of life, as we think of comforts. Miss Collins and Miss Drummer hated to have so much more than the poor people they had come there to help, so they never told of the discomforts. It was not until one of the white women sent out by the Board went there and wrote back about what these colored women were putting up with that any one at home knew. A comfortable two-story home, with plenty of room, was then built for them, and they could not help enjoying it.

But though their home is at the foot of the

mountain in this high country and commands a
beautiful view, it is neither as healthful nor as
comfortable as it would be in a different climate.
The heavy African rains pour down for months
until the land is saturated with water, and every
valley and little hollow becomes a marsh. Here
insect pests breed by millions, carrying not only
grave discomfort, but disease and even death. So
heavy are the rains that it takes nearly the whole
of the dry season for the swamps to disappear.
Then the rains come again, and the marshes begin
once more to form.

Not long after Miss Drummer reached Quessua
an epidemic of fever broke out. She herself
nursed thirty-eight cases, bringing thirty-seven
back to health. The suffering from disease, so
much of it preventable, and from the ignorance
which makes sickness even more dangerous, she
still finds among the hardest things to bear. In
her trips through the heathen villages, she takes
as many simple remedies as she can, never knowing what she may have to face. On a recent trip
she heard a baby screaming with pain. The child
was ill, and the mother had sent for the witch-
doctor, the only doctor she had ever known about.
He had cut the baby's head in ugly gashes and
given the mother a mixture of green leaves boiled
together to rub into the wounds. Poor ignorant
soul! She sat there torturing her baby in the
belief that she was doing the only thing that could

save its life. Another baby had a great boil on its neck which would not come to a head until Miss Drummer's magic salve brought relief. The mother was sure the owner of the magic stuff was a god. The witch-doctors were the most wonderful of human beings, she knew; and no witch doctor could do a thing like that; it must be the work of a god!

After five years in Africa Miss Drummer wrote to a friend, "I hardly think you could enjoy the hardships here. I fit in like a cup in a saucer; but you see I've always had things hard. . . . I'm not reaping where another has sown, so I'm getting a taste of real heathenism. They think it folly to teach a woman anything but farm work. They think we ought to give them presents for letting us feed and teach a girl. . . . You have no conception of their heathenish customs. . . . I am glad from my soul that I came. Last Sunday I spoke to over two hundred people in one yard. We have all our services at the mission station in the morning, so the afternoon can be used for village work. All my services are outdoors.

"My regular work is in the orphanage with forty girls. This is our family. My co-worker has spent twenty-one years in Africa. She is a fine house-mother. We have six children under six years and two just on their legs for the first time and into all sorts of mischief. One has just poured a cup of sand in the middle of my clean floor. But they are nice, if they are naughty some-times. I have learned that everything human is human.

"I put a great part of my earnings in my work. I started to ask the Lord for twenty-five desks for the school; but I got ashamed and got up to an-swer the prayer myself. I am negotiating now. If my fifty dollars won't cover buying and freight, I will ask the Lord to raise what is lacking. Pray for me. I am engaged in the best of services, for the best of masters, and on the best of terms."

Miss Drummer has served not only her own people, but any who were in need. When she came home in 1911 she said she had nursed people of twelve nationalities. A Portuguese officer, out in the wilds, brought his young wife to this mission-ary nurse's home as the only place where medical care could be secured for her. When the wife went back home, Miss Drummer went with her to care for her and the baby through the hard journey. The officer wanted her to stay with them a while and rest; but her work called her. After paying his wife's expenses, he gave Miss Drummer fifty dollars personally as an expression of his grati-tude. At that time she had some more prayers on hand to answer herself, so she spent ten dollars for a silver watch and gave the rest of the money to the orphanage.

In 1918 Miss Drummer came home on furlough again and spoke at many white missionary gatherings with telling effect. She did not like their prayers, she said, so one day she told them about it. She said they all prayed for China and Japan and India and the islands of the sea and Mexico and South America, "and all the rest." It was that "all the rest" she was tired of. "There isn't any 'all the rest' but Africa," she said. "Call it by its name. Say 'Africa' when you pray, and then maybe you will think to pray for it oftener."

In Boston she made so strong an appeal for her medical work that a thousand dollars was given her from the floor before she could sit down. She made them *see* her people, the suffering old folk, the poor, hopeless mothers, the little children, as ready to learn kindness and happiness and to grow strong and healthy as any of the children of the world.

When she returned to Africa, she bought a donkey for near-by trips, as riding would be cheaper than going in a hammock. He was such a solemn donkey that she named him Jeremiah. He was very gentle and went beautifully on dry land, but he refused entirely to cross a stream or to step in a muddy place. He was gentle, but inflexible. So she had to sell him, saying that "a stubborn donkey without rubbers" was not much help in mission work in such a new country.

Trips make up a large part of the work of a missionary in Africa. The longer ones must be taken in the dry season and often occupy several weeks. Where it is possible, two missionaries go together, with five or six bearers apiece for their hammocks and baggage. Much of their food must be carried in a box as nearly insect-proof as possible. This box is all the furniture, except the camp-beds, they have with them. After they take out their food and granite plates, they sit on the chest while they eat. If they forget the salt or anything else, they must both stand up while they hunt it out. Men, women, and children crowd about them while they eat, touching them, feeling their clothes, peering at them, and talking about their looks, their food, and the way they eat it, until meal-time is an ordeal gladly ended.

At first Miss Drummer felt she must share her food with all these curious and sometimes hungry folk, but she found she could not possibly carry enough for the throngs of even a single village; she had to keep the contents of her box for herself or give up all thought of missionary journeys. And after all, she found this enforced eating in public a very good way of advertising her presence and attracting a crowd to hear the story she had come so far to tell.

The instant the plates are back in the box, and before the people begin to scatter, Miss Drummer gets them to sit down on the grass and begins to sing a hymn, teaching it to them line by line. "Jesus loves me" is usually the one she begins with, and they are quick to learn it. Then she reads and explains a few verses from the Bible and closes with a short prayer.

One evening she and her helper came to a village called Ngala. The chief gave them the biggest half of his two-room hut to sleep in. He and his family took the smaller room, and the missionaries put their camp-beds in one end of the other, curtaining off with the hammocks a place at the other end for their ten bearers to sleep on mats. The chief's goats and chickens slept in the room also, and plenty of rats—no, the rats didn't sleep! That was their time for exercise. The missionaries got some eggs and sweet potatoes in the village and cooked their supper on a little outdoor fire. They had a prayer-meeting in the hut. Miss Drummer and her helper sat on the bed, one holding the candle, the other reading the Bible and talking. The room was packed with young and old, all straining to catch a word. Nor would they go away when the meeting was over until the candle was put out and there was no more chance to stare at the strangers.

Next morning nearly two hundred of the villagers went a couple of miles with them on their way, begging, as they so often do, for some one to come and stay with them and teach them "the new way." Miss Drummer finds that everywhere she goes, the songs that they like best are those that tell of the great Friend, and of the love of God. They need a Friend so much!

One night she came to a village where the only shelter to be had was a hut with only two-and-a-half sides to it. The bearers stretched the hammocks around the open part to keep out wild animals. Just as they were dropping off to sleep after the meeting, they heard terrible noises—a hyena attacking a cow. The government does not allow the natives to have firearms, so the whole village got out of bed to make noise enough to scare the hyena away. They screamed and ran about with fishing-spears and with feathers and horns stuck on their heads. They were afraid the visitors had made the hyena so bold, for while there are many all about, they do not often come right into the village as this one did and kill a hog and attack a cow. Miss Drummer was afraid the people would not come to her meeting in the morning, but they did, and afterward they went along the road with her for quite a distance.

One great trouble on these journeys is the difficulty of finding water. They must get down by a wayside stream to do their washing, for they can hardly carry enough clothes to last without laundering on these long trips. Sometimes as they scrub things in the stream, they hear a panther or a hyena howling near by and decide it is best to move on. On reaching the villages, they may find the nearest water is a mile or two away, and when they go to it, it may be covered with green scum. Thirsty as they are, they cannot

MISS MARTHA DRUMMER (AT THE LEFT) AND THE GIRLS' SCHOOL AT QUESSUA

drink it, but they boil it and make tea or cocoa and drink that.

The women in these villages work very hard. They do all the work in the fields, from planting to harvesting, as well as all the work in the homes. One heavy task is the making of flour. For this they dig and dry the root of the manioca, a plant which grows in great abundance, and pound it fine. No wonder they do not have time to think about the way they look. There are mats to be woven for the houses, baskets to be made for bringing in the crops, skins to dress, and so on. Usually the men fight and hunt, but occasionally they work. Once Miss Drummer found an old chief crippled with leprosy setting an example of industry to his people by making rope. But perhaps if he had not been crippled, he too would have been hunting or fighting.

Some things we spend a good deal of time on, these people make very short work of. For instance, think how mothers in this country comb and brush their own and their children's hair every day. An African woman does the family's hair to last for months or even years. She powders up a red stone, mixes it with oil, and rubs it in until the hair is all dyed red. Then she does it up in funny little tight braids all over the head, and that child's hair is off her mind for good. Our notions about hair seem very peculiar to them. Once a white missionary went on a trip with Miss

Drummer. They crowded into the room, as usual, and they thought the missionary's hair the very queerest thing their eyes had ever beheld. It was so straight and funny, with such a queer, big knot. They said she looked like a "hoje," or lion, with a big mane. So you see our being accustomed or unaccustomed to things has a great deal to do with our thinking them ugly or pretty.

One day when Miss Drummer was nearing a village she met the chief and some of his people going hunting. They turned back and went to the village with her, saying to each other they didn't dare not to, for the gods had come and would be angry with them if they didn't listen to them. The chief said he would call his people in his other villages. This he did by means of a telephone of real African make. They brought out a "drum," which was a hollow log with holes all down the sides, and they beat it with little wooden mallets. The sound carries for miles, and it means, "Come quick. It's the chief's orders." It would be a very bold man who would disobey a summons like that. They can send other messages, too, for they have a code of long and short taps that can be made into all sorts of sentences.

In one of the many villages where the people begged for teachers they said, when Miss Drummer told them there was no one to send, "Oh, surely you can find one person to send! And if you will, we will build a hut for her. Send us just one." And think of all the people here in America who are not doing anything to really help other people, and who could so easily go!

The people in Africa are ready to learn. On her way back from one of these long trips Miss Drummer met some men from a village she had been to a couple of weeks before. They were out hunting. They told her they had been keeping Sunday since she had been there. They wanted a teacher, too. Some miles further down the road the missionaries heard some little children singing "Jesus loves me," and came upon a company from another village who had heard in some way that the missionaries were coming on their way back home. The old crippled chief was with them, hobbling along on his cane. He said they had been in such a dangerous country he had expected them to be killed by the natives, and he was so glad they had escaped. They had had no trouble at all, God had taken care of His children who trusted Him.

It is no easy task being a missionary in Africa. But Martha Drummer has found out that "everything human is human." May God give us each an understanding heart, that need in any guise may draw us, and that we may recognize our brothers and love them wherever and whatever they may be!

XI

SURE FOUNDATIONS

IN Wake County, N. C., James Dunston was born, before the war, but born free, as his father had been, before him. His father's parents had been set free by their owner before his father's birth; but why the thing was done, he does not know.

Before the Civil War, there were almost half a million of "free people of color," as they were called, in the United States. Most of them were in the South, and the causes of their freedom were numerous. Frequently a master allowed a very efficient or favored slave to take charge of himself. Such a man, usually skilled in some trade, would hire himself out, paying his master a stated sum each year and keeping the rest for himself. In this way, not infrequently, slaves saved enough to buy themselves; and sometimes they were able to buy their wives and children too.

Many were set free because their masters did not believe in slavery. George Washington's will provided that all his slaves should be set free at his wife's death; but Mrs. Washington, we are told, as soon as she learned of this provision insisted on their being set free at once. Some masters, like John Randolph, of Virginia, not only set their slaves free, but bequeathed money to buy land for them in a free state and to transport them thither. In this way several prosperous colonies were planted in the Middle West.

Some slaves were set free in gratitude or affection, after especially faithful service. A few won their freedom by some deed of courage or sacrifice. There is the famous case of the slave in Charleston, South Carolina, who saved St. Michael's Church from the flames. This quaint and ancient Episcopal church, one of the oldest in the country, whose bricks were brought from England in colonial times, and in which many of the state's most distinguished men have worshiped, is dear to all South Carolinians regardless of church affiliations. The story goes that a fire which swept a whole section of the city was stayed by herculean effort before it reached the church; but just as it was thought to be safe, a great gust of wind blew a bit of burning timber high against the old wooden steeple, where it caught and lodged. A groan went up from the crowd. The church seemed doomed, for human hands could never reach that dangerous peak. The people stood in silent sorrow, watching. Suddenly, from a slit-like window on the side of the steeple there appeared a man who began to climb up towards the brand. The crowd below, thrilled by his heroism, expected every second to see him fall to his death; he was attempting the impossible. Yet, as if by miracle, he went on. Higher and higher he crept. At last he reached and seized the brand and flung it clear of the beloved building, down to the churchyard, harmless. A great shout went up—to be stilled instantly. Could the man possibly come down safely? Must he pay with his life for the church? The people watched, breathless, till he reached the window again and disappeared inside. A sigh of relief swept over the crowd. Who was he, this hero? They searched one another's faces to see which of their everyday companions was absent, turned hero in an hour. The church door opened—and a Negro slave came forth. The story, as told long after by the old sexton, goes that when he stepped out, for a moment Charleston gasped—then it cheered! The mayor ran forward and caught the black man's hand, and after the mayor came the crowd. The slave's master, who was among them, then and there gave him the freedom he had so bravely earned.

But these fortunate freedmen were the exception. The lot of such people was often harder than that of slaves. With no white people to look to for protection or to care for them in sickness or old age, often looked upon with suspicion by their white neighbors, envied, perhaps, and yet despised by the slaves, unable to mingle freely with their own race, and exploited by unscrupulous white people from whom they had no protection, life was indeed difficult for many of this class.

James Dunston's parents found it so. His father rented land from a white farmer and worked as hard as he could. But the land was poor, nothing was known about scientific agriculture, and farm machinery was a thing of the future. The family was large, and the task of filling the hungry mouths was almost more than the father and mother could manage. They lived in a poor little cabin and knew nothing about the most ordinary comforts of life. But both parents were devout Christians, and they brought up their children with Christian ideals of honesty and kindness in all their doings.

James had one great ambition: he wanted to learn to read. But at that time there were no schools for Negroes anywhere. Had he been a slave, he might have been fortunate enough to find among "his white folks" somebody—his Christian mistress, perhaps, or one of her daughters—who would have gratified his great desire and started him on the path to knowledge. But who was there to teach a free Negro, a bit of driftwood on the current of life, for whom nobody cared, and whose existence mattered to nobody? He knew what a wild dream his was, and yet he clung to it.

With poor food and poorer shelter as work's utmost reward, he grew up working on his father's rented place. When he was fifteen he became a Christian and joined the church. This was in 1866. Not long after, a wonderful thing happened: in a log hut not very far away, a school was opened for Negroes! And the school-teacher was a Negro—miracle number two! James was tremendously excited about it. He was going to that school whether he had anything to eat or not. He was going to learn to read.

The boy got a blue-backed spelling book and started in, as eager a scholar as ever a teacher had. But it was only a little while before his hopes were all in ruins. He found that he already knew as much as his teacher did. He had come to the end of that road. The poor "teacher" did not even know his own ignorance. He knew the alphabet and a few words and could spell out some others. What more in the way of learning could one aspire to!

James, however, was determined to read the whole Bible right straight through, like—well, like white folks. Now that he had the key to words, he meant to unlock the Book. If he couldn't have a teacher to help him, he must work it out for himself, for read he must and would. And he did.

He clung to his blue-backed speller and his Bible until he mastered both. It took him years to do it in the brief times of rest between his long

hours of work in the field. He married, mean-
time, when he was about twenty years old, and
he and his wife started in on the same treadmill
life his parents lived—renting a few poor acres
and a little cabin and working from sun-up till
dark for just enough to keep them alive.

But after a while James Dunston faced the
astonishing fact that he was getting a little ahead
—a few dollars left at the end of the year and
never a cent of debt! New vistas opened before
him. He really had the gift of farming as some
have the gift of music. For one thing, he dearly
loved it and felt the life of the earth very close
to that of the God he loved. No trouble was too
small or too great for him to take with growing
things. He used his wits, too, and profited by
his own experience and that of others, as far as he
could learn it. While he was still very young,
he began to be called a good farmer.

"The white folks called me that," he said, with
a smile as shy as a child's. "I hope you won't
think I'm boasting—I don't mean it that way—I
just worked hard, and I got the name of doing well
with the land."

Seven years from the time he was married,
Dunston bought his first land, four whole acres
of it, and all his very own! To this poor freed-
man of the third generation it must have been a
wonderful day. He still rented a place and made
a little more than a living on it, but his own land

was clear profit. Before long the four acres had grown to thirty-five. He felt that he had now mastered adversity, and the future lay plain before him, so far as material things were concerned.

In other respects it was not at all clear. He was studying his Bible harder than ever, for he had learned to read it all at last and knew much of it by heart. The simplicity and sincerity of his faith made it easy for him to see how simple a thing our Lord's way of living is. He wanted with all his heart to tell other people about it.

"But how could I preach?" he asked, that curious child-look again in his eyes. "I was so ignorant. I'm ignorant yet. And for me to set up to teach my people! I was ashamed of myself for even thinking about it. I kept telling myself it wasn't the Lord calling me, it wasn't anything but my own foolishness. The Lord *couldn't* want anybody like me to preach. I would put it clean out of my head. And then it would come back. I couldn't get away from it. It kept on that way for years.

"At last I gave in. I was always ready to give in if the Lord really wanted me, of course, and at last it looked to me like maybe He did, and I'd better try it and do the best I could. That would be all He'd ask."

Mr. Dunston began to preach in 1882. He kept right on with his farming all the week—he had to do that to live—but he began to preach to his neighbors right there where he lived, and they gave him two hundred and fifty dollars a year. All this time he was taking care of his wife, who was an invalid until her death, a few years ago.

"We went through bad times here in North Carolina after the War—reconstruction times, folks called them. It was bad, and it stirred up trouble that lasted a long time. There were some white folks wanted to use the colored folks, especially about election time. It was too much politics; and it wasn't for our good. Our folks were so poor and so ignorant, and they kept expecting somebody to come along and do something for them or give them something instead of their getting right down to work and doing something for themselves with what muscle and sense the Lord gave them. I made the condition of my people a subject of prayer for years, and their relations with white people, too. And I saw what they needed: they needed to work, to fix up their houses, to educate their children, and quit depending on politics."

After Dunston understood what was needed, he tried to settle some of the Negroes on land they could buy for themselves. He wanted to help them to own their homes and be independent. He secured two thousand acres, and let the people pay for it as fast as they made the money. By this time he owned three hundred acres himself and began with nothing, so he knew others could do the same if they would.

"But how could you finance so big a project?" he was asked.

He gave a little chuckling laugh, whether of amusement at the simplicity of any one who could be puzzled over a matter so clear or of happiness in the help which had been given him, one could not tell.

"Why, the Lord tended to the finances, ma'am: I just had to do the part I could manage. I knew three white men who had plenty of money, and they knew me and trusted me. They wouldn't have lent the money to the men I wanted to help —they didn't know them like I did. But they lent it to me. Then I picked men I knew I could depend on. Every man on that two thousand acres owns his farm and house now." The farms run from fifty acres to a hundred and sixty. His own land was right alongside, and he lived with the men, plowing and working and running his farm, and of course showing them everything he knew and could learn about right ways of farming. On Sundays they all went to Mr. Dunston's church—that first church he took when he began to preach, and where he has been preaching ever since. They built up a good, strong community of Christian people, happy and prosperous, right there on their own land.

Of course, they had to have a school. It was a long time ago when all this was started, and school money was then hard to get even for white people, and much harder for colored people. The county board of education agreed that if they would get the land and bear half the cost of the building, the county would bear the other half. The matron at Shaw University, in Raleigh, had some lots in the village. She gave enough land for the school, and the people gave their part of the building, some in money and some in work. As they became able to do so, they improved the school.

As time went on other villages in that section of the county grew, and the pastor felt the need of more churches. He persuaded about twenty of his members at Shiloh, the original church, to form a new society at Mebane, which was nearer their farms than the old church. There he built up a second membership, dividing time between the two churches on Sundays and working on his farm and with his neighbors during the week. At Mebane he preached the same doctrines that had proved so effective at Shiloh: that religion meant living right every day in one's home and with one's neighbors; and that it also meant honest work, thrift, and a fair chance for the children.

In time, after the same, manner, a third and a fourth church were added to his charge. Then, the two thousand acres being bought and paid for, he secured fourteen hundred acres more, which is still in process of being paid for by the settlers.

"But I'm not farming myself now," he said, with a touch of what would have been regret if he had not been so sure that everything in life happens just right for the man who trusts in God. "You see, I'm seventy years old now, and I'm not—well, not exactly able to work quite so hard. I did my own plowing as long as I could walk between the handles, but for three or four years now I've had rather to oversee things and tend to my preaching, and have somebody else do the real work. I've been farming ever since I was a little boy, but now I've got to where most of my farming is done."

"You've helped a lot of people with your farming," it was suggested.

"Yes'm, I have, with the Lord's help. And I've been able to help with money, too. 'Tisn't so much, and yet in all these years it counts up, too. Three or four years after I began to preach, I promised the Lord I'd give a tenth of all I made to His work, and I've always had a little something ready when it was needed—twenty-five dollars or maybe fifty; I've never had more than fifty at one time, but then after a while I'd have some more, and in thirty-five years it's right surprising how much it all comes to."

I was talking to him after service at one of his four churches. I had gone eighteen miles in the country from Durham to see the man whom hard-headed business men of his race speak of as though he were of different clay from the ordinary run of people. "The best Christian I ever knew," said one of them; and another, whose own religion is respected and believed in by men of both races, said in a tone which lent wonderful meaning to his words, "I wish you could *see* him"— as if nothing short of that would enable one to understand quite what he was like.

So I went to one of his churches, where he had been holding a ten days' meeting. It is a well-kept building, freshly painted, and seating about two hundred people. It was well over half full, this week-day morning. As I went up the steps, I heard through the open windows the quiet, earnest voice of the preacher. He had closed his meeting the night before and baptized his converts. This was just a little farewell talk with the new Christians before he went on his way. They sat on the two front benches, with a goodly gathering of young people behind them and the older members on the sides, while he stood behind the altar railing and told them what being a Christian means.

He may not know very much about books, but he knows the Book—he was saturated with it. He said nothing about creed or doctrines, he was talking about the life of Christ in the heart. He stood there in his spotless linen and worn, well-brushed

clothes, an upright, gray-haired old man with a
fresh, young, unlined face, and a look of one long
acquainted with God and joyfully at peace with
Him.   There was something child-like about him
—his simplicity, his lack of self-consciousness.
When the service was over and I spoke to him,
he talked with me with a sort of gentle shyness
which had in it neither distrust nor self-depre-
ciation.

The people, young and old, gave him all their
attention; the entrance of a white stranger passed
almost unnoticed.   They were country people,
but they were all comfortably and nicely dressed,
clean, healthy, prosperous-looking people.   There
were a number of men in middle life in the congre-
gation—men who had left their farms in working
hours to hear this old man talk about his Master.
When he finished and went down to the front
benches to shake hands with the new members and
bid them Godspeed, the whole membership rose
and followed his example.   It seemed to the on-
looker, as they filed past, that in the older faces
was reflected something of the preacher's look.
One old woman, especially, had almost the same
air of shining peace.

Somehow the old man seemed typical of Christ's
work for men in all countries and races and
through the centuries.   Most of the service men
need cannot be given by learned or gifted people
—there are not enough of them to go around.   No

REV. JAMES H. DUNSTON AND ONE OF THE CHURCHES HE MINISTERS TO

unusual equipment is necessary to really help—no unusual gifts; only an unusual faithfulness in the use of ordinary gifts, such faithfulness as any of us may bring to our service if we will. And when we bring it, He uses it like this. All over the world it is love of Him in somebody's heart that has laid, and is yet laying, foundations of character, of opportunity, of higher ideals, of cleaner, happier, everyday living among poor and hitherto unfriended folk, lifting them from whatever depth they may be in toward that high end for which mankind was made.

It was this simple, loving, faithful service from some who had come to know God that first lifted our own savage ancestors, and many another wild race, and set their feet on the long road toward Christian civilization. All over the South to-day, among the poorest, this force is at work. It is like the lifting power of light, silently, the world around, drawing unnumbered tons of cold, dark earth into the beauty and glory of green leaves and flowers and food for a hungry world.

This old man, James Dunston, as he goes from village to village, with the peace of God in his face, is one of the real builders of America's prosperity and progress. It is people of his spirit who lay the real foundations of race or national life—the only foundations that can endure.

XII

A SEED OF FLAME

WHEN Negro literature is mentioned, most white people think of Paul Laurence Dunbar, the great Negro poet whom William Dean Howells discovered, and of whom he proclaimed to all America that, Negro or no Negro, here was a writer "of innate distinction" whose "refined and delicate art" attained "a very artistic completeness." Dunbar has been widely read, and his gifts as widely acknowledged. To many white people he still represents the whole of Negro literature. Others, however, add a few names to his. No one who has read Dr. DuBois's *Souls of Black Folk* will deny that it is literature of most unusual quality, or will they soon forget its haunting beauty. Readers of the *Atlantic Monthly* know Chesnutt's stories and the poems of Braithwaite, whose work has also appeared in the *Century*. Mr. Braithwaite is distinguished as both poet and critic, having served in the latter capacity on the staff of the *Boston Transcript* for many years. Since 1913 he has issued a yearly anthology, giving the best poems of the year which have appeared in American periodicals. He edits the *New Poetry Review* of

Cambridge, and is general editor of the series of *Contemporary American Poets.*

Of these four men, Dunbar, born in 1872, was the youngest. Of the still younger generation of Negro writers, few white people are aware. One reason for this is that the younger men, growing up in a new time, are passionately concerned for justice to their race. They have chosen between protest and literature, and men like James Weldon Johnson and others of his class, who could undoubtedly achieve distinction in the latter field, are pouring their gifts and energies into other channels. There will be those after them, they say, to write essays and novels and poems; their work is something more pressing.

But this story is of none of these. It is the story of one who barely crossed the threshold of manhood, of a poet most of whose poems were still unwritten when his long struggle with suffering ended in the fulness of life and light.

There was no struggle against hardship in this boy's youth, no fight for an education against odds. His father had waged that fight and won it splendidly before the boy was born. The son opened his baby eyes in a home of comfort and refinement and grew up a boy of brilliant promise, an only son, and the idol of his parents.

His father, Joseph S. Cotter, for whom the boy was named, was the son of a slave who was herself the daughter of free Negroes, but in some way she had been bonded as a slave. She must have seemed a strange woman, with much of her life beyond the understanding of the slaves about her. She worked hard, but she sang a great deal, improvising her songs as she worked. She made up plays and acted them before her admiring fellow-slaves. She was a deeply religious woman who was sometimes caught up into religious ecstasies. There was plainly something in her quite different from those about her. In thinking of her and of her son and her grandson, in whom her own strange spark of life flamed up, one is reminded of Browning's lines:

. . . God drops his seed of heavenly flame
Just where He wills on earth.

Looking at the slave woman, "the naked unpreparedness of rock" seems best to describe the barren circumstances into which the seed had fallen for her. For a long time life seemed little more propitious for her son. He learned to read when he was four years old, but forgot all about it, being long unused to books; so that when, in his early twenties, he entered night-school, he had to learn the alphabet all over again.

But he used some of his gifts in those lean years, nevertheless. At ten years of age he was working with boys and men in a brickyard in Louisville, Kentucky. He was set upon by the bigger boys and much tormented. Knowing the hopelessness of physical resistance, Joseph set his wits to work. He noticed that in the noon hour the men gathered around those of their number who could tell a good story. Why shouldn't boys do the same? And something within him told him he could furnish the stories. So he tried it and found it worked like a charm. The boys forgot to tease and crowded round him with growing respect and interest. The men, noticing their absorption from day to day, began to stroll over to investigate, and before long there was only one group at the noon hour—boys and men gathered around the little black boy, listening to the tales which he daily fashioned for them out of his own fancies.

At the age of twenty-two, hunger for an education stirred within him, and he went to night-school, beginning with the alphabet. In two years' time he was prepared to teach, and from that day to this he has been a student. He became principal of the Louisville Coleridge-Taylor school, named in honor of the great Negro musician who lives in London and is ranked as one of the foremost composers of our time. Mr. Cotter's work, however, is not confined to the school. When Louisville, first of all Southern cities, opened playgrounds for colored children, this older Joseph Cotter gave them a story-hour. He does the same thing at the two colored branches of the Louisville Public Library, and is helping to inspire and train in the same fine art young teachers and the children who will one day teach. He owns a comfortable home and a library especially rich in poetry. He has his mother's love of poetry and her gift, with a finer power of expression. A poet himself, he first made Dunbar known among his own people in the South, quick to acknowledge in another the gift he himself shared.

Into this home came Joseph Cotter, Jr., in September, 1895. He and his sister Florence, who was two years older, grew up together, devoted friends and chums. Florence taught Joseph to read. When he started to school at the mature age of six, he had read about thirty books, including the readers of all the eight grades of the public schools and parts of the Bible.

The parents, seeing how eagerly their children learned, very wisely held them back. They were both rather delicate, and their father and mother felt that sound bodies were of the first importance. Several times they refused consent when the children's teachers would have given them more rapid promotion; yet even so, Florence graduated from high school at sixteen with first honors, and Joseph, two years later, graduated at the same age, with second honors. He was first in scholarship, but some bit of mischief had forced his teachers to discipline him, and so he was given second place.

He seems to have been a real boy, for all his

physical delicacy and his voracious love of books. He worked hard as a newsboy, and while he was still a little fellow, he and his friends formed a grass-cutting club and made it pay. He did not waste the money he earned, but showed self-control and good sense in managing it. He was interested in doing all he could for himself.

The boy was an enthusiast in athletics and distinguished himself in them. He was especially fond of football, which he played well despite his slight physique. He always said it took brains rather than muscle to play football anyway, and the handicap he would not yield to could not block his way. While he was in high school, his jaw was broken by a base-ball and had to be wired in place. For two weeks he could not open his mouth, and was fed liquids through a straw; but he kept on attending school, doing his work well.

He was a quiet chap, with gentle and courteous manners; but if he felt it necessary, he would fight, giving his entire interest and attention to the matter in hand. He was popular because he thought of others. One of his great gifts was the power to draw people out, and he was always ready to help them discover the best in themselves.

Joseph was as fond of books as of people. The books of poetry in his father's library especially appealed to him, and he drank deep of this great spring of literature and of life.

That he should be particularly well-informed on the race question seems a matter of course; the significant thing is that his interest was never confined to it. His alert and eager mind went out to the whole world, to everything that concerned the Race of Man, to which all races belong. He was a keen student of world history and world movements, and this explains the poise and balance of his outlook on the problems of the race with which he himself was identified. This attitude is well shown in the following poem which is not only filled with a courage that looks facts and the world squarely in the face but is saturated with serenity of soul:

The Mulatto to His Critics

Ashamed of my race?
And of what race am I?
I am many in one.
Through my veins there flows the blood
Of Red Man, Black Man, Briton, Celt, and Scot,
In warring clash and tumultuous riot.
I welcome all,
But love the blood of the kindly race
That swarths my skin, crinkles my hair,
And puts sweet music into my soul.

"And puts sweet music into my soul." That is especially the dower of African blood. It pours out in kindly laughter and friendly human cheerfulness amid circumstances which would turn Nordic blood to gall or flame. It wells up to God in the strange, soul-moving melody of the "spirituals" out of slavery itself. White slaves have

Photo by Evans Studio, Louisville, Ky.

JOSEPH S. COTTER, JR.

attained spiritual vision—Epictetus is undying witness to that, but did ever a whole race of slaves lift their hearts in song before? When the races of men are all developed and the contribution of each to the Race of Man can be defined, that of the African race will be based on this very quality—that it "puts sweet music into my soul."

After finishing at high school, Joseph followed his sister to Fisk University at Nashville. He was there for a year and a half when he developed tuberculosis and was forced to come home. For six years he fought a good fight, his soul conquering, his body going under, slipping down toward the last surrender in increasing weakness and pain. As long as he could move, he worked. He was associate editor of the Louisville *Leader,* a position which suited him and which he filled with ability.

In December of the year in which Joseph left the university, his sister Florence was stricken with the same disease and came home, as he had done, to go under the doctor's care. She died just a year later, in December, 1914.

This was a heavy sorrow. The family was a deeply affectionate one, and the tie between the brother and sister was unusually close. It was while visiting her grave, some months after her death, that the impulse came upon him to express his grief in verse, and he wrote there the lines, "To Florence," which began his career as a poet. He recognized clearly that it was a question of but a short time before his own body would be laid beside hers, but he went on, meeting life as best he could from day to day, with failing strength but with a valiant heart. He had the best of medical care, and the white physician who attended him said that for courage, patience, and cheerfulness, he was, during the six years of his illness, the most remarkable patient he had ever had.

One of his special friends in the grass-cutting club of his boyhood was Abram Simpson, the youngest colored captain in the World War, and now a banker in Louisville. While he was facing death in France, Joseph, his friend, was facing it here at home in the silence of his quiet room.

But no one who suffers much and yet turns to those about him a steady and cheerful spirit can achieve that victory without times of fierce inward struggle. Yet in the little book of poems published a year before his death there is but one hint of discouragement. It is this short poem:

Supplication

I am so tired and weary,
  So tired of the endless fight,
So weary of waiting the dawn
  And finding endless night,
That I ask but rest and quiet—
  Rest for the days that are gone,
And quiet for the little space
  That I must journey on.

Next to this, however, we find the following:

The Goal

I have found joy,
   Surcease from sorrow,
From qualms for today
   And fears for tomorrow.

I have found love
   Sifted of pain,
Of life's harsh goading
   And worldly disdain.

I have found peace
   Still-born from grief,
From soul's bitter mocking,
   And heart's unbelief.

Now may I rest,
   Soul-glad and free;
For, Lord, in the travail
   I have found Thee.

That his pure joy in the beauty of the world about him was fresh and keen this lyric witnesses, almost singing itself:

Rain Music

On the dusty earth-drum
   Beats the falling rain,
Now a whispered murmur,
   Now a louder strain.

Slender silvery drumsticks,
   On an ancient drum,
Beat the mellow music,
   Bidding life to come.

Chords of earth awakened,
   Notes of greening spring,
Rise and fall triumphant
   Over everything.

Slender silvery drumsticks
   Beat the long tattoo—
God, the great musician,
   Calling life anew.

The little book of poems published before his death takes its name, *The Band of Gideon,* from the first poem in the book, a weird fancy of storm-driven black clouds, which seems akin to some of the old "spirituals." The book is manifestly the work of youth and as such, immature. "A Prayer" voices his own consciousness of this, and his desire to work out in well-wrought lines that which he sees with the eyes of his soul but cannot yet fully express.

A Prayer

As I lie in bed,
Flat on my back,
There passes across my ceiling
An endless panorama of things—
Quick steps of gay-voiced children,
Adolescence in its wondering silences,
Maid and man on moonlit summer's eve,
Women in the holy glow of motherhood,
Old men gazing silently through the twilight
Into the beyond.
O God, give me words to make my dream-children live.

The strongest poem in the book, with one exception, is a sonnet, "To the Negro Soldiers." Confined to his bed by suffering, he was now often too weak to write or to think, but his heart was with his comrades who had gone to the front, and with them he hoped most passionately that the loyalty and sacrifice of Negro Americans during the war would win for the race a better justice here at home and fuller respect as citizens.

To the Negro Soldiers

They shall go down unto Life's Borderland,
  Walk unafraid within that Living Hell,
  Nor heed the driving rain of shot and shell
That round them falls; but with uplifted hand
Be one with mighty hosts, an armèd band
  Against man's wrong to man—for such full well
  They know. And from their trembling lips shall swell
A song of hope the world can understand.
All this to them shall be a glorious sign,
  A glimmer of that resurrection morn
When age-long faith, crowned with a grace benign,
  Shall rise and from their brows cast down the thorn
Of prejudice. E'en though through blood it be,
There breaks this day their dawn of liberty.

Joseph Cotter's best work was done for the most part after the publication of his book. It is found in a sequence of nineteen love-sonnets of remarkable beauty and workmanship for so young a man. They are published in the A. M. E. *Zion Quarterly Review* for the third quarter of 1920. The last one, especially, of the little child

Who never was, nor is, nor e'er shall be.

is of a moving and haunting beauty. He left these sonnets, with a few short poems and one-act plays, unpublished at his death.

He sank toward death for years, fighting at every step. At the last, sight and hearing failed him, yet his whispered words were still of courage and cheer. He died in his father's arms on the third day of February, 1919.

Considering his youth and the heavy handicap

of illness during those few years, when, even in full vigor, his powers would but have been putting forth their first buds, his literary achievements are full of promise—a promise which in God's own time will find fulfilment in a broader life than this. One quality of his work is its direct and full sincerity. This quality blazes through what is, to the writer, the strongest of all his poems. There is no bitterness in it, nor was there any in his life, yet he knew the facts —knew them better and knew more of them, doubtless, than we white people ever do. And what he knew he felt. He was fully identified in his own heart and will with the Negro race—his people, entirely his people, though strains of many races mingled in his life. But feeling as he did the injustices from which his people suffer, he asks without rancor or reproach of his white brother:

And What Shall You Say?

Brother, come!
And let us go unto our God.
And when we stand before Him
I shall say—
"Lord, I do not hate,
I am hated.
I scourge no one,
I am scourged.
I covet no lands,
My lands are coveted.
I mock no peoples,
My people are mocked."
—And, brother, what shall you say?

The longer one thinks of it, the deeper that

question presses in, the more one feels its quiet, inescapable power. The words fit the thought and the thought the truth—the truth as regards a whole great section of American life—as a glove fits the hand. It is a question which will eventually compel its answer, and as it is answered, will the fate of America be. This book, put forth by the Council of Women for Home Missions and the Missionary Education Movement in the interest of justice and kindness between the races, is itself one of many indications, small and great, that in these later years the Christian mind is turning toward the right answer.

For too long white Christians felt that individual kindness and justice to individual Negroes was the full measure of Christian obligation. In the great awakening now upon the South is seen and felt the birth of a new consciousness and a new conscience—a sense of collective responsibility for community conditions. The North, industrially a generation in the lead, came by a social consciousness and a social conscience before the South. But North and South, there is needed a fuller awakening as regards both justice and kindness to our Negro brethren as a race. The individuals who have understood this are drawing together all over the country, and in every state their numbers grow. A new public opinion is creating new alignments, and old prejudices and foolish fears are "crystallizing out" in the process. True racial integrity is seen to involve the self-respect of each race and mutual respect between the races. To keep each race separate and pure no man of either race must hate or scourge or mock or despise the other. All such enmity must cease. The young people coming on as well as those who are now leaders must, in the presence of God, settle the question,

"And, brother, what shall you say?"

In Black and White

Bishop W. R. Lambuth of the M. E. Church, South, and Prof. J. W. Gilbert of the Colored M. E. Church, on their 900-mile tramp through Africa to locate a joint mission for their respective churches. "In all the dangers and hardships of of the journey," says the Bishop, "Gilbert never failed me. Daily he proved himself every inch a man and a Christian." The mission located, Prof. Gilbert reduced the speech of the savages to writing, compiled a grammar, and is translating the Bible into the Batatela tongue. (Courtesy of the Board of Church Extension, M. E. Church, South.)

In Black and White

AN INTERPRETATION
of SOUTHERN LIFE

By

L. H. HAMMOND

Author of "The Master-Word"

With an Introduction by

JAMES H. DILLARD, M.A., LL.D.,

*President of the Jeanes Foundation Board, Director of
the Slater Fund*

NEW YORK   CHICAGO   TORONTO

Fleming H. Revell Company

LONDON   AND   EDINBURGH

New York: 158 Fifth Avenue
Chicago: 125 North Wabash Ave.
Toronto: 25 Richmond Street, W.
London: 21 Paternoster Square
Edinburgh: 100 Princes Street

To my mother and my father,
both slave-owners in earlier life,
whose broad thinking and selfless living
first taught me the meaning of human
brotherhood,
I dedicate this book,
with a gratitude deepened by time,
and a love undiminished by death.

Introduction

THE problem of the South to-day is how to find voices and hearings for her best thoughts and sentiments. Especially is this true in regard to the relationship between the races. Public sentiment rules. It rules the attitude of individuals. It makes and unmakes the laws. It enforces or neglects the laws that are made. Public sentiment is mainly dependent upon the thoughts and sentiments that find expression in the constant utterances of pulpit, press, and political campaigns. On this question of race relationship the pulpit in the South is remarkably silent. The point is not raised whether or not the province of the pulpit is to discuss public and social problems. The fact is that the pulpit in the South is remarkably silent on the race question, even on the side of religion and religious duties. With few exceptions the direct contributions of the Southern clergy in establishing public sentiment on this question have amounted to little, and may almost be left out of count. It is the editor and the politician who, more exclusively in the South than in any other part of the country, influence public sentiment on the race question as well as on other public questions. The men of letters, the educators, the educated business men, have not counted appreciably in moulding public sentiment. I said editors along with politicians, but it is not so much the editorial writers as it is the managers who direct what news shall appear, and regulate the tones and head-lines of what appears. It is these and the politicians who are most responsible for public sentiment. For reasons that run back to the awful mistakes and hardships and outrages of the reconstruction period, the men who deal professionally in politics and public questions, and these include the newspaper men, have taken and still continue to take, not all of them but a large majority, an attitude of hostility and repression towards the Negro race. It is natural that it should be so.

But is it not time for a better note? The Negro is here, and so far as human vision reaches, he is here to stay, and to stay mainly in the South. He is not only here, but he is improving wonderfully in education and in the acquisition of property. There are exceptions. There are in fact large masses of

Negroes who are not improving in their conditions; but the figures of statistics are beyond contradicting the fact that the race as a whole is making forward strides away from gross illiteracy and dependent poverty. Shall the white people wish it to be so? It seems to me that they should wish it to be so. It seems to me that our material prosperity depends upon the spread of intelligence and thrift among all the people, even the humblest. It seems to me that our public health demands this, because filth and disease extend their evils high and low. And how dare we say that humanity and religion do not demand it? If humanity and religion mean anything, they mean good will to man and the application of the eternal principles of justice and righteousness now and always.

It does not follow that any amount of good will and desire for righteous dealing does away with the fact of race. The Frenchman is not a German, nor the Jew a Gentile, and the difference of the Negro and the white is most of all distinctly marked. The problem of their living and working side by side in the same region is a problem, which no amount of optimism can deny. The problem is a problem which calls for neither a blind and hopeless pessimism nor a weak and watery optimism. The call is for facing facts, and dealing with them in the light of wise statesmanship and the holy principles of religious faith. Some advanced spirits would ignore the universal fact of race, and in the highest sense they are right in the sight of law and religion ; but in the practical living of our lives there is no reason to ignore racial any more than other natural distinctions and affinities. There is a segregation which is perfectly natural and inevitable, and will surely take care of itself. Negroes as naturally and inevitably flock together as do the whites, and in my opinion their leaders oppose any denial of such natural segregation, and frown on offensive efforts to ignore the fact. Many doubtless question the truth of this attitude of the Negroes, but my experience leads me to the conviction that, however much we may think to the contrary, it is essentially and almost universally true.

For the white people the main point is that, with all recognition of racial feelings, we are bound to acknowledge the common rights of humanity. We are bound to acknowledge that all men are human, and have human rights and claims to life, liberty, and the pursuit of happiness. Are we not, we whites of the South, also bound by peculiar claims both of nearness and necessity? The Negro served us as a slave; in the providence of God he is now by law among us as a man. For his good, for our own good, is it not well for us to be helping him on to useful manhood? Grant that in the mass he is low down, can any low class, black or white, lie in the ditch and all of us not suffer?

It is because Mrs. Hammond's book strikes the good note that it is to be greatly welcomed at this time. I believe that our press and public will welcome it as a sincere, earnest, and able effort to tell the difficult truth. All may not agree with all she says, but that is not so important as to recognize that her book is one of the utterances which are needed at this time, and that she is seeking to help us all, North and South, to think rightly on this problem.

JAMES H. DILLARD.

Contents

Illustrations

I

IN TERMS OF HUMANITY

THERE is nothing except love itself which so adds to the richness and charm of life as a sense of wide horizons. One breathes in freedom under a wide sky, catching the proper perspective for life, and setting large and small in their true relations. The burdens and hindrances which press so close in a narrow, personal atmosphere drop away, and dwindle to their true size in those far spaces which include all human life. We never understand them till we see them so, set against the background of a world-experience, translated into terms common to all mankind.

We were made to be world-dwellers; members of our own small circle and section of country, loving and loyal to them all, yet members too of the whole human brotherhood: of our own race intensely; yet just as vitally, and more broadly, of the great Race of Man.

The best that can be said of an isolated

man, cut off from his wide human relations,
is that he has a capacity for life.   A human
stomach, or liver, or heart, may be cut out of
the body it belongs in, and yet be kept
" alive."   It serves no end of use or beauty,
poor unrelated thing, and is practically dead
in its cold, colourless abiding place.   Yet it
has a latent capacity for living, if only it be
placed again in vital connection with a human organism, and receive life from a working connection with the whole.

So many of us lead cold-storage lives, and
find them, naturally, dull enough.   So many
more are vitally connected with but a fragment of life—our family circle, our neighbourhood or section.   It is as if a heart beat
in a mutilated body, legless or armless, perhaps without sight, or deaf to the far, sweet
voices which call to the freest and happiest
things in life.

We are made far-sighted.   Scientists tell us
that our increasing need of glasses is due to
the fine, near-at-hand work imposed by civilization on eyes planned by nature for far-
sweeping vision, for the wide look which goes
from verge to verge of the high-arching sky.

It is much that we have acquired near
vision; we would be savages still without it.
Close observation, thought of little things,

the constructive spirit at work upon details —these, inch by inch, through the ages, have built the road over which the race has advanced. Long sacrifice has gone into them, untold patience and endurance, the endless drudgery out of which character emerges, like a winged thing from its cocoon.

But we need not lose the wide look, nor work at details knowing nothing of their relation to the big world-life of man. How could we understand them so, or understand ourselves? How should we bear our griefs, or meet our difficulties, or work in hope and with joy? Life is such a dull puzzle to near-sighted folk; and so many of those whose lives touch theirs are sealed books to them, uninteresting because unknown. And ignorance breeds prejudice as a dunghill breeds flies.

The commonest prejudice of all, perhaps, is the near-visioned belief in the superiority of the people of one's own small corner to all the rest of the world. This frank and childish egotism is the hall-mark of the separated life, whether lived by Anglo-Saxon or Patagonian, Chinaman or American. We are the people, and wisdom will die with us! That is the world-cry of unrelated man; and it arrogates a superiority which implies antagonistic criticism of all dwellers without the small charmed circle of the crier's understanding.

This unsympathetic criticism betrays itself as ignorance by the very fact of its existence; for sympathy cannot fail if only one understands deep enough. It is the surface view, always, which breeds antagonism. If one could understand to the uttermost one would inevitably love to the uttermost: one's compassions, like God's, would be new every morning. It is because it is ordinarily so apart, cut off from sympathy, that criticism is so often shorn of renovating force. Its only chance for constructive service lies in being passed through the alembic of a living sympathy, which alone can transmute the inorganic matter of criticism into food for assimilation and growth.

For love, and not intellect, is the vital force; and no man is shut out by lack of knowledge from the widest human life. Things dim and confusing to the mind are clearly apprehended by the heart. If I venture to offer this partial interpretation of the life of that corner of the world which is home to me, it is not because of a belief that peculiar powers of any kind have been given to me, entitling me to speak of my people, or to them.   It is because I am so truly one of the mass, living a small life in a small place, walled in by circumstances, like my brothers.   For any sharer of the common lot whose deepest desire is to walk in love towards all the world will find, with the years, a way opening into the very heart of life, and will come upon the reasons for many of the things which perplex us, for much of the wrong we bear and the wrong we inflict, much which hedges us in, much which makes our brothers of a wider circle misunderstand and misjudge us.   What is said must be incomplete, and partly incorrect.   One life may mirror the race life ; yet the waves of personality inevitably refract the reflected rays. It is offered only for what it is : an attempt to translate some fragments of Southern life into world-terms ; to set our sectional problems in their wide human relations, and so to see them as they really are.

When one lives on a little hill, all closed in by mountains, one cannot possibly see " the lay of the land " ; and most of us begin life in a place like that.   Some of us climb later to a mountain top, and live there with wide views, and heads near the stars.   But the valleys look deep and dark from up there,

the hills seem small, and the mountains fill
the world. It is beautiful and splendid, and
true, too : but it is only the half of truth—
that most dangerous of all lies—until the
mountains, too, are set in their wide relations.
When men make them wings like birds, and
fly high enough, they see something bigger
than the mountains, and that is the earth to
which they all belong. One can love the
mountains after that without any childish
pride in them, or childish scorn of the valleys
and hills.

It is so with the races of men, and with
that great, underlying humanity which binds
them all in one.

Long ago, when I was young, I knew so
many things that aren't so. I could label all
the deeds of men as fast as I heard about
them ; and what was far more amazing, I
could label the men who did them. Labelling deeds is really not a very complicated
process. Even a child, for instance, can dis-
tinguish lies of a fairly simple type. But to
put the right label on the man behind the lie
—that is a different and most difficult matter.
He may be a man who would die for the
truth, who daily sacrifices for it as he understands it He may be all hedged in with in-

heritances from which he has no way of escape—an example of "invincible ignorance." He may be just at the beginning of things : so many of us tell lies because we are not out of the kindergarten yet, and life exists for us only in relation to our own exuberant personalities. And he may be—though it isn't likely—a deliberate lover of lies. To label his deed is easy ; but how shall one label him ?

Yet youth has a passion for labels. It is such a fascinating way of displaying one's knowledge to a supposedly admiring world. And the more recently acquired our knowledge is, the more superficial, the more, in our youth, it refreshes our souls to display it, and to criticize the little folk of the family, who are still in those depths of ignorance so recently occupied by ourselves ; and to criticize the old folks, whose knowledge has so fruited into wisdom that we cannot trace its connection with our own brand-new buds at all.

Dispensing information concerning its own shortcomings to a world that lies in darkness is, in fact, one of the natural and unforgettable joys of adolescence. Nobody ought to begrudge it to anybody. It is part of the glamour of youth, and dear, at one stage of life, to every soul alive. As we grow older we should remember, and smile. Poor young things, they beat against the walls of their ignorance so soon!

But one's wisdom must be ripe and garnered for this understanding. It is not to be expected of the younger young folks, whom older adolescence is so very hard upon. Their knowledge has achieved little more than a pair of cotyledons as yet, perhaps, and wisdom waits on the years. But they will be as big as the biggest soon, and know as much, or more: the younger ones "sass back."

That is the way quarrels start in families, as all long-suffering parents know. And I think something very like that has happened between the North and the South—between the big brother and the little one. For races are men writ large, and men are but larger children.

Sometimes we see twins whose individual development indicates a difference of years between the two. One had measles, perhaps, or scarlet fever, "with ulterior consequences," as the doctors say, and it has set him back a long time. His digestion was impaired, and lack of nourishment has stunted his growth. The other boy is full fed and vigorous, glorying in his strength as every boy

must, and claiming the earth as his birth-
right. He wants to be nice to his little
brother, but the child can't live his big-boy
life at all; and he's grouchy, too—always
getting his feelings hurt. It isn't the big
boy's fault he's no bigger; and he's pig-
headed and mean, anyway: just see the way
he picks on folks that are weaker than he is!

The war was our measles; and we have
hardly recovered from the ulterior consequences yet. But our Northern twin kept
right on growing. He came to adolescence
first: and in the last twenty-five years or so
he has reached that later period of youth
when one begins to look soberly out upon an
ever-widening world, and to see a man's
work and a man's responsibilities shaping
themselves from dreams.

I am sure that when I was a girl of fifteen,
and first began to explore the purlieus of
some Northern tenements, hardly any of my
well-to-do, educated, and entirely respectable
and Christian acquaintances cared anything
whatever about them. Our rector was a man
of visions and dreams, and he stirred his people to open a mission in what was considered
the worst section of the city. I was a member of its regular working force until my marriage, a few years later. But to nobody con-

nected with that mission did it exist for any purpose whatever except to save the souls of the tenement-dwellers out of this world into another one, and, incidentally, to show personal kindness, as occasion offered, to individuals of the district. Nobody dissented from the doctrine that whatever was wrong in the general tenement-house environment was merely the outward and visible sign of the tenement-dwellers' inward and spiritual lack of grace : if all their souls could only be saved there would be nothing left wrong with the tenements. There was no sense of responsibility on landlords, on the health authorities, the employers of labour, or the public at large. There was, in every one I was thrown with, a vigorous personal conscience ; strong personal sympathy for individuals, who were to be got out of the general tenement-house mess if possible ; much personal sacrifice ; and a deep sense of personal obligation to be individually kind, and to save all the souls that were savable. But that was all. There was no glimmering of community consciousness, of community conscience, or of community sin. The North was growing fast, but it was still a many-individualed North. It responded keenly, as growing children will, to those stimuli which pene-

PRESTON STREET COOKING SCHOOL, LOUIS-
VILLE, KY.

trated the area of its awakened consciousness.
It was eager, alert, questioning, learning, im-
measurably more stimulating mentally than
my own beloved South : but it had not yet
reached that stage of growth where a social
conscience is possible. In the presence of
appalling social wrong there was no response
to stimulus whatever.

For myself, I was in wild revolt : but the
only way out then conceivable to me was for
the poor all to get saved in a hurry, and die
and go to heaven. God might have known
what He was about when He made slum people : but His reasons passed my understanding.

Just then I came upon some old English
magazines containing Miss Hill's earlier arti-
cles on housing, and God was cleared of the
charges I had brought against Him. The
evils in the tenements were man-made; and
if enough people would do the loving thing
they could be stopped. It was all personal
still—work, responsibility, and righted wrong;
but saving souls included the changing of
physical conditions.

But good people were not interested.
Those to whom I talked considered Miss
Hill's ideas visionary. They did not believe
it possible to redeem slums—only to redeem
some slum-dwellers' souls. I labelled them

all on the spot, and " stupid " was the nicest word in the list. The indictment grew longer and blacker as the years went on. I was back in the South now—the beautiful, Christian country, where there were no slums, nor child labourers, nor sweat-shops, nor white slaves. It never occurred to me that we were too young and small, industrially, to develop these things ; or that, like the North, we had to travel through the country of indifference to the evils we did have before we could grow old enough to care.

When Stead wrote "If Christ Came to Chicago" it was the last straw : respect for the North was gone. They had money up there ; they claimed to be Christians ; and they knew. Yet nothing was done. The imprecatory Psalms made excellent reading.

And then, out of that vast welter of indifference, the emergence of a social conscience in the North ! There had been already, here and there, a point of light—a man or a woman flinging an isolated life against embattled social wrongs. But now began a gathering of little groups ; here and yonder one heard a word caught up by other voices until it rose into a cry : and now the sound of marching feet, and a thunder which begins to shake the world !

The North is a glorious big brother : and as the hatred of newly-realized old wrongs grows within him, as that which is highest in him is more and more committing him to the doctrine and life of brotherhood, it is part of the law of youth and growth that he should have scant patience with those who are indifferent to conditions which touch him to the quick. The one unforgivable thing to him is that a people should be lacking in social conscience ; the one inexplicable audacity, that without it they should dare to call themselves Christians. Our brother of the North is deep in the labelling stage.

And we Southern folk ? If the big brother's contempt has scorched and burnt us, have we had no contempt for those who are younger than we ? We had no smaller child in the immediate family to outlaw with labels ; but providence has not been altogether unkind. For there is the cook's black baby : and it is so long since we were babies ourselves we can't be expected to remember that stage of our growth. Anyway, there is the baby ; and the labels show up on him beautifully.

The North, of course, thinks it had a social conscience fifty years ago : but that was a

social conscience about other people's sins—
a delicate variety for early forcing merely, as
I know by my own experience. I once had
a deal more social conscience about Northern
conditions than about those of our Southern
Negroes,[1] though my personal conscience
about the Negroes was in a flourishing state.
Besides, we had a conscience about slavery
ourselves—a true social conscience in the
germ. One of our sorest sore points is our
Northern brother's irritating inability to grasp
this fact, which is matter of common knowledge in the South. Thousands of slave-
owners, like my own parents, thought slavery
wrong, and confidently expected the time,
not far distant, when the states would themselves abolish it. The South did not fight
for slavery. We have seen the day, down
here, when we would have enjoyed putting
that fact into our Northern brother's head
with a pile-driver: and it really does seem,
sometimes, that no lesser agency will ever
get it there.

What the South fought for was its consti-
tutional right to get out of the Union when
it no longer desired to stay in it. We still

[1] The word Negro is printed with a capital throughout this
book in obedience to the rule which requires all race-names to
begin with a capital letter: *e. g.*, Indian, Teuton, Zulu, Maori,
Anglo-Saxon, Filipino, etc., etc.

believe the point was open for debate, though we have long since ceased to regret that the " Noes " won it.

As for the Negroes, we were developing a social conscience about them, a healthier growth, perhaps, though a slower one, than the vicarious conscience of the North.   And because of that conscience, as well as because of natural human kindliness, the relations between black and white were in the main kindly and understanding.   I make no excuse for slavery, nor for the terrible things allowed by it : but those things were the exception and not the rule.   The conduct of the Negroes during the war proves that. They are a patient, gentle folk ; but they are far from being superhuman.   If the main product of slave-relations had not been kindliness the Southern armies would have disbanded to protect Southern homes.

These kindly relations were not shaken by Negro freedom.   Nobody held it against the Negroes that they were free.   And in the white men's hearts kindness was reinforced by gratitude for the faithful care the Negroes had given to the women and children of the South.   In the ruin of the old order, and the desperate poverty of the new, readjustment would have been slow and difficult.   It would have been, doubtless, many years before the polls would have been open to any considerable number of Negroes. But there were matters more vital than votes; and the readjustment, if slow, would have progressed normally, in mutual kindliness and patience.

But the North, with its social conscience about home conditions yet in embryo, and its social conscience for other folks, like a clock without a pendulum, working overtime, was bent on growth by cataclysm. If it could only have taken a world-look for a minute it would have seen growth never comes that way; but being so very busy doing things, it had no time to look. The North was a child as yet, and lived in a world fashioned out of its own thoughts. A child can take blocks of wood and put them into a barn or a castle or a ship: it is as easy as making fiat money. But when the blocks are men the fiat process never works: they will not stay put.

That was our great disaster—ours, and the Negro's and the North's. Children ourselves, how should we know the big, strong, overbearing North was but a child too? And we had all a child's keen sense of injustice, and keen resentment of it. We thought the North understood as well as we did what it was doing; we even thought the Negro understood. Hate sprang full-armoured in a night. The North called it reconstruction: it was destruction of a very high order. And in all that ruin of our dearest possessions the most precious, the most necessary thing destroyed was the old-time friendship between white and black. It shrivelled in the fires of hate; and from the ashes rose suspicion and injustice, all wrong inflicted and sustained, to curse both races yet.

The shock of those anarchic days is deep in the South's nerves to this day. Much which the North calls by a harsher name is a resurgence of an almost physical hysteria.

When I was a child my nurse put me to bed, and was supposed to sit by me till I went to sleep; but she never did. She was a white woman, by the way, and quite well educated: the older children's black mammy had stayed. She had a sweetheart waiting in the kitchen; and as soon as she tucked me in bed she put out the light, and left me with the assurance that a lion and a tiger were under my bed, both friends of hers; and if I ever dared to get up to call my mother, or told her I was left alone, they would claw me under the bed by my feet and eat me up.

That was fifty years ago.   But to this day,
as soon as the light goes out my well-trained
nerves try to jump me into bed.   When I
am least thinking of it there descends that
sudden sense of impending claws.

We are like that about Negro domination.
We know it is a foolish fear ; yet we are so
ready to start at it, both as regards our
political and our social life.   Governor
Northen, of Georgia, spoke the truth when
he declared that "Social equality is a delusion set up by the demagogue" for his own
ends : but demagogue or nurse, children are
easily frightened.   And the South really felt
the claws once ; and the memory is deep in
every nerve.

Beyond this, we have never yet set the
Negro in his world-relations, any more than
the North has so set us.   We have looked
upon our "Negro problem" as a thing apart,
our strange, peculiar burden, the like of which
the world has never seen ; and our dominating thought about it is that this excrescence
on Southern life shall never again threaten
the existence of our civilization.

That this should be the main aspect the
problems of our poorer classes present to us
we owe partly to our memory of claws ; yet
largely too to that irresponsible, but inevi-

table, selfishness of youth, a phenomenon of growth not to be averted or shortened, which sees all life from a purely personal standpoint. We are just beginning, as a people, to touch that period of later adolescence where one glimpses the fact that a standpoint purely personal cannot, in the nature of things, be either kind or just, or true to our own best selves.

But while we are learning to admit this, to ourselves and to others, there are some things our kinsmen of a wider circle should remember. They should not forget that the first effect of sorrow is always isolation. After sorrow is assimilated, become food for expanding life, one may emerge and take one's place again, with no trace of past struggle except in a deeper sympathy with humanity, and a broader understanding of it. But assimilation takes place in the wilderness; and life passes one by at a time like that, an unheeded, alien, far-off force.

For years we lived in that wilderness, with no thought nor care for the wide world-life climbing, expanding, outside. Two things we had beside our sorrow: a struggle for bare existence which absorbed the energy of every fibre; and the pride of a high-spirited people who had been humbled in the dust.

Sorrow, poverty, and pride : can any other three things produce such perfect insulation as these?

How should we have a social conscience? No nation has ever developed community consciousness while its members were battling for daily bread. A class possessed of a little leisure must be developed before that can appear, and must bear and rear children educated to a somewhat wider outlook than their fathers' bitter struggle made possible. The South is barely at this initial stage.

We knew the world—the polite world— pretty well before we had the measles. We were a cultivated folk. But the world of those days knew no more about a social conscience than it knew about "movies," or automobiles: it hadn't gone that far in the book. Individuals, it is true, were spending their lives, here and there, in the preparation of a soil where later a social conscience might germinate; but they were thought of, so far as they were thought of at all, as individual saints or individual cranks. The housing movement had a few disciples, both in France and in England; but they were not in the public eye. And the voice of the socialist was heard in the land only to mark him as a fit subject for the madhouse. England, foremost of all nations, had entered, half unwittingly, upon her magnificent and long-to-be-continued course of social legislation ; and men like Kingsley and Maurice were calling passionately to that void where a social conscience was soon to be. But these were but the local affairs of a foreign nation, as we and the rest of the world saw them. There was nothing in America to parallel the conditions which had called their protest forth ; and to us, as to the great mass of the privileged everywhere, nearly all of human life was foreign.

It was during the years of our sojourn in the wilderness that the privileged of earth began to discover humanity as a brotherhood, and shot beyond us. But our time of separation is ending. We have learned and achieved much in these years. Our sympathies are broader, our minds more mature, our hearts nearer a full awakening. But we know very little as yet about this new old world to which we have returned. We haven't learned about slums, or a minimum wage, or mending criminals instead of manufacturing them, or the abolition of poverty, or the connection between under-nourishment and the poorhouse. Even our churches are still inclined, many of them, to look askance

at social service as an adulteration of the
" pure gospel," and to regard the saving of
souls out of this world into another one as
the full measure of Christian duty. Some of
us think if anybody says social service and
Negroes in the same breath he must mean
" social equality," and reach for a gun at
once.

But the time of isolation is past with us.
We stand ready to take our place in the
world, and the powers of youth and health
stir within us. We are ready for life in the
open, for world-connections and a world-
view.

What will we do with the Negro, our peculiar and heavy burden, our puzzle, almost our
despair ?

If we will quit thinking about him as peculiar he will cease to be either a puzzle or a
despair.   Are we the only folk on earth responsible for a " submerged tenth " ? Burdens are peculiar in details, fitted to the individual or the race ; but in essence they are
the same for all mankind, and call for the
same courage, the same sympathy, the same
patience and hope and strength. National
trials and difficulties are like personal sorrows and hardships : when we regard them
as peculiar to ourselves they overwhelm us.

Who are we, to walk in an unblazed path, to solve a problem new in the experience of mankind, to bear what man has never borne before? Human nature turns coward at the mere thought of it, and excuses its failure with the plea that it cannot be expected to be stronger or wiser than all the world.

But if the burden is not peculiar? If it is our part of a world-wide task? If everywhere men living under such conditions as do the majority of our Negroes are reacted upon by their environment just as the Negroes are? If we have mistakenly counted our poverty line and our colour line as one? If in every nation long neglect of the poor and the ignorant has piled up just such a weight of weakness, unthrift, unreliability and crime for a clearer-visioned generation to transform? If men in all lands, the best and finest, are spending themselves to solve problems such as ours?

When we see our problem in that light—see it as it is, see it in its wide human relations—we will set ourselves to its solution. We never have been "quitters" in the South. If this be our part of a world-task we will achieve it.

And our part of a world-task we will find it, as soon as we compare our poorest with the poorest of other countries and of all races. Skins differ in colour, heads are shaped differently ; one man's mind runs ahead of his sympathies, perhaps, and another man's mind may creep while his emotional nature runs rampant. But under all outward differences their fundamental humanity is as much the same as is the earth under the mountain and the hill. The same things poison the minds and bodies of white and of black alike; the same elements nourish both. Honesty, purity, love, self-reliance and self-respect—who dare claim a monopoly of these for themselves? They are human, not racial, and to be built up in all races by the same processes: else Christ were a dreamer whom it were madness to follow.

We need to take the long look, as well as the wide one. We say—a church paper in the South said it only a few weeks ago—that in a whole long fifty years of freedom the Negro has advanced so little that his condition " is not encouraging." If that be true it is a grave indictment of us white folks : for the Negro has these fifty years accepted the conditions we have furnished for him, and been subject to us in all things. He has lived beside us, done our work. If there were no encouraging signs after our management of him for fifty years, the difficulty might lie with the management.

As a matter of fact, the statement was made without a proper knowledge of facts. Facts show remarkable progress, and under difficult conditions. But what is fifty years in the development of a race?—or two hundred and fifty, when it starts from savagery?

If we could go back to the skin-and-club days of our own puissant ancestors we would probably find that they made less progress from savagery in two hundred and fifty years than the Negroes have done in that time. Of course they had less outside help: they had to evolve many of their own forces of advance. But for centuries no one seeing then could have dreamed of the world-service waiting in the ages ahead for those wild Britains, who lived like beasts in their lairs. If we could go back and spend a few months with our forefathers, two hundred and fifty years after Roman civilization first touched them, we would probably be glad enough to get back to our black folks again: they would never be quite so black any more.

The truth is, we know nothing about what Negroes were made for or what they are capable of, except on the broad general ground that every human race has human

power of development in some direction.—
When any one says a thing like that old
memories stir instantly in some of us, and we
suspect the argument of carrying the sting of
social equality in its tail. If we just could
rout that old bogey out of our imaginations,
and turn our minds from claws! Nobody
can force on anybody associations undesired.
And whatever Negroes may become, they
will certainly not be white folks. They will be
just themselves; something that will balance
the white race and the yellow and the red,
and that will render a racial service all its
own. The higher they rise the more Negro
they will be, the more the tides of their own
race life will fill and satisfy and lift them—
along their own path. To doubt that they
have, beyond our vision, some world-service
yet to render, something enough worth while
to justify their long suffering and our own,
would be to rule God out of history, and to
put the thinking mind "to permanent intellectual confusion."

I would not appear to overlook the existence of race consciousness and of race
prejudice, nor to blink the fact that the latter
gravely complicates our portion of the world-
problems of the unprivileged. Yet race

prejudice, though necessarily local in its manifestations, cannot be charged upon the South alone : it is as wide as humanity, and as old as time. It is not confined, in the South, to either race. A thing so wide-spread, so deeply human, so common to all races, should move no man to bitterness, but to patience. And we are not denied the hope that humanity will one day rise above it.

Race consciousness is another matter. In every highly-developed branch of the great human race-stocks there exists a desire for the integrity of that stock, an instinct against amalgamation with any very-distantly-related race. It is true that with the majority of any such people the instinct shows itself chiefly as race-antagonism and race-prejudice ; yet it is shared by those who are free from these lower manifestations of it. Despite individual exceptions this law holds good, the world around ; and its violation, in the marriage of individuals of widely-different race-stocks, involves disastrous penalties.

An instinct so wide-spread and so deep may be safely credited to some underlying cause in full harmony with the great laws of human development. The instinct for racial integrity, with its corollary of a separate social life, will doubtless persist in a world from which race prejudice has vanished. If one believed in an Ultimate Race which would be a blend of all races—a belief frequently adopted when one first recognizes the real oneness of humanity—one would necessarily regard this desire for racial integrity as but another manifestation of race prejudice, doomed, as such, to pass. But the wider and deeper one's association with life the more clearly seen is the law of differentiation in all development. In the light of this law the ultimate physical oneness of human races becomes as chimerical as the ultimate oneness of all species of trees, or the disappearance of the rich diversity of winged forms of life in favour of an Ultimate Bird.

Life does not develop towards uniformity, but towards richness of variety in a unity of beauty and service. Unless the Race of Man contradicts all known laws of life it will develop in the same way; and whether white, or yellow, or black, they who guard their own racial integrity, in a spirit of brotherhood free from all other-racial scorn, will most truly serve the Race to which all belong. What we white people need to lay aside is not our care for racial separateness, but our prejudice. The black race needs, in aspiring to the fullest possible development, to foster a fuller faith in its own blood, and in the world's need for some service which it, and it alone, can render in richest measure to the great Brotherhood of Man.

II

THE BASIS OF ADJUSTMENT

IN a newspaper of a Southern city I read recently a report of the court proceedings of the day before. The first case tried was that of a white man, some thirty years of age, who had violated the white slave law. He had abducted a girl of sixteen from her home, and was using her for immoral gain. The judge, in sentencing him, had dwelt at length on the preciousness of that of which the child had been robbed; but added that he had decided to make the sentence a light one, because the law was new, and not very widely understood. He gave the man one year in prison.

The next case, according to the paper, was that of a Negro boy of twenty. He had stolen eleven dollars and forty-six cents. The evidence was convincing; but the judge said he would give him also a light sentence. His reason was not, as it might have been, that the law against the offense was new. It is just as new as the other one, having been formally promulgated at the same time, on a mountain in the Sinaitic peninsula.   But the judge's reason for mercy, he said, was that the evidence clearly showed that the boy had never had any chance in life.   His parents had both died in his infancy, and nobody else had wanted him.   He had grown up, no one knew how, beaten from pillar to post, uncared for, untaught.   So the judge decided on mercy, and gave him three years.

I do not at this time raise the question of the wisdom of time-sentences, in these or in any cases ; that will be taken up later.   The point is that the value of a child's honour and a mother's happiness, when stolen by a mature white man, was assessed at one year in prison ; and the value of eleven dollars and forty-six cents, when stolen by a young Negro waif, was assessed at three years in the same place.   The judge is a man who has, I believe, a sincere desire correctly to administer the law in his high office ; and law and justice are to him synonymous words.   He thinks in terms of law, not in terms of humanity.

Some months ago I was visiting friends when a son of the house, a university student, came in with a story of a morning spent in the city court.   Some case was pending in which the students were interested, and a body of them had been in attendance all the morning. A number of cases concerning Negroes had been disposed of before theirs was called.

"I tell you," he said, summing the morning up, "a 'nigger' stands no show in our courts."

He was evidently shocked by the fact, and so was the family. They are people far above the average in intelligence, in loving-kindness, in culture, in self-sacrificing personal service to the individual poor, both white and black. But courts of law were without the pale of their personal responsibility : their personal conscience, quick and beautifully responsive in any individual matter, merely condemned this wrong and laid it aside. There was no sign of a social consciousness ; of any sense that if anybody stood no show in their courts it was a community sin, for which all members of the community were responsible, and which the community could change if it would. They did not see that they had any duty in arousing the community to consciousness of social wrong. If any individual one of the many Negroes known to them had been brought before the court that morning, they would have done just what I have done in days when I had no more social

conscience about Negroes than they had:
they would have seen him, or his family, beforehand, and asked some good lawyer, a
personal friend probably, to see that the
Negro had justice.   The lawyer, who would
probably not be in the habit of taking such
cases, would do so cheerfully and without
remuneration, partly to oblige a lady, but
largely too for the sake of protecting a Negro
who had become individually known to him,
and who therefore appealed to his personal
conscience.

Cases of both kinds are common all over
the South.   A Negro who gets in jail will
send for "his white folks" first thing, if he is
fortunate enough to have any.   And they
come, man or woman as the case may be,
practically without fail.   And often, when
they come, the Negro gets less than justice in
the courts in the sense that he is let off with
a reprimand or a small fine when the law
would call for something more.   But none of
us are sorry for that, for our penal laws, like
those of most of the rest of the world, are
archaic survivals, and recognize no relation
between cause and effect where crime is concerned.

But the very great majority of Negroes who
come before the courts have no white folks to

send to.   Our criminals, like the criminals of
every country, come chiefly from the economic
class which lives on, or over, the poverty line
—from our "submerged tenth."   Nearly all
those in this economic class in the South are
Negroes—a fact which has resulted in our
confusing the poverty line with the colour
line, and charging Negroes racially with sins
and tendencies which belong, the world over,
to any race living in their economic condition.   But it is just the Negroes who belong
in this economic class, these Negroes who
form our submerged tenth, and who furnish
the most of our criminal supply, whom we
white people do not know, and who conse-
quently have no white folks to send to, to see
that they are protected in the courts.—Oh,
there is the Negro problem, and the solution
of it !   The poorest, the most ignorant, the
ones least able to resist temptation, the folk
unhelped, untaught, who are born in squalor,
who live in ignorance and in want of all
things necessary for useful, innocent, happy
lives—they do not know us, nor we them !
There is no human bond of fellowship between
our full lives and their empty ones ; no making of straight paths for these stumbling feet,
no service of the outcast by those who are
lords of all !

In that one sense the Negro problem is peculiar. Otherwise it is an integral part of the world-problem of strength and weakness dwelling side by side, with the great Law overhead laying upon them both the necessity of working out a state of civilization which shall embody the spirit of human brotherhood, and secure justice and opportunity for all. There is nothing peculiar in that. The call to this duty is world-wide : the obligation we share with all the privileged of earth. The peculiar thing is that we alone, of all the privileged of Christendom, have no wide-spread sense of obligation to achieve this task. We even, many of us, look on the handful who respond to this world-call by service to our neediest as people half disgraced, who dishonour their high heritage in going where Christ would go, and in doing His will with all He has left on earth to do it—human feet and hands and hearts. That is peculiar.

For we honour the privileged of other places who do this very thing. Any of us would have been proud to know Tolstoi, not just as a writer of books, but as a great man willing to forego greatness, and to give his life to ignorance and squalor and want. We are proud of Miss Jane Addams, formerly of

Chicago, Illinois, but now this long time of the United States of America, North and South.   But a Jane Addams among the Negroes—the slum Negroes, folk of that very economic class for which she spends herself at Hull House ——— !   There is no more to be said.

Ah, but there is !   We are only at that border-line of adolescence where a social conscience may stir in the heart's soil, and begin to reach upward to the light.   We will know our slum folk yet.   And that knowledge will be part of the basis of the adjustment which is to come.

A recent incident told me by a friend, one of the chief actors in it, throws light on present Southern conditions at several points.

This friend lives alone with her servants on her old family plantation, a few miles from one of our greatest cities.   Her cook's husband, a trifling Negro and a steady drinker, had hired himself to a near-by farmer for whom the whites of the neighbourhood had scant respect.   The man kept a plantation store where his "hands" could obtain provisions and whiskey as advances on their wages, settling with their employer at the end of the week, or the year.   Until poor

SOUTHERN WHITE TEACHERS, LOUISVILLE, KY.

folk learn coöperative buying, after the English and continental method, these master-owned stores are a necessity in the South, as they are elsewhere; and here, as in Western lumber camps or Eastern mines and mills, monopoly tempts some to extortion. In such cases the Negroes are never out of debt, from year to year, their own fondness for whiskey being often as potent a reason for that fact as the storekeeper's greed. The storekeeper usually furnishes the whiskey which keeps them such unremunerative labourers; but his profit on the whiskey makes up for that.

The farmer in question appears to have been an employer of this type; and the Negro, whose poor wages fully paid for the work he did, was soon deep in debt. He decided to hire out somewhere else, and his contract troubled him no whit. He told his second employer of his debt to the first; and the man, according to custom, agreed to stand for it to the creditor by withholding part of the Negro's wages while in his employ, and paying it on the debt. Ordinarily this would have released the Negro, as few people try to get work out of one, contract or no contract, who is unwilling to give it. But the first farmer needed his "hand," and had, apparently, not even a personal conscience, or a rudimentary respect for law. So he kidnapped the Negro on his way to his new employer, gave him a hard beating, and set him to work on his own farm, threatening him, the Negro said, with far worse if he left the place again before the year was out. He even kept him at night until my friend, finding where he was, sent the farmer orders to allow the man to come home every night as soon as his day's work was done.

She is a frail little body, but accustomed to being obeyed; and the farmer did as he was bid. The Negro, however, shirked his work, and once more roused his employer's ire. This time the farmer came to the cabin in my friend's yard one night after she had retired. He brought a rope with him, without expounding his reason therefor, and ordered the Negro to get up and come with him. My friend went out and delivered, as her ultimatum, a demand that the Negro be formally released from his contract on the spot. Her simple fearlessness forced the white man's consent; and she gave him, in return, her personal check for eighty dollars—the amount claimed on the Negro's indebtedness.

The story shows the lengths to which the Southern personal conscience will go in befriending even a trifling Negro; and the fact that everybody settled down in peace as soon as the white man let the black one alone throws light on the state of our social consciousness. It is true my friend said the white man was practically ostracized by his own race ; but that fact was the aggregate result of the action of many individuals, rather than the action of a community with a sense of community responsibility to uphold law.

The story naturally brings up the question of peonage, which is a logical outcome of our attitude to the Negroes since the destructive days of " reconstruction."

Country Negroes of the better type, hardworking, honest and thrifty, are pretty sure, sooner or later, to own their own farms and be their own masters. Negro ownership of Southern farm lands increased one hundred and fifty per cent. between 1900 and 1910— clear proof that the race is advancing rapidly, no matter how much that is undesirable may remain for future elimination. Proof, also, that notwithstanding mob barbarities and much unjust discrimination, Southern whites are better neighbours for black folk than some of our Northern brothers fear.

By this steady promotion of the best Negro tenants and labourers into the class of landowners, those left available for labour on white farms tend constantly to a lower level of character and efficiency. It would be hard to exaggerate the shiftlessness and unreliability of many of them. The farmer who has employed them by the year may find himself deserted at the most critical period, and his year's work little more than a disaster. It is for protection against this danger that a number of men have resorted to the expedient of keeping the labourers forever in their debt, and, by agreement with other farmers, preventing their getting employment elsewhere until that impossible time when their debt shall have been cancelled.

It is a surface remedy, which penetrates the skin of the difficulty only to set up inflammation. The basis of adjustment here necessitates an entire readjustment of thought and action, on the part of the whites, to the country Negro and his needs.

The two great assets of any country are the land and the people ; and the people necessarily include those engaged in the basal industry of agriculture. The land produces increasingly as the people who till it gain in health, in morals, in intelligence, in the freedom and joy of life. It grows barren as they are debased. No man, however intelligent himself, can make a free man's crop with peon labour. For many years the South squandered the fertility of her fields. We are learning of late years, slowly and painfully, to build up the impoverished soil, and restore it to its former richness. But we have overlooked the other half of the problem—the squandered fertility of labour. Until we build up the worker the material on which his work is spent will never yield its normal return. The houses of very many farm labourers are more than enough to sap their vitality, to destroy ambition and self-respect, and to foster immorality and disease. Conditions like these filch from the community its capital of human productiveness.

Added to this is our habitual neglect of the farm-hand's recreational life—the danger-place of all people of all races and all ages whose inward resources are limited, and whose power of self-control is not highly developed.

Even a locomotive, a thing all steel and brass, has to have its periods of cared-for rest—its recreational life—if it is to live out in usefulness the normal lifetime of such an engine : and no man, of any race, will or can do first-class work if he is regarded as a machine while at work, and as a nonentity

when his work-hours end. Drunkenness
and immorality are the only resources of
many of our farm-hands when not at work
in the field. Peonage is no cure for debase-
ment like this.

The Negroes need to be built up, like the
soil. In cities and factories we are finding
that it pays, in dollars and cents, to care for
"the [white] human end of the machine."
It will pay in the country, too, and when the
human end is black. Christ's law of brotherhood is universal in its working, or it is no
law at all. A Negro of this class, given a
decent house and let alone in it, would soon
bring it to the level of his former habitation.
But if with the house he were given a friend
—who according to Emerson's fine definition
is "one who makes us do what we can";
if he were helped to start a chicken-yard
of his own on intelligent principles, or a
garden-patch; if the educational methods so
successful at some points in the rural South
were universally applied, relating the children rationally and happily to the land; if
the schoolhouses were secured as social centres for older Negroes, and the better classes
of coloured people were encouraged to cooperate in the movement; if the white men
of the neighbourhood, farmers, pastors, school-

teachers and doctors, met them there occasionally to lecture on matters of community interest, and also to give them some real outlook in life, some glimpse of the wide relations of their narrow toil ; if the white people would look into their religious life a little and do what so many white people did before the war—superintend their Sunday-schools and teach their Bible classes ; if these simple and entirely possible things were done, the labourer would be built up along with the soil, and peonage would be seen for what it is— the device of selfish ignorance for meeting a situation which is caused by our own neglect of our poor, and is to be controlled only by service in a spirit of brotherhood.

It would not be as easy to do as to read about, of course. There would be discouragement and failures. There always are when a thing is really worth doing. And we must expect, moreover, to pay a heavy premium for our fifty years' neglect of this simple duty to our country poor. The Negroes do not love us as much as they did fifty years ago, nor trust us as they did. No Southern white can turn in sympathy to the service of the poorer Negroes without being often startled, and sometimes sharply hurt, by suspicions and mistrusts which peer at him from hidden places, and sometimes threaten to bar his way. But that is our heritage from our own past, and it only emphasizes the danger of further neglect. It may go against our pride to recognize the fact, but we white people, if we really win our way with the mass of the Negroes, and pay in honour our share of the world-debt of the strong to the weak, must live down much of the record of our last fifty years.

But the lower class of Negroes, whether in city or country, do not present the only, nor, I often think, the most serious aspect of our Negro problem, so called. We have many classes of whites in the South, the lowest of which are little, if any, above the lower Negroes in education or morality. This class is not a large one, but it is widely scattered ; and it is the most unstable element in our civilization. It is the nitrogen of the South, ready at a touch to slip its peaceful combinations, and in the ensuing explosion to rend the social fabric in every direction. It is the storm-centre of our race-prejudices, and generates many a cyclone which cuts a broad swath through much that the South cherishes. I know of no solution for this white side of our " Negro problem " but the one to be applied to the black side also—the gradual upbuilding of character by training and personal service, and above all by the example of just living in every relation of life.

But control of a situation need not wait on the solution of its problems. The existence of this dangerous white class is no excuse for the deeds its members are permitted to do; it but constitutes our duty and our reproach. There are a hundred law-abiding Southerners—oh, far, far more !—to every one of these lawless firebrands; yet individualistic as we are, unorganized by a social consciousness, half a dozen of them can sway the weak, the excitable, the unformed among us, can fire the mob spirit, and lay the honour of thousands in the dust.

We have lately had, in one Southern state, an extreme instance of this kind. A peculiarly atrocious murder had been committed by five Negroes, two of whom were lynched, the remaining three being hung by process of law. Some lawless white men, evidently too poor themselves to need the Negro's labour, then undertook to drive all Negroes from the country. Notice was served on the white people, in city and country, that dire and summary punishment would be meted out to all whites employing Negroes in any capacity after a certain date. The Negroes were warned that working for white people meant death, and were ordered to leave the country at once.   A friend of mine who lives in the county town, which numbers several thousand inhabitants, told me the Negroes were pitiful to see.   They went out in droves, young and old, often in rickety little wagons piled high with household goods ; went out, not knowing whither, and leaving gardens behind them, and often homes of their own.

And the white people—the law-abiding majority of the population ?   They were thoroughly indignant from a personal, but not from a community standpoint.   They condemned the outrage publicly, as individuals ; and as individuals they each protected those Negroes personally known to them. Men carried pistols to protect their Negro chauffeurs, none of whom were molested as soon as that fact became known.   Servants came to the white people's premises to sleep, and brought their relatives with them.   It was the Negroes who had no " white folks " who suffered.   Finally the matter dropped out of the newspapers.   A year later two of the Negroes ventured back to their homes, which were promptly dynamited, though fortunately without loss of life.   The two houses, the papers stated, were owned by white men ; and the governor offered five hundred dollars reward for the perpetrators of this latest crime. They have not yet, however, been apprehended.

The papers of the state, like the whites of the outraged community, were outspoken in condemnation of these barbarous proceedings ; yet there was no community conscience to weld the law-abiding majority of town or state into one strong will, fired with a determination to stop a hideous injustice, or to give the weak the protection of law which was their due, instead of the haphazard personal safeguards afforded by the circumstance of acquaintance with some white person.

It is scarcely a step from deeds like this to the murder, by mob law, of human beings. To a thinking mind there is nothing so sinister in our Southern life as the swift debauching of many of our people through yielding to the mob spirit. Time was when a Negro was lynched for one crime only ; and the fearful provocation is still adduced, at least as the reason, if not as the excuse, for this savagery among us. But this lawless element has long since fallen below the point where such offense is necessary to set them baying for some Negro's life like bloodhounds on a trail. The curse of their own sins is upon them, and they drop nearer the beast's level every year.

But we of the law-abiding majority cannot lay on their shoulders our part of a community sin. If they do the deed, we, who could prevent it, permit them. There are, however, signs of a wide awakening. The individual consciences of the South are yearly more deeply stirred by these outrages. The outspoken condemnation of a few men and newspapers, years ago, is the common attitude to-day. And more than that, far more, is the stirring, by more signs than one, of a true community conscience at this most vital point. A few weeks ago the citizens of a town just disgraced by mob violence met in public assembly, confessed openly their sense of community shame, and pledged themselves as a people to see that the law was upheld in their midst henceforth. When the real South, the law-abiding majority, catches the contagion of that social consciousness mobs will be heard of among us no more.

A law has been proposed by some Southern man, whose name I am unable to trace, which would go far towards checking mob violence. It would automatically remove from office any sheriff who failed to protect a prisoner in his charge, and would render him ineligible for reëlection ; and it would make the county liable for damages to the family of the murdered man. It would, in the writer's opinion, be wise to add to these provisions a requirement that the county tax for education be largely increased for a term of years following such a crime.

It was with the deepest thankfulness that I sat in a body of Southern women, gathered in Birmingham last April, when resolutions against lynching were brought in and unanimously passed. The overwhelming majority of Southern women have always repudiated the need of mob-murder for their protection ; but it marks a great advance towards social consciousness when an organization representing over two hundred thousand Southern white women delivers a public protest against it. The occasion was the annual meeting of the Woman's Missionary Council of the M. E. Church, South. The resolutions " deplore the demoralizing influence of mob violence upon communities, and especially upon the youth of both races, who are thereby incited to a contempt of law resulting in moral degeneracy and the overthrow of justice." They state " that, as women engaged in Christian social service for the full redemption of our social order, we do protest, in the name of outraged justice, against the savagery of lynching ; " and " call upon lawmakers and enforcers of law, and upon all who value justice and righteousness, to recognize their duty to the law, and to the criminal classes. We appeal to them to arouse public opinion against mob violence, and to enforce the law against those who defy it." The resolutions end by pledging the women " to increasing prayer and effort in behalf of those classes, the very environment of whose lives breeds crime."

Here is one vigorous development of social conscience in the South as regards the Negro. The Sociological Congress showed others. It is as contagious, thank heaven, as tuberculosis itself, once the patient's condition is ripe for it ; and when we break out with it, as we presently shall, we shall have a notable case. We never have done things by halves.

But the evil effects of the past are still with us. It is true that the crime of lynching is decreasing among us. It is also true that the number of Negroes lynched in the years made darkest by this wickedness was almost negligible as compared with the total Negro population. Negligible, I mean, not from a

human, but from an arithmetical standpoint;
and somehow, by that curious mental process
of self-exculpation common to all men in the
presence of embarrassing or shameful facts,
many of us who yet abhor mob violence
have unconsciously sought refuge from the
horror in the arithmetical point of view. "It
is horrible," we say, "wicked, shameful, in-
human; but at least, thank heaven, the crime
is infrequent: the millions of Negroes never
in danger proves that. As a race they are
safe, and they know it."

But they do not know it; nor would we in
their place. We have failed to use our imagination at this point. Every one of our millions of black citizens knows that every time
this fire of death has flamed up from those
depths where savagery still lurks in human
hearts it has burst forth in a fresh place, without warning, dealing individual death, and
sometimes suffering for many not even ac-
cused of crime. Lynchings do not come in
the same place twice: if they did they could
be avoided. The volcano bursts forth from
what has been, in the memory of man, but a
peaceful hillside. It is true the eruption
seldom takes place: the awful thing to the
Negro is that it *may* take place at any time,
anywhere, even upon trivial, or, conceivably,

upon unconscious provocation. That is lynching from the Negroes' point of view, which would probably be our own in their place. The possibility of illegal violence, the fear of it, is an ever-present thing in their lives. It hangs, a thick fog of distrust, between their race and ours. Through it they grope, misunderstanding and misinterpreting many of our most innocent deeds and ways. Individual whites they trust; but I think few of them really trust us as a people. They know that nearly all of us feel kindly to them, that very few of us would ever harm them: but they also realize, taught by frightful experience, that when the very small lawless white element rises against them they cannot certainly rely upon protection from the rest of us.

This sense of evil possibly impending, with the deep distrust engendered by it, colours all the Negro's relations with us. It makes him shifty, time-serving. All of personal good that he plans or desires too often appears to him to be subject to the one imperious necessity of getting along with white folks—not of deserving or obtaining the respect of the better classes among us, but of avoiding the anger of individuals of our smallest and most dangerous class. To live in an atmosphere like that without moral deterioration requires a strength of character rare in men of every race.

Nor does the administration of criminal law in our courts always tend to lessen this distrust of white people. At each session of the Southern Sociological Congress Southern men high in office among us—judges, professors in our great universities, Y. M. C. A. leaders, and others, have stated that, despite individual exceptions, the trend of our courts is to mete out heavier punishment to black offenders than to white. It is not, they say, that Negroes are illegally sentenced; but that, for similar offenses, the Negro gets one of the heavier sentences permissible under the law, the white man one of the lighter. More than one Southern governor has defended his wholesale use of the pardoning power on the express ground "that the proportion of convictions is greater, and the terms of sentence longer, for Negroes than for whites." One Southern judge, a speaker at the Sociological Congress in Nashville, after stating that the white man too often escapes where the Negro is punished for a like offense, added the warning "that if punishments of the law are not imposed upon all offenders alike it will breed distrust of administration." Yes: and distrust of the race behind the administration. It will, and does.

A Southern bishop told me recently that at a banquet where several prominent Southerners were present, this judge among them, some of the guests questioned the accuracy of his statement in regard to discrimination in the courts. "And he just turned on us," said the bishop, "and gave us chapter and verse. He told what he had himself seen, in different courts. And he convinced his audience ; when he finished nobody had a word to say."

It is not only the Negro's well-being that is at stake in this matter : it is the civilization of the South. Through all the ages, the country which denies the poorest equal justice is the one foredoomed to fall. It is doubtless true that our Southern courts are no more unjust to the very poor than are the courts of many other sections of our country, especially in our great cities. The poor immigrant without a "next friend" is liable to fare as badly as the Negro without any "white folks" ; but that does not lessen our danger, or our responsibility. It ought to draw North and South closer together in the bonds of a common patriotism and a common public duty. It is because our poor are made conspicuous, and advertised, as it were, by

their difference in colour that we seem to all
the world greater sinners at this point than
themselves. But while I would offer this suggestion, that others outside may feel more
human sympathy for us while yet condemn-
ing our human sin, I would not have us at
all excuse ourselves on the score that our sin
is common to mankind. A social conscience,
like a personal one, regards the moral quality of one's own deeds, and not what one's
neighbours do, or fail to do. If we fail to
achieve justice for the poorest, our doom is
written in the stars : and we are neither
helped nor hindered by other people's shortcomings.

Last of all in this connection, yet in their
practical prevention of good feeling between
the races not least, are the annoyances, discomforts and hardships laid upon the better
class of Negroes by our failure to see under
their black skins a humanity as dear to justice and to God as our own. There are many
points for illustration ; but one will suffice
here—the matter of " Jim Crow " cars.

We who believe that the races should be
kept racially, and therefore socially, distinct
cannot advocate their mingling in the enforced intimacy of Pullman cars. It is enough
for us to put up with ourselves under such

conditions—and sometimes almost too much. But that does not at all excuse the travelling conditions which are forced upon Negroes of education and refinement, (I use the word advisedly), throughout the South. They pay for a straight railroad ticket exactly what we pay, and we force them to habitually accept in return accommodations we would despise one of our own people for putting up with. —And we say the Negroes are dirty! Miraculously, some of them are not, notwithstanding all the provision we make for confirming them in that condition.

Last year a young Negro girl came to the school of which my husband is the president —a school, by the way, founded, maintained and officered by Southern whites; and after she had been there some time she confided to one of her white teachers the fact that when she came to the city she had ridden in "the white folks' car."

"Were you with white people?" she was asked.

No, she was not. She had paid her full fare, as usual, and had taken her place in the "Jim Crow" car, filthy with tobacco juice and incrusted dirt, foul with smoke both new and old, and containing a number of Negro men of the baser sort—the kind of car, in short, in which Negro women and girls, and clean, educated, well-to-do Negro men are so frequently expected to travel. There were no women that day, and only these rough men ; and they began to molest the girl almost at once. Shrinking back in her seat in terror, she felt a sudden hope as the white brakeman came through the car : but he passed through, as unheeding as though dogs were squabbling over a bone. She stood it a few minutes longer, and then dashed frantically into the next car, the white day coach, dropped into the last seat, and burst into tears. Thus the conductor found her. On hearing her story he told her to stay where she was ; that if any of the white people in the car objected he would explain her presence, and they would be willing for her to stay. No one objected, however, and she rode to her destination in peace.

Not all conductors are so humane. And it is practically impossible, as may be seen at a glance, for one white man, often a mere boy, to keep order among a car-full of Negroes like that, roused to evil by the presence of a girl evidently above their own social class. A white boy-conductor would be risking his life in such a case ; and even if he saved it, if he started any " race row " on a railroad train by defending one Negro from another he would lose his job. So most of them harden their hearts and turn their eyes the other way—a performance for which I, for one, am slow to blame them. We have no right, as a people, habitually to permit impossible situations, and then to throw the responsibility for them on one man's, or one boy's, shoulders.

Last Christmas a coloured kindergartner, employed by some Southern white women in settlement work among her own people, went home for the holidays. There are several day trains, but some important home happening made her presence there necessary the morning after her work closed at the settlement; so she took the night train, a thing she had never done before. The young woman is a college graduate, refined in speech and manner, modest and sensible in her relations with people of both races, and a strong and wholesome force in the lives of the poorer Negroes among whom she works. She took the Jim Crow car, of course, expecting to sit up all night, but with no idea of the experiences before her. The car was full of half-drunken Negro men off to enjoy one of the very few pleasures open to Negroes in the South—a regular old Christmas spree.

There were one or two other women in the car, and they huddled together and endured the night in frightened silence. The train men, passing through, took no notice of the insults, or oaths, or vile talk.

When she told the white women who had employed her about it, ten days later, she trembled as she spoke.

" I had never seen Negroes like that in my life," she said. " I knew there were such men ; but my mother had spent her life keeping me away from them.—Why can't the white people see it ? " she burst out passionately. " Will they think forever that we are all like that? Why can't they let us be decent when we want to be ? "

While my husband was Secretary of Education of the Southern Methodist Church, part of his work was to lay the matter of Negro education on the conscience of his denomination. One of the teachers at our one school for Negroes was a coloured man of unusual gifts and character, an honour graduate of a Northern university, and a man high in the respect and friendship of Southern whites in many states. To bring " the Negro question " closer home to our people the Methodist Board of Education paid this man's salary and travelling expenses; and for four years the white man and the black one travelled the rounds of our annual conferences, presenting the cause of the Negro to our white preachers and laymen, and finding, as time went on, much prejudice giving way to sympathy.

The conference meetings are nearly all crowded into three months, several being held each week. When a secretary attends them his days are given to the conferences, his nights to travel; and it is a time of physical strain, even with all the comforts of modern travel. My husband, strong as he is, came home tired out at the end of each annual round.

" How Gilbert stands it, physically or religiously, I cannot see," he said. " He goes half the time without lying down to sleep. If I were not with him, to dash into some white restaurant and buy him a cup of coffee and something to eat, he would often go hungry. And I have never once heard him complain, or seen his Christian composure ruffled. He is doing us white people a great service, freeing us from some of our worst prejudices: and we require him to do it at this cost!"

I know a Negro woman, the wife of a doctor, whom white doctors of the city tell me they respect both as a man and as a physician. He has a large charity practice, but a large paying one also. He is a man of considerable means, and owns an automobile. His home is thoroughly comfortable; and his wife is as amply provided for as the wife of a white man in similar circumstances would be. She is a refined, sensible, good woman, whose influence among her own people is of the best.

She told me not long ago that she went on a visit which necessitated a day in the usual Jim Crow car. I had asked her about the matter or she would not have mentioned it. We do not suspect the reserves of pride in Negroes of this class; and I count it a chief proof that my life among them is not a failure that they will speak to me frankly, as to a friend.

There had been no insult or terror in her case; simply filth, tobacco juice and smoke, coarse talk among other Negroes, and blinding, choking dust. When she reached her destination, she said, no one could have told the colour or texture of her dress or hat.

Somehow the hat gripped my sympathies. Women do so cherish their hats! I am never happy myself until the porter brings me a bag, and my head-gear is safe beyond reach of dust, with a hat-pin thrust through the gathered opening of the bag into the back of the opposite seat, to keep its precious contents from being waggled about. I can wash my hair ; but a soot-filled hat is irretrievable ; it can never look impeccable again.

Why should this other woman, who loves cleanliness as much as I do, and who is quite as willing to pay for it, be forced to travel in that disgusting filth ? I know if I were forced to do it my husband and my children and all my friends would feel outraged about it, and would never have any use for the people who made me do it. Why should these people feel differently? It is nearly always the smaller matters of life which make its bitterness or its sweetness for us white people. We can bear great things greatly, often ; but our courage and kindness and sympathies fail before the annoyances of life. Shall we expect more of Negroes than of ourselves ?

A Southern state, a few years ago, required the railroads to provide equal accommodations for whites and Negroes in that state. They replied by a threat to take off all Pullmans for white people, as they could only be operated at a loss for Negroes: and the matter was dropped.

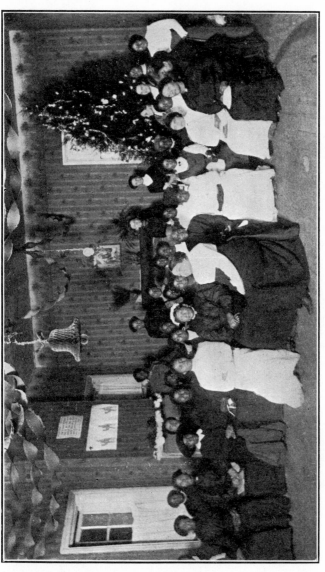

CHRISTMAS CELEBRATION, BETHLEHEM HOUSE, NASHVILLE.

But day-coach accommodations are rarely equal. Even where the cars were originally alike, the habitual neglect of those in use for Negroes soon reduces them to a condition revolting to people of cleanly habits. The fact that many Negroes are unclean in their habits is no excuse for the condition of the cars. When white people are unclean, as they often are, the railroad is not excused from keeping the cars in a fairly decent condition, at worst. They may have to spend a little more for soap and water ; but they must take their chances on that when they sell tickets.

The Jim Crow cars come under no one general description. I have occasionally seen a car for Negroes as clean as any day coach for whites. Similarly, I have known personally of Negroes riding through Southern states all day and all night in a Pullman section, their presence known to all the white passengers, none of whom voiced any objection to them. But neither occurrence is the rule.

Sometimes there is a clean day coach for Negroes, and also a separate place for Negro men to smoke—usually a cut-off end of the smoking-car for whites. This is the best accommodation on the best roads. Sometimes this half of a smoking car, with its single toilet, is the only part of the train open to Negroes at all. Sometimes there is no place for Negroes except in the car with white smokers, though this again is unusual. The average conditions, undoubtedly, are far below those provided for white passengers paying the same price: and the spirit manifested by this treatment of Negroes is one people of any race or any class have the right to resent.

If whole Pullman cars cannot be profitably provided, one end of a first class day coach could be fitted up as a Pullman, and put in charge of the men on the white people's Pullman; and the other part of the car could give the Negroes what they now so often lack—day-coach accommodations equal to those for whites.

I believe the railroad people themselves have little idea of the number of Negroes who could and would pay for first-class accommodations. We know little about the educated, prosperous members of the race. As fast as they enter this class they withdraw into a world of their own—a world which lies all about us white folks, yet of whose existence we are scarcely aware. It is largely the inefficients, the failures, or the immature and untrained who remain with us. As they rise

out of this class they disappear from our
view. There are more prosperous Negroes
who would pay for Pullmans than we imagine.

But if the railroads claim that they really
cannot provide decent day coaches and comfortable sleeping accommodations for Negroes, a commission should be appointed to
look into the matter : and if their contention
proved just, fares for everybody should be
raised by law to a point which would allow
the roads to maintain standards of comfort
and decency for all their passengers. We
cannot afford, as a people, to let the Negroes
pay for our cheap fares : for that is just what
it amounts to when the railroad takes the
same amount of money from both of us, and
gives us better accommodations than it can
afford to give them. We are not paying for
all we get in our day coaches, evidently ; and
if the Negro isn't footing the bill for the def-
icit, who is ? As for the Pullman company,
if half the published tales of its dividends be
true, it could furnish cars for Negroes and
pay its employees a living wage, and yet be
in no danger of bankruptcy. Public utilities
should be subject to public control.

It should be pointed out that not one of
the Negroes whose cases I have cited, nor

any Negro I ever spoke to on the subject,
had any desire to share cars with white people. They have their pride, too; and they
are not going where they are not wanted.
They want safety, cleanliness, and comfort,
not white company; and they are willing
and ready to pay for them.

There is another grave injustice, wholly
different from any I have touched upon,
which I believe has had a profound effect for
evil upon a large class of Negroes; yet
scarcely any one, white or black, thinks of it
as injustice at all. We Southern white
women are greater offenders in the matter
than the men; and I myself must plead
guilty to the common charge. Yet I scarcely
see how a woman very far from strong could
sometimes do differently; and if one be excused on the score of illness, it looks ugly to
call her neighbour lazy for the same offense.
We demand too little in the way of honest
work of the Negroes in our employ. Shirk-
ing, untidy habits, petty, and often serious,
pilferings—we wink at all of them, and continue to pay honest money for dishonest
work. We do not like to discharge Negroes.
It grates on our pride to be talked about by
a "darkey": and talk about us they certainly

will, frequently with scant respect for truth. And as to discharging them, where will we get a better one, we ask; they are all alike. And you can't possibly do the work yourself; yet if you make them mad they may keep you out of a cook for weeks. And besides, "darkies" are "darkies": white people always have put up with them, and always will.—So we mourn in secret over the departed flour, and sigh for the lard that used to be in the bucket, and tell Jane or Lucinda how nice her cake was last night, and give her the cold biscuit to take home to her grandmother, and a few cookies for the children. And when Eliza Ann brings in the wash with three of the best towels gone, and half the handkerchiefs, and tells us blandly that she know she done brung back ev'y las' thing she took out, 'cause she hung 'em on her own line an' dey ain't been nobody near 'em but her an' de chillun, we falter meekly that it doesn't matter, and that the tablecloths look nice; and we give her a pair of stockings with just one tiny hole in them, and the dress she has scorched in two in the back breadth to make over for little Susan; and we pay her the full week's wages.

In our hearts we feel that we are " quality," and so cannot afford to hold Negroes to a strict account. For fifty years we have trained those of them with whom we have come in contact to rate both our friendship and our gentility in exact proportion to what we put up with from them, and what we give them without expectation of return. They think none the less of Northern people who require a return in well-done work for money received ; but Southerners are " our white folks," and such exactions from them arouse instant distrust in the average Negro's breast, the least of his suspicions being that his employer has no connection with the " quality."

A year or two ago I had a bright little coloured girl about sixteen years old as extra help while company was in the house. I never have locked things up. I would rather have a dishonest servant steal from me than hurt an honest one's feelings : so I take my chances. But things did so vanish out of the pantry ! Cake and fruit just melted into air. The cook was as honest as I was ; and my little housemaid was getting fat. Finally, when a basket of high-priced peaches lost two-thirds of its contents before appearing in the house at all, I knew, like Brer Rabbit, that something had to be done. I talked to the child seriously about honesty as an asset of character. She turned on me with round-eyed wonder, and with what I still believe to have been genuine scorn.

"Well, if ever I had white folks talk to me like that!" she exclaimed. "*Honest!* I been honest all my life! I ain't never worked anywhere since I was born"—she had been at it, by spells, ever since she was ten—"where white folks grudge me what I et before. Ef it belongs to my white folks hit belongs to me, an' I takes it. I ain't goin' to work for no other kind." And she put on her hat and went home : I was beneath her services.

I felt ashamed. I had put up with her pilferings a long time before I spoke ; and I and others like me had been training her, and tens of thousands more, to shiftlessness and dishonesty ever since they were born. The wonder is not that so many of them are worthless, but that there are so many honest, painstaking, trustworthy ones among them. They have attained to honesty with little help from us.

I once praised a cook of mine for her exquisite cleanliness, and the economy with which she evolved the most delicious dishes. She really was a jewel of a cook. She laughed amusedly when I spoke.

"I worked up North twelve years, an' I

learned things," she said. "If I was dirty, or wasted, I lost my place. And I'd have lost it in a minute if I'd taken things. Yankee women don't put up with nothin'; they fire you an' do the work themselves."

She turned on me suddenly.

"It's you white people's fault we coloured people are so triflin'!" she burst out. "You-all scold us, but you put up with us. We don't need to do any better, because we get along just as well as if we did honest work. You-all say 'Oh, what can you expect of darkies?' But we can be honest, and up there they make us. I wasn't no manner of account till I went North. An' if the Yankees had some of these other servants 'round yere they'd learn 'em somethin'. We can do better—if we must!"

Now in all these matters, great and small, and in dozens more which may not here be touched upon, what basis for living does white example furnish? Outside of personal and often unreasoning kindness, where we are prone to take the attitude of feudal lords who give *largesse*, what is there in our treatment of the Negro to inspire him with respect for justice and the law? If we will lay aside our preconceived notions for a little, and go over all the complex web of racial relations in the South as they might appear to a gentleman from Mars, for instance, newly landed on the earth, what is there, outcome of the fifty years, commensurate with the obligation of a strong people to a weak one? What have we done to bind them to us? What to lift them up? What foundation have we as a people laid for dwelling with them in honour and mutual good will?

I do not mean to imply that no basis of justice exists : if it did not, our civilization would be falling of its own weight. It does exist between many individual lives, both white and black. But as a people for a people the foundation is yet to be sought : and other foundation than justice there is none.

There is no sense in mincing matters. We are no longer children. It is the first step that costs, always ; but the first step is very plain. It is to put away childish things—unreasoning prejudice and unreasoning pride —and to look truth squarely in the face, as men and women who love it at all costs. There is no truth in a detached view of the Negro, or of any human being. Everybody on earth is human first and racial afterwards. We must see in the Negro first of all, deeper than all, higher than all, a man, made in the image of God as truly as we ourselves. If in the race that image be less developed than in our own, in some individuals of the race it is certainly more highly developed than in some individuals of ours. And whatever grows is growable.

The only basis of living between man and man, whether low or high, which is safe for either is justice. And where there is less than justice, the danger is ever greater for the oppressor than for the oppressed. If white civilization is to endure, in the South or anywhere else, it must strike deep roots into the soil of our common humanity, and reach down to that bed-rock of justice which makes the framework of the world.

And one thing more is needed. For justice is a hard, cold thing; stable and strong; yet must it be softened to nourish a people's growth, and pass through the alembic of life itself before it can mount to light and warmth, and flutter brave banners in the sunshine, for the joy and refreshment of mankind.

There are some elements of the inorganic world so diverse that they can never join hands for useful work except in the presence of another element which, in some way beyond our knowledge as yet, removes the unseen barriers, and allows the two to meet.

We call it catalytic action, by way of labelling our ignorance; and that which allows the unrelated fragments to exert their latent power for common service is a catalyser.

We are not left without a catalyser in our diverse human life. In an atmosphere of sympathy, of human brotherhood, of care for all for whom Christ died, the races of men—all races—may come together, for service of that great Race which climbs upward to the light.

My only fear for white supremacy is that we should prove unworthy of it. If we fail there, we shall pass. Supremacy is for service. It is suicide to thrust other races back from the good which we hold in trust for humanity. For him who would be greatest the price is still that he shall be servant of all.

III

HOUSES AND HOMES

LONG ago, when I was a child, a grown-up cousin took me driving one afternoon behind a pair of his thoroughbreds. As we swept over the long shell road through autumn sunshine, with the pine trees singing overhead and the wind whitening the waves in the harbour beyond, I came on one of those experiences known to us all, when something long familiar yet never noticed stands suddenly forth, challenging eye and soul in a manner never to be forgotten.

Beside the road was a one-roomed Negro cabin, built of logs and chinked with mud. Its one door swung wide, and showed the rotted floor within. At the side was an unglazed opening like an eyeless socket, through which I glimpsed a tumbled bed and a broken cook-stove. A woman stood by the door, a little child beside her. Their rags were thick with dirt. The child looked at us with the wonder and interest of life yet in his young eyes; but the woman's black face was expressionless, her murky eyes unquestioning, unexpectant. She saw us because we crossed her field of vision, just as an animal might see a passing bird.

The day was glorious, our swift flight intoxicating; the swaying pines called to the blood, and the sea sang of wonders yet to be; but the stolid woman and her eyeless home blotted out everything else. I had looked at the like a thousand times; but somehow that day, in my riot of physical and mental exaltation, I had eyes to see; and the shock of it made me gasp.

"Why must they live like that?" I demanded. "Why do I have everything, and they nothing?"

My elderly cousin laughed a little, and then, realizing my excitement, spoke soberly.

"Don't take other people's troubles too seriously, my dear; try to understand how much being used to things means. If those darkies had to live in your house they'd never rest till they got it as dirty and broken up as what they're used to. Then they'd be comfortable. They like what they've got: they're made that way."

I considered this comfortable doctrine in silence. Then:

"Why didn't God make them another way —some clean way? It would have been just as easy."

"That's too deep water for a person of your inches," he replied. "You must take God and folks like you find them. But that little darkey has as much fun as you do— maybe more: don't worry your head over nonsense."

A year or two afterwards my father's business took us to a great city of the North; and I was soon hard at work, on Saturdays and Sundays, at a church mission in the tenement district. Not content with the class work at the chapel I visited my small pupils in their—no, not their homes; I could never call them that; their dens. There were long stairs slippery with dirt, where blows and curses from the foul, dark rooms assailed my ears; there were rooms with one tiny window, and rooms with no window at all; there were beds and tubs and stoves and sewing-machines and babies and rags and tin cans and children and dirt and noise in one horrible confusion.

My mother was dead, and I kept my expeditions to myself. But I turned back to what my cousin had said about the Negroes for comfort. Did these white people like the

way they lived? Were they made that way too?

The more I saw of them the more dubious I became; but my sociological researches, becoming known to the family, were summarily put a stop to. So I dropped the biological method and took to books.

But through those early experiences I came unconsciously to regard slum-dwellers as of one class. There were people of many races in those tenements; but their differences sank out of sight before the common degradation of their lives. And always with the thought of these came the memory of that Negro woman and her not-yet stolid child. They were human too; and there was something in them deeper than being Negroes—something that was kin to these emigrants of the tenements, and to me, and to all the world. They were a part of human life, like the rest: their fundamental needs and their fundamental reactions to environment were the same in kind. Whatever differences existed, they were differences in degree.

It is this recognition of human oneness that opens the door of understanding into the Negro slums. One slum interprets another; each slum-dweller helps to explain all the **rest**, whatever their nationality, **wherever**

their abode. We can see this when we get
rid of the deadening influence of the old
political economy, and recognize the Negro
slum for what it, and all slums, are—the joint
product of ignorance, greed, and the mon-
strous old doctrine of *laissez faire.*

The old political economy was a science of
investigation, not one of construction, and
still less one at all concerned with morality.
It observed the methods of human business
intercourse much as one might examine the
ways of earthquakes, or any other natural phe-
nomena, with a view to deducting therefrom
certain fixed laws as inherent in the nature
of things, and as unmoral, as the attraction of
oxygen and hydrogen. Thus, for example,
the old doctrine concerning wages—that the
employer would inevitably drive the workman
as close to the edge of starvation as he possibly could while still keeping him alive to
work; and that the workman would resist as
much as he dared with the fear of losing his
job before his eyes—was accepted as a basal
law of a world where, apparently, whatever
was was right. In such a world, the law of
gravitation was no firmer or more respectable
a fixture than the law that the landlord should
get the highest rent he could for the cheapest
shelter the poor could be induced to accept.

The watchword of the old political economy was that business is business—a territory roped off from human considerations, and governed by laws of its own. When human beings got into this district they were subject to the law of the land, which gave a chance only to him who could snatch and hold it. Religion and philanthropy might stand without if they would, and more or less liberally anoint the wounds of those who were worsted in the struggle, but otherwise they had no concern in the fray.

This conception of human relations had governed the world for ages before Ricardo formulated his "iron law." Its mark is deep in our life and thought to-day; and nowhere is it plainer, the world around, than upon the houses of the poor. In all countries where there is enough of civilization for society to have become divided into groups, the poorer folk, often without a sense of wrong on their part or injustice on the landlords', have been huddled together in a manner to bring property-owners the largest returns, regardless of other consequences.

Those other consequences have none the less left their mark also deep in human life. They are the same everywhere, regardless of country or race.

Cleanliness of body and of habitation is a fundamental preparation for cleanliness of mind, and water and fresh air exist in abundance to furnish it; yet the houses of those who most need cleanliness, and to whom it is most difficult by inclination and occupation, are largely cut off from these two necessities without which human life cannot be normal. A well-to-do child, with generations of bath-tubs, outdoor sports, and sunny rooms behind him, might retain through life moral and even physical health under the conditions of the world's slums; but his children would show signs of breaking; and their children would be as truly of the slum as their neighbours. Generations of gain could be lost in one man's lifetime. Yet of the mass of the Negroes, who live in the slums we have built for them, where water is hard to come by and adequate ventilation impossible, we say that they are dirty by nature, and that to provide better things would result only in a waste of money.

We know little, as yet, in this our dawn of social consciousness, of the slums of the rest of the world. Our slum-dwellers are to us a race apart, a separate fragment of life, unrelated, a law unto themselves. They make their slums, we think, as a spider spins his web, from within. We all know, of course, that very many Negroes are far above the slum-dwellers. There are few communities in the South, however small, without a few Negroes whom the whites respect and trust. But we regard them, not as the natural outcome of a more normal chance in life, but as exceptions to the law of Negro development, through some personally-inherent exceptional quality, probably an infusion of white blood.

We need a wide horizon for the understanding of our slum-dweller. When we set him in his world-relations we see that in all mankind slum conditions produce slum results. Waterless, ill-ventilated houses, crowded beyond the possibility of decency because of low wages and high rents, make impossible the physical basis that is necessary for even the poorest home. And with this kind of housing go other evils, all working together to produce in any people, the world around, those characteristics which we believe to be racial and Negro. In a population racially homogeneous, like that of Rome or of Pekin, or racially heterogeneous like that of Chicago or New York, or in a bi-racial population like our own, the results are the same. Bad housing conditions, in-

sufficient or un-nourishing food, vicious surroundings, a childhood spent unprotected in
the streets, produce, in Europe, Asia, and
America, ill-nourished bodies, unbalanced
nerves, vacant and vicious minds, a craving
for stimulants and all evil excitements, lack
of energy, weakened wills, laziness, thriftless-
ness, unreliability in every relation of life.

As life rises, it differentiates. Anglo-Saxon
and Chinaman develop along different lines ;
and the higher their development the less
alike they are. Each brings his own race-
contribution to the great Race of Man. But
in those lowest depths, where men are thrust
back towards the level of beasts, acquired
characteristics are in abeyance, and the old
brute longings dominate once more. Men
are wonderfully alike on this level—as alike
as are vegetable and animal on their lowest
plane : and yellow or white or black, there
is little for any to boast of. But when
normal conditions of growth are furnished,
men of each race will come true to type ;
and the higher they rise the greater their
differences will be. Just what the highest
type of the Negro race will be nobody
knows ; for as a race they have not yet had
normal conditions, nor time for full development. But whatever it may be, it will not

be a white type, nor a red nor a yellow one ; and it will be something needed for the perfect development of the Race of Man.

These things being so—and a wide world-look is convincing—the places where our poorest live, our weakest and most tempted folk, take on new aspects and suggest new implications. Our slums are not the product of a race unrelated and incapable of development ; they are our part of a world-wide morass where life capable of higher things is sucked under and destroyed.

The old political economy took no account of such matters ; it accepted as a universal law the policy of exploitation, of individualistic commercialism, of cut-throat competition. It saw, not human beings, but profit and loss.

The new political economy is shifting the thought and the business of the world towards a basis of human brotherhood. It puts human rights above profit and loss, and holds conservation a wiser policy than exploitation. As to the human morass, it would drain it. And all this not as a matter of charity, not because Christ said men are all brethen ; but because we *are* all brethren, and so lose more than we gain, in the long run, if we run things on any other basis. That thing Christ said is true !

When one sees in the slum-dweller a brother, what is one to do? If he really is a brother it will pay to treat him like one. Laws—the real ones—never do contradict one another. No law of true prosperity can be infringed upon by obedience to the law of brotherhood, if brotherhood is a real fact. It will work with any other real law there is.

A woman saw that, fifty years ago, and set out to demonstrate it in this very matter of housing.

" The people's homes are bad," she wrote, " partly because they are badly built and arranged; they are tenfold worse because the tenants' habits and lives are what they are. Transplant them to-morrow to healthy and commodious homes, and they would pollute and destroy them. There needs, and will need for some time, a reformatory work which will demand that loving zeal of individuals which cannot be legislated for by parliament. The heart of the English nation will supply it. It may and should be organized; it cannot be created."

Might not that have been written of the very poor of New York or St. Louis, instead of the very poor of London? Or of the very poor of Atlanta or Birmingham, who happen to be black?

In 1866, three years after Ruskin's three thousand pounds made the beginning of her work possible, Miss Hill wrote again :

"That the spiritual elevation of a large class depended to a considerable extent on sanitary reform was, I considered, proved. But I was equally certain that sanitary improvement itself was dependent on educational work among grown-up people. . . . It seems to me that a greater power is in the hands of landlords and landladies than of school-teachers—power either of life or death, physical and spiritual.

"The disciplining of our immense poor population must be effected by individual influence ; and this power can change it from a mob of paupers and semi-paupers into a body of self-dependent workers."

It can change it because it did, and does ; and Mr. Ruskin, "who alone believed the scheme would work," was repaid in good English money for his investment, as were the many others whose renting properties she and her trained assistants managed during the fifty years between her first experiment in 1863 and her death in 1912.

After twenty years of work she wrote, in 1883 :

"I have no hesitation in saying that if a

site were handed over to me at the [usual] price, I would engage to house upon it under thoroughly healthy conditions, at rents which they could pay, and which would yield a fair interest on capital, a very large proportion of the very poor."

And what was Miss Hill's scheme? Just a combination of the law of brotherhood with a sound business policy in collecting rents. With Ruskin's money she acquired three houses "in a dreadful state of dirt and neglect." This was remedied, and an ample water supply provided. She herself undertook to collect the weekly rent. At first her tenants regarded her as a natural enemy. Sometimes, when she went on Saturday nights for her rent, she found them lying on their filthy floors, dead drunk. The rent would often be thrust out to her through a crack in the door, held fast against her entrance. The stairs were " many inches deep in dirt, so hardened that a shovel had to be used to get it off." The people were the poorest renting class, just above vagrants; they lived on the edge of crime, and all too frequently passed over the fatal line. " Truly," said Miss Hill, "a wild, lawless, desolate little kingdom to rule over."

" On what principles was I to rule these

people? On the same that I had already tried, and tried with success, in other places, and which I may sum up as the two following: firstly, to demand a strict fulfillment of their duties to me—one of the chief of which would be the punctual payment of rent; and secondly, to endeavour to be so unfailingly just and patient, that they should learn to trust the rule that was over them.

"With regard to details, I would make a few improvements at once—such, for example, as the laying on of water and repairing of dust bins; but, for the most part, improvements should be made only by degrees, as the people became more capable of valuing and not abusing them. I would have the rooms distempered and thoroughly cleansed as they became vacant, and then they should be offered to the more cleanly of the tenants. I would save such repairs as were not immediately needed as a means of giving work to the men in times of distress. I would draft the occupants of the underground kitchens into the up-stairs rooms, and would ultimately convert the kitchens into bath-rooms and wash-houses. I would have the landlady's portion of the house—*i. e.*, the stairs and passages—at once repaired and distempered; and they should be regularly

scrubbed, and, as far as possible, made
models of cleanliness; for I knew from former
experience that the example of this would, in
time, silently spread itself to the rooms themselves, and that payment for this work would
give me some hold over the elder girls. I
would collect savings personally, not trust to
their being taken to distant banks or saving
clubs. And, finally, I knew that I should
learn to feel these people as my friends, and
so should instinctively feel the same respect
for their privacy and their independence, and
should treat them with the same courtesy,
that I should show towards any other personal friends. There would be no interference, no entering their rooms uninvited, no
offer of money or the necessaries of life. But
when occasion presented itself I should give
them any help I could, such as I might offer
without insult to other friends—sympathy in
their distresses; advice, help, and counsel in
their difficulties. . . .

" When we set about our repairs and alter-
ations, there was much that was discourag-
ing. The better class of people in the court
were hopeless of any permanent improvement. When one of the tenants of the shops
saw that we were sending workmen into the
empty rooms, he said considerately, 'I'll tell

AN ALABAMA SCHOOL IMPROVEMENT LEAGUE.

A GEORGIA COUNTY SUPERINTENDENT VISITING
NEGRO SCHOOL.

you what it is, Miss, it'll cost you a lot o'
money to repair them places, and it's no
good. The women's 'eads'll be druv through
the door panels again in no time, and the
place is good enough for such cattle as them
there.' But we were not to be deterred.

"On the other hand, we were not to be
hurried in our action by threats. These were
not wanting. For no sooner did the tenants
see the workmen about than they seemed to
think that if they only clamoured enough,
they would get their own rooms put to rights.
Nothing had been done for years. Now,
they thought, was their opportunity. More
than one woman locked me in her room with
her, the better to rave and storm. She would
shake the rent in her pocket to tempt me
with the sound of the money, and roar out
' that never a farthing of it would she pay till
her grate was set,' or her floor was mended,
as the case might be. Perfect silence would
make her voice drop lower and lower, until at last she would stop, wondering that no
violent answers were hurled back at her, and
a pause would ensue. I felt that promises
would be little believed in, and besides, I
wished to feel free to do as much, and only
as much, as seemed to me best ; so that my
plan was to trust to my deeds to speak for

themselves, and inspire confidence as time went on.

"The importance of advancing slowly, and of gaining some hold over the people as a necessary accompaniment to any real improvement in their dwellings, was perpetually apparent. Their habits were so degraded that we had to work a change in these before they would make any proper use of the improved surroundings we were prepared to give them. We had locks torn off, windows broken, drains stopped, dust-bins misused in every manner ; even pipes broken, and water-taps wrenched away. This was sometimes the result of carelessness, and a deeply-rooted habit of dirt and untidiness ; sometimes the damage was willful. Our remedy was to watch the right moment for furnishing these appliances, to persevere in supplying them, and to get the people by degrees to work with us for their preservation. I have learned to know that people are ashamed to abuse a place they find cared for. They will add dirt to dirt till a place is pestilential, but the more they find done for it, the more they will respect it, till at last order and cleanliness prevail. It is this feeling of theirs, coupled with the fact that they do not like those whom they have learned to love, and whose standard is higher than their own, to see things which would grieve them, which has enabled us to accomplish nearly every reform of outward things that we have achieved ; so that the surest way to have any place kept clean is to go through it often yourself. . . .

" I mentioned our custom of using some of the necessary, yet not immediately wanted repairs as a means of affording work to tenants in slack times. . . . When a tenant is out of work, instead of reducing his energy by any gifts of money, we simply, whenever the funds at our disposal allow it, employ him in restoring and purifying the houses. And what a difference five shillings' worth of work in a bad week will make to a family ! The father, instead of idling listlessly at the corner of the street, sets busily and happily to work, prepares the whitewash, mends the plaster, distempers the room ; the wife bethinks herself of having a turn-out of musty corners or drawers—untouched, maybe, for months—of cleaning her windows, perhaps even of putting up a clean blind ; and thus a sense of decency, the hope of beginning afresh and doing better, comes like new life into the home.

" The same cheering and encouraging sort of influence, though in a less degree, is exer-

cised by our plan of having a little band of
scrubbers.

" We have each passage scrubbed twice a
week by one of the elder girls.   The sixpence
thus earned is a stimulus, and they often take
an extreme interest in the work itself.   One
little girl was so proud of her first cleaning
that she stood two hours watching her passage lest the boys, whom she considered as
the natural enemies of order and cleanliness,
should spoil it before I came to see it.   And
one woman remarked to her neighbour how
nice the stairs looked.   'They haven't been
cleaned,' she added, 'since ever I came into
this house.'   She had been there six years!
The effect of these clean passages frequently
spreads to the rooms, as the dark line of de-
marcation between the cleaned passage and
the still dirty room arouses the attention, and
begins to trouble the minds of its inmates.

" Gradually, then, these various modes of
dealing with our little realm began to tell.
Gradually the people began to trust us ; and
gradually the houses were improved.   The
sense of quiet power and sympathy soon
made itself felt, and less and less was there
any sign of rudeness or violence towards ourselves.   Even before the first winter was over
many a one would hurry to light us up the

stairs, and instead of my having the rent-book and money thrust to me through the half-open door, my reception would be, ' Oh, can't you come in, Miss, and sit down for a bit?' Little by little houses were renovated, the grates reset, the holes in the floors repaired, the cracking, dirty plaster replaced by a clean, smooth surface, the heaps of rubbish removed, and we progressed towards order.

"Amongst the many benefits which the possession of the houses enables us to confer on the people, perhaps one of the most important, is our power of saving them from neighbours who would render their lives miserable. It is a most merciful thing to protect the poor from the pain of living in the next room to drunken, disorderly people. ' I am dying,' said an old woman to me the other day : ' I wish you would put me where I can't hear S—— beating his wife. Her screams are awful. And B——, too, he do come in so drunk. Let me go over the way to No. 30.' Our success depends on duly arranging the inmates : not too many children in any one house, so as to overcrowd it ; not too few, so as to overcrowd another ; not two bad people side by side, or they drink to-together ; not a terribly bad person beside a very respectable one. .   .   .

" On Saturday evenings, about eight o'clock, the tenants know that we are to be found in the club-room . . . and that they may come to us there if they like, either for business or a friendly chat.

" Picture a low, rather long room, one of my assistants and myself sitting in state, with pen and ink and bags for money at a deal table under a flaring gas-jet ; the door, which leads straight into the court, standing wide open. A bright red blind, drawn down over the broad window, prevents the passers-by from gazing in there, but round the open door there are gathered a set of wild, dirty faces looking in upon us. Such a semicircle they make, as the strong gas-light falls upon them ! They are mostly children with di- shevelled hair, and ragged, uncared-for clothes ; but above them, now and then, one sees the haggard face of a woman hurrying to make her Saturday evening purchases, or the vacant stare of some half-drunken man. The grown-up people who stop to look in are usually strangers, for those who know us generally come in to us. ' Well ! they give it this time, anyhow,' one woman will exclaim, sitting down on a bench near us, so engrossed in the question of whether she obtains a par- ish allowance that she thinks ' they ' can mean no one but the Board of Guardians, and 'it' nothing but the much-desired allowance. 'Yes, I thought I'd come in and tell you,' she will go on; 'I went up Tuesday ——' And then will follow the whole story.

"'Well, and how do you find yourself, Miss?' a big Irish labourer in a flannel jacket will say, entering afterwards; 'I just come in to say I shall be knocked off Monday; finished a job across the park: and if so be there's any little thing in whitewashing to do, why, I'll be glad to do it.'

"'Presently,' we reply, nodding to a thin, slight woman at the door. She has not spoken, but we know the meaning of that beseeching look. She wants us to go up and get her husband's rent from him before he goes out to spend more of it in drink.

"The eager, watchful eyes of one of our little scrubbers next attract attention: there she stands, with her savings-card in her hand, waiting till we enter the sixpences she has earned from us during the week. 'How much have I got?' she says, eyeing the written sixpences with delight, 'because mother says, please, I'm to draw out next Saturday; she's going to buy me a pair of boots.'

"'Take two shillings on the card and four

shillings rent,' a proudly happy woman will
say, as she lays down a piece of bright gold.
A rare sight this in the court, but her husband has been in regular work for some
little time.

"'Please, Miss,' says another woman, 'will
you see and do something for Jane? She's
that masterful since her father died, I can't
do nothing with her, and she'll do no good
in this court. Do see and get her a place
somewheres away.'

"A man will enter now: 'I'll leave you
my rent to-night, Miss, instead o' Monday,
please; it'll be safer with you than with me.'

"A pale woman comes next, in great
sorrow. Her husband, she tells us, has been
arrested without cause. We believe this to
be true; the man has always paid his way
honestly, worked industriously, and lived
decently. So my assistant goes round to
the police-station at once to bail him, while
I remain to collect the savings. 'Did he
seem grateful?' I say to her on her return.
'He took it very quietly,' is her answer; 'he
seemed to feel it quite natural that we should
help him.'

"Such are some of the scenes on our
savings evenings; such some of the services
we are called upon to render; such the kind

of footing we are on with our tenants. An evening such as this assuredly shows that our footing has somewhat changed since those spent in this court during the first winter.

" My readers will not imagine that I mean to imply that there are not still depths of evil remaining in this court. It would be impossible for such a place as I described it as being originally to be raised in two years to a satisfactory condition. But what I do contend is, that we have worked some very real reforms, and seen some very real results. I feel that it is in a very great degree a question of time, and that, now that we have got hold of the hearts of the people, the court is sure to improve steadily. It will pay as good a percentage to its owners, and will benefit its tenants as much, as any of the other properties under my management have done. This court contains two out of eight properties on which the same plans have been tried, and all of them are increasingly prosperous. The first two were purchased by Mr. Ruskin.

" It appears to me then to be proved by practical experience that when we can induce the rich to undertake the duties of landlord in poor neighbourhoods, and ensure a sufficient amount of the wise, personal super-vision of educated and sympathetic people acting as their representatives, we achieve results which are not attainable in any other way. . . . It is not so much a question of dealing with houses alone, as of dealing with houses in connection with their influence on the character and habits of the people who inhabit them. . . . The principle on which the whole work rests is that the inhabitants and their surroundings must be improved together. It has never yet failed to succeed.

" Finally, I would call upon those who may possess cottage property in large towns to consider the immense power they thus hold in their hands, and the large influence for good they may exercise by the wise use of that power. . . . And I would ask those who do not hold such property to con-sider whether they might not, by possessing themselves of some, confer lasting benefits on their poorer neighbours?

" In these pages I have dwelt mainly on the way our management affects the people, as I have given elsewhere my experience as to financial matters and details of practical management. But I may here urge one thing on those about to undertake to deal with such property—the extreme importance of enforcing the punctual payment of rents. This principle is a vital one. Firstly, because it strikes one blow at the credit system, that curse of the poor; secondly, because it prevents large losses from bad debts, and prevents the tenant from believing he will be suffered to remain, whatever his conduct may be, resting that belief on his knowledge of the large sum that would be lost were he turned out; and, thirdly, because the mere fact that the man is kept up to his duty is a help to him, and increases his self-respect and hope of doing better.

" I would also say to those who, in the carrying out of such an undertaking, are brought into immediate contact with the tenants, that its success will depend most of all on their giving sympathy to the tenants, and awakening confidence in them ; but it will depend also in a great degree on their power of bestowing concentrated attention on small details. . . .

" It is the small things of the world that colour the lives of those around, and it is on persistent efforts to reform these that progress depends ; and we may rest assured that they who see with greater eyes than ours have a due estimate of the service, and that if we did but perceive the mighty principles underlying these tiny things we should rather feel awed that we are entrusted with them at all, than scornful and impatient that they are no larger. What are we that we should ask for more than that God should let us work for Him among the tangible things which He created to be fair, and the human spirits which He redeemed to be pure?"

I have quoted at length from Miss Hill's little book, partly because her work is so little known in the South; partly because her own words make so clear the basis of human sympathy on which the success of all such work must depend. That sympathy is a world-principle, a world-need, and a world-power. If she proved with these people—as she did for fifty years—that business success is entirely compatible with a spirit of brotherhood; that housing reform and the reform of immorality and vice go hand in hand; that paupers and semi-paupers can be changed into a body of self-dependent workers; then surely there is hope for slum-dwellers elsewhere.

The Octavia Hill plan has been tried in a number of cities in England and Scotland; and in New York, Boston, and Philadelphia. The work has been to a remarkable degree both financially and humanly successful.

Mme. Montessori's work in Rome is among this same tenement class. Her Houses of Childhood are in re-made tenements, where good business and brotherhood go hand in hand. The children who have astonished the world are from this same class of paupers, semi-paupers and criminals. Until opportunity was offered these who had been denied it, who could have guessed the measure of their response?

The Negroes of this same economic class need what their class needs the world around. They will respond in the same way. The colour of one's skin, or even the shape of one's head, cannot change the working of a principle. The trouble in lifting up this lowest class of Negroes is that we have not yet paid the price. Things worth doing always cost ; and to do this thing among us will take, in somebody's heart, that same passion for justice and opportunity for the weak that it takes everywhere else.

But the doing of it need not wait until that passion rises in all hearts, else one might well despair. Prove that a thing pays—in money—and it goes. Men and women who cared little for humanity were glad to turn the management of their tenement property over to Miss Hill as soon as they found returns by her methods were better than by theirs. She was so overwhelmed with offers that she and her assistants had to refuse much of what the owners urged upon them. Many of the great manufacturers of this and other countries frankly admit that their reason for the extensive welfare work they carry on among their working people is purely a business one : they have found that it pays, in money, to care for "the human end of the machine."

That is the way the world moves. The people with love in their hearts, the seers, pay the price, open the new way, and prove it better than the old ; then people walk in it, because it is proven good.

There is nothing to do with many of the shanties for Negroes, in city and country, but to condemn them by law and tear them down. As our social conscience becomes aroused this will inevitably be done. Many houses now in use would do very well if given a water supply and some extra windows, provided the rent-collecting were done, not by an indifferent or contemptuous real estate agent, but on the Octavia Hill plan.

Negro women of force and character should be trained under white auspices to do this work. Two or three owners of Negro renting property could together employ such a rent collector for what the real estate agent would cost, or less. Their property would improve as well as their tenants ; and the frightful waste of humanity that goes on in our slums, the drifting of wreckage into prisons and poorhouses, would not only be checked, but these now broken creatures would become a community asset, as every real worker is.

We need an experiment station in the housing of Negroes of this class. An ordinary city block, two-thirds of it covered with decent little houses, could carry the interest on the whole investment, though one-third be given over to a playground, on a corner of which should stand a community house with rooms for clubs and industrial classes, as well as a decent meeting place for young people in the evening. Such a plant would demonstrate that healthful housing of the very poor could be made a paying investment ; and the income from it, if made available for such a purpose, would provide for the training, under the best of white management, of the Negro social workers so sorely needed in the homes of our poor.

Calls for such workers are already coming from white people in several Southern states.

The owner of a lumber camp in the South-west, who has long carried on welfare work among his white employees, has tried to get a Negro woman to help his coloured employees; and similar efforts have been lately made by several others. A Southern white woman wrote me recently of conditions in a camp of Negroes where electricity was being developed from water power. The workmen had their families with them—fourteen hundred black folk in all, herded like cattle there in God's clean mountains, and living as untaught, helpless people will. Drinking, vice, and immorality were rampant. The women knew nothing of home-making, had homes been possible. The children were born like flies, and grew or died in moral and physical filth. A breeding-place for criminals! And the right kind of Negro woman, properly trained, and backed by a corporation merely selfishly intelligent, could have brought outward order and decency, lifted the workers to a far higher efficiency, and created many real homes there, each one a point of contagion for life and hope and health. It would pay in dollars and cents.

It is impossible to speak of housing for Negroes without a word about the better classes among them, and the fight these must make for decent homes.

The thrifty working people, who constitute a large and ever-growing class, make heroic sacrifices to own their own homes. This is easier to do in the country than in the city, and the home, when won, is far safer; for if one owns even a very few acres one need not fear the placing of a saloon next door, or a low dance-hall, or a vice resort for white people—evils which constantly threaten every Negro owner of a hard-won city home. Sanitary conditions, too, are under one's own control, and with intelligent parents it is possible for children to grow up in robust health, which they can scarcely do in those parts of our cities open to Negro homes. The country is the place for poor Negroes, not because they are Negroes, but because they are human, and of like needs with the rest of the world.

But before they will be permanently content in the country they must have what any race of people must have under like conditions: perfect security for life and property; and such education as will relate them to country life in an efficient, social and joyful way.

Neither of these things is beyond attainment. The trend towards better education

in the Negro rural schools is noted elsewhere ; and the effects of this movement will
be powerfully reinforced by the decision of
the United States Government to use its eight
hundred Southern farm-demonstrators for
work among both races. There is also a
strong element in the Southern state universities which favours the inclusion of gatherings of Negro farmers in the agricultural
extension work of their lecturers and demon-
strators. When these things bear fruit, and
when not merely a large part of the South,
but absolutely all of it, is as safe for Negroes
as for white people, the housing of the
country Negro will be a problem practically
solved.

The city dwellers are in a harder case.
The poorest share the fate of slum-dwellers
of all races. They live in those sections
which are morally and physically the least
desirable, and are neglected habitually by the
city health authorities. Cleanliness and decency are alike beyond them. But in addition to these things, in far too many of our
cities, both the respectable working man and
the prosperous, educated Negro are forced to
live in surroundings from which men of any
other race, of their economic status, would
be allowed to escape.

It is even worse than that. When by their own efforts a few Negroes secure a respectable neighbourhood, families of the better class building up a little community of their own, they are peculiarly liable to have saloons and houses of ill-fame thrust upon them by a low class of whites whom the upper classes do not restrain. The Negro owner of a city home, whatever his education or business success, whatever the sum invested in his property, cannot be sure, from month to month, of retaining for his family surroundings compatible with moral health and safety.

I know a Negro, an honour graduate of Brown University, a winner there of the fellowship in the American School at Athens, Greece. He is a man of wide attainments, of blameless life, of modesty and good manners. He is in full sympathy with the best Southern thought concerning race relations ; and his wide influence among his people is a thing for white Southerners to be thankful for. He has turned aside from money-getting, all these years, to serve his people in return for a very simple living. By what effort one can imagine he bought a little home. It is far from his work, on the outskirts of the city, placed there in the hope that his children might grow up in safety.

His home attracted other homes, until the neighbourhood became good enough for a white man's house of ill-fame, which he found was to be erected on the lot adjoining his own. He has three daughters, the oldest barely grown. He saved himself by buying the lot, at a cost of long saving and strain.

"But I am not safe any more," he said. "There are still vacant lots there; and I can't possibly buy them all."

If I were a Negro I should do just as Negroes do—resent with all my heart our stupid white assumption that when they attempt to buy property in our own desirable sections they are trying to force themselves upon us in impudence, and to assert their belief in and desire for "social equality."

What these Negroes of the better classes want is first of all a neighbourhood of assured moral decency in which to rear their children. Their passionate desire for character in their children we do not begin to understand. Next to that they want sanitary conditions, and avoidance of the lower classes of their own people, just as we do ourselves. To get these things some Negroes are willing to thrust themselves, if they can, among white people, and to endure their resentment and contempt.

"If you white people could only understand!" a Negro woman said to me not long ago, her face fired with feeling. "We don't want our homes where we're not wanted. But we want to be decent, too. And it's the same all over the country—anything will do for a 'nigger.' You think we're all alike, and you don't care what happens to us just so we're out of your sight. My husband and I were living in Denver; and we had money to pay for a comfortable house. But there wasn't a place for rent to Negroes that a self-respecting Negro would have. And how will my people ever learn to be decent if they must live in the white people's vice district?"

We have no right to treat people like that. In one large Southern city, with high taxes and a big revenue and an expensive health department, a white friend of mine counted one morning twelve dead cats and dogs, in various stages of decomposition, in one short Negro alley. It was not an uncommon sight, except that the corpses were rather numerous. The outhouses are vile beyond description, a menace not merely to the Negroes but to the entire community. Yet if a Negro tries to buy a home in a healthful part of town we think his one motive is to thrust himself upon us, socially, just as far as he dares.

The way out of a situation like that is so simple, so plain! What is needed to solve the problem is not a segregation law, to force those who would be clean back into the bog we ought to drain out of existence ; it is just to put ourselves in the Negroes' place and do as we would be done by. If we white people could only have a Negro's consciousness for a day or two it would clear up so many things. As it is, we can at least use our imagination.

If the city's health laws were enforced where they are most needed, punishing those who break them if necessary, till they learned better ; if streets could be set aside in a district capable of being made attractive, and a fair share of city improvements put there ; if the Negroes who built good homes there were protected as well-to-do white people are from the fear of saloons and other vice resorts ; if it were all done not in contempt, but in a spirit of justice and human consideration, there would be no need for segregation laws. Negroes, like white people, like to live among their friends. The overwhelming majority of them believe, as we do, in the social separation of the races ; and beyond that, they do not want their children to grow up among those who look down upon them.

I am told that a well-to-do Negro in Kansas City, understanding his people's feeling, bought a considerable tract of land there, some distance out, and improved it as white men do for white buyers. The lots were sold under restrictions which guaranteed the neighbourhood morally, and went, my informant said, "like hot cakes." The place is to-day the most desirable for Negro home-owners in Kansas City. The man who bought the land originally made a handsome profit. His example could be followed by real estate men, white or black, in any large Southern city with an assurance of success. It is really not bad business to do justice.

I have dwelt at length on this matter of Negro homes because it is fundamental to justice, and therefore to any lasting adjustment between the races. No people can rise higher than their homes. And we criticize unsparingly the Negro's weakness and faults, yet fasten upon him living conditions which, the world over and among all races, breed just those things for which we blame him most.

IV

AN OUNCE OF PREVENTION

THERE is practical unanimity in the South regarding the low moral standards of the Negro race as a whole. We admit that there are exceptions to the rule ; we always know a few personally. But the overwhelming concensus of opinion is that Negroes generally are dirty, untruthful, and immoral; and beyond and above and below everything else, they are by nature dishonest.

However exaggerated such statements may be as applied to the whole ten million Negroes in America, very many of whom are practically as unknown to us whites as though they lived in another country, they are dangerously true of a large part of that class with which we come most frequently in contact. But have we ever asked ourselves why ? Have we gone into their homes to find what drives them ? Do we know anything of the wants in their lives ? Have we any idea of the tremendous forces of wreckage which gather in those great empty places

where human need cries with none to answer?

If we would look a little into the lives of
those who live below the poverty line in
communities where there are no black people, we would find that there is a certain degree of pressure under which human character, in the mass, tends to break.   The ideal
of humanity is the man who will meet all
tests, endure all pressure, surmount all difficulties, suffer all loss, and pass out at last
still pure in heart, unspotted, undefiled.
However we fail ourselves—nay, because we
fail—we cling to this ideal as the standard by
which men should be judged.   Whatever soil
of sin be on us, we know, in our inmost hearts,
that men and women were meant to be like
that.   It is for this that we honour our heroes
and martyrs, who, wherever they have come
to birth, belong first of all to humanity, and
not to any one race.   It is not for what they
bore that we love them most, nor for what
they have achieved : they are to us revealers
of our own possibilities.   We see in them
the heights to which we ourselves, and all
humanity, were meant to rise.

But is a child's power of resistance to be
tested like an adult's ?   We are learning that
premature burdens will strain young muscle

beyond the possibility of future vigour.   We
found out long ago that young colts and
calves must be shielded from undue strain :
we lost money unless they were.

Later, and more slowly, the world is waking to the money loss involved in straining
children's muscles too soon.   We find that a
child's muscles are a national asset, or ought
to be, as well as a colt's.   But character is a
more precious asset still.   It is a driving-
force scarcely to be measured in national life,
a productive source of wealth, as well as of
happiness, beyond any other one thing.   It
is of far slower growth than muscle, and
strain is more fatal, care more vital to it.
Even the highest races are still so undeveloped morally that in any heavy, wide-
spread stress the cartilaginous honour of
thousands will give under the pressure, until
men hitherto counted blameless seem little
better than beasts.   Times of war disclose
conditions like that, invariably ; and times of
wide-spread panic, or famine, or disaster of
any kind.   The San Francisco earthquake
furnished a recent and spectacular example.

Now when these things are true of favoured
folk, of those who have had something of a
normal chance in life, we may be sure, even
before we look to see, that those cut off from

PLAYGROUND AT STORY HOUR, LOUISVILLE.

a normal chance will not, in the mass, develop much power of resistance to undue strain. They, of all men, have least to bear strain with. Their moral muscles, undernourished and over-strained from birth, are uncoördinated with one another, or with their wills. The will itself hangs loose and undeveloped, shaken by vagrant desires and passing storms of passion. These are the people, the world around, who strew the path of civilization with wreckage. Crime is but the extreme manifestation of conditions which create vast swamps of incapacity, shiftlessness and immorality, in which human character is engulfed as in a quicksand, and out of which crime emerges as the topmost blossom of its rank and fetid growth.

What are some of the main causes of this human ruin and waste? Not here in the South, but everywhere. We have no peculiar laws of life down here, any more than we have peculiar laws of physics. If an apple falls to the ground in England because of the attraction of gravitation, one will fall in Maine, or in Georgia, or in Kamchatka, for exactly the same reason. And if certain conditions in New York wreck physical and moral health in human beings, and result in all unhuman ruin, those same conditions will produce similar results, in any climate, upon any fragment of humanity exposed to them.

We are a pious people here in the South— perhaps, like our brethren elsewhere, more pious than we are Christlike. There are very many of us who, when the effect of conditions on character is asserted, begin at once to defend God's almightiness, and the power of grace to save to the uttermost. To some among us it seems a reflection on grace to suggest that men ever need anything else, or need grace itself anywhere but in their own lives. But they do need it elsewhere, nevertheless—in the hearts and lives of other people, and expressed in the conditions which surround them. One of the best women I know, one of unusual intelligence and education, said to me not long ago, in a hesitating, doubtful voice :

" And you heard her say, that doctor, just as I did, that when she examined the blood of those thirty fallen girls the average for the thirty was less than three million red blood-corpuscles where five million were normal ; and that blood so impoverished lowered the vitality, starved the nerves, lessened their resistive power to temptation and impaired their wills, as well as their energy and ability to work. She said they were not fallen

women : they were felled women—felled by
social conditions to which we Christian women
assented.—It did sound reasonable, I know,
and dreadful. I felt like a criminal myself, almost. But doesn't it leave out God, and salvation ? Where does sin come in when you
look at society like that ? And surely God is
almighty ; and His grace ——" She looked
at me, a puzzled frown between her eyes.

I do not doubt God's almightiness ; nor do
I pretend to understand why, being almighty,
He has chosen to so limit His own power that
His own will cannot possibly get done in this
world until men are willing to do it. I do
not doubt that He can do a great many things
which I feel sure He never will. He never will,
for instance, enable a man to make two hundred bushels of corn to the acre on land un-
cleared of weeds : and He will not return to
any people, or any church, a harvest of
"saved souls" in bodies whose living conditions defy all His laws of health and growth
and decency, moral and physical. ·A few ears
of corn may come to maturity, even among
the weeds ; and a man or woman here or
there may rise to newness of life despite
surroundings which deal death on every
side : but the law holds good, all the same.
It would be quite as effective, and fully as

religious, so far as I can understand, to kneel beside the untouched weeds and pray for a bumper crop of corn as it is for us Christians to pray for the souls' salvation of the poor, and go comfortably home to dinner without one rudimentary intention of furnishing them surroundings in which love and righteousness can flourish. To look at community life like that does not, to my mind, do away with sin. It fixes it on us, the supposedly righteous, who know and do not, rather than on those who neither know nor do, and whom we fail to enlighten or protect.

I know the feeling is very strong in the South against any attempt at regeneration by man-made law instead of by spiritual processes; and I would not seem to fail in reverence to that best and greatest of all miracles, the redeeming life of God in the soul. I believe, in the brave words of Dr. Wines, spoken at the International Prison Congress after forty years of labour for prison reform, that "reformation is never accomplished until the heart has been reached and regenerated by the grace of Almighty God." I also believe that our neglect of the living conditions of the poor has raised barriers between them and that grace which can no more be removed by prayer alone, or by faith not "made whole with deed," than weeds could be removed from a corn field by the same process. To destroy those barriers by arousing a community conscience, and recording its awakening in community action expressed in statutory law, is more religious by far than any amount of prayer for the salvation of the poor offered by folk who go home to idleness. We have thrown on the poor, and on God's grace, responsibility for the results of our own sins of neglect : and until the churches shoulder their share of responsibility for community conditions which defy the Bible law of human brotherhood here and now, I do not believe they will make any great headway, in the world outside their borders, in preaching the fatherhood of God or salvation for the world to come.

Where, then, should one apply the hoe in order to earn the right to pray unashamed for a harvest of salvation among the poor ?

The matters of housing and sanitation have been already touched upon ; inadequately, yet enough, I trust, to set wiser minds than my own to thinking, and stronger hands to work. Next to it, and closely connected with it, is the fundamental question of recreation.

The negations of life are the deadly things. Overt acts of wrong have inflicted untold miseries in every age; yet for blight upon humanity at large they cannot compare with the steady, persistent, accumulated results of perfectly respectable neglects. And the neglect of the human desire for recreation, age-long, world-wide, has been so often not merely respectable, but a virtue of the highest standing! We have talked much of the universal instinct for God, so evident even among savages; and we have based on it one of our strongest arguments for the existence of a God: to such universal need, we say, there must be somewhere an answer; the existence of the need demands it. But in this universal play-instinct, common to all races and all time, we have found no proof of a need that demands an answer, no trace of a wise Creator's handiwork, nothing at all of design. For centuries it was merely an elfish trick of youth, to be as nearly suppressed as possible, being dangerously akin to the devil and all his works. And even now many affectionate and otherwise intelligent parents regard it as a part of their children's childhood and youth merely, to be lived through until that safe stage of maturity be reached where children become sober and sensible, and put away childish things. Many provide dolls and balls because they enjoy giving their children pleasure, but with little idea that the love of play is almost the greatest formative power in a child's life, and that by it he may be shaped to the highest ideals, the widest usefulness, or be degraded to the level of the beast.

It is not merely that a child coördinates his muscles and mind in play ; he coördinates his entire being with the world about him in play that is wisely directed. He finds himself as a citizen of his world. In team-play, in the give and take of success and defeat, in fair play and respect for the rules of the game, he learns self-control, respect for the rights of others, the adjustment of his own personality to those about him, and a deep regard for law and justice.

All these things are fundamental to a law-abiding, honest life. In families of several children, where the mother is willing and able to share the play life of the children, they may learn these things at home, even in cramped quarters and under unfavourable conditions : but few poor children have mothers of leisure. There is no place for their play in the cluttered house, or in the diminutive yard some poor people are fortunate enough to own. In the cities the streets are the playgrounds of the poor. They are such for our poor, the Negroes. There is little play possible there, even in smaller cities, that fits their need. Besides, few of them know how to play, in city or country. The play-instinct has been perverted or suppressed so long that its natural outlet, with many of them, seems closed. They are not peculiar in this: they have simply suffered the deprivation of a deep human need, as children of the very poor have done elsewhere; and they react under the unnatural condition exactly as does all the rest of humanity in a similar situation.

There are certain laws of spiritual physics which are universal in their operation, and which seem closely akin to the physics of matter. One can compress the air, guide it according to its own laws in prepared channels, and work with it miracles of usefulness. One can compress it with no outlet at all, and defy the law of its nature up to a certain point. After that, something goes to smash. Those are facts at the North Pole, and at the South Pole, and everywhere in between. Similarly, one can take this race-wide play-instinct, and guide it according to its own law of development to the building up of body and soul far above the danger-line of human ruin. Also, one can suppress it with impunity—for a certain length of time. But like the air, it has to go somewhere ; and if it cannot go the safe way, it will take some other : the energy which creates it must be expressed. To this crude young need with no adequate outlet all sorts of illicit adventures proffer their irresistible lure—petty thefts, trials of brute strength, the aping of older folk in obscene talk and vicious deeds, " crap-playing " in the streets, the smoking of cigarettes, surreptitious drinking, the stealing of older people's " dope."

We understand here in the South, those of us who are somewhat interested in such matters, that these are proven facts concerning the gangs of young toughs in Northern slums. It is perfectly reasonable to quite a number of us that a baseball ground and a boys' club, or an organization of Boy Scouts, will transform a crowd of budding white criminals into decent young humans who delight to obey the law and to require their companions to do likewise : but it does not seem to occur to us, as yet, that this law of the gang is operative except where humanity has a white skin. So instead of buying playgrounds for our poor with our taxes, and

furnishing trained directors of play for them,
we take many times the sum needed for this
simple provision for a normal need, and build
great court-houses with it, filled with expensive machinery, human and other, of what
we are pleased to call justice; and put up
endless local jails, every one of which is
guaranteed, by every law of spiritual dy-
namics, to poison the folk put into it, and to
smother their impulses towards a better life.
And then we sit down and commiserate ourselves for being burdened with a people so
bent by nature towards crime.

In the summer of 1912, in a Southern city,
afternoon playgrounds for Negro children
were opened by the combined efforts of a few
people of both races. Negro women of force
and ability were engaged to supervise them,
and the whole venture was under the direction of a Southern white woman, a graduate
of her own state university and of Columbia.
The children gathered in the playgrounds
like flies. None of them knew how to play,
but they were still plastic with childhood,
and responded as childhood everywhere does
from the North Pole to the South. But older
children came too—gangs of adolescent boys
whose only idea of "fun" was to torment
folk weaker than themselves, and to smash

up whatever afforded others pleasure.   They were a whole battalion of thorns in the flesh all summer long.   The white women concerned, having exhausted their own resources, appealed to the local Y. M. C. A., and to the pastors of several of the churches, for a white man who would take the gang in charge and organize its members as a constructive force in their community.   But though the Y. M. C. A. director and the pastors tried diligently to find a man to undertake the task, nobody was forthcoming; and the group continues its boisterous career towards the chain-gang, where so many of us believe Negroes gravitate by their own nature rather than by our neglect.

But children are only the beginning of the story.   The play instinct is not an evanescent appurtenance of childhood: it is deep down among the primal needs of life, as real and as persistent as the need for air or food. We educated white people are perfectly aware of our own need for recreation.   We turn to the woods and the mountains, to golf and tennis, fishing and camping, whenever we can possibly afford it, and just as long as we live.   In between whiles we go to the theatre and the " movies," to baseball and football games, to the parks, on motoring trips—any and everywhere that promises us a break in the monotony of life, a bit of relaxation, a little laughter. We begin to understand that the need of these things is bedded so deep in the nature of white people that wage earners are actually more profitable to their employers, in dollars and cents, if they get their bit of vacation in summer time. It has long been customary in the North, and grows yearly more common with us, to give clerks and salespeople two-weeks' playtime a year, with pay; to close department stores at noon on Saturdays in summer; to let everybody off on holidays. We are learning to do it not simply because we want other people to enjoy themselves, but because our enlightened selfishness is becoming convinced that a workman who never plays can never do the most efficient work.

But it has not occurred to us that natural laws have no special editions for skins of different colours. There are, of course, as many kinds of pleasure as there are individual natures; and some of them require not only certain temperaments, but certain stages of intellectual advancement, for their enjoyment. No one would claim that a slum Negro could be interested for a moment in much that would give a cultivated white man the keenest pleasure. But a need common to all humanity has somewhere an answer suited to each man's stage of development ; an answer clean, healthful, and life-giving : and they who withhold it do so to their own peril as well as to the injury of him who needs.

The poor of every nation need play more than any other class, and are more injured by the lack of it. What else drives New York's wage-earning girls, by scores of thousands, to the low dance-halls of commercialized pleasure ? They would rather go to decent places, as is shown by the way they crowd the few which are provided : but recreation they must have, or snap under the daily strain of work. Young men flock to the same places, decent fellows to begin with, often, pitifully eager to meet "some nice girl." But the associations are too much for their unguarded youth. It is the exhilaration of the liquor they drink which lures them, not its taste. They want that glorious sense of freedom which is its first effect, that power to rise in a tumult of life and energy above all that cramps them in their sordid daily lives. It is the excitement of gambling that draws them—the ecstasy of bated breath, of pulses that throb and thrill. They never intend to wreck their lives ; only to bring into their poor dull colourlessness a little of sheen and glamour and fire. The lower they are in the economic and the moral scale, in every city of every land, the bleaker and duller their empty lives, the more fiercely this need drives them. A man with a few of the comforts of life, a few inward resources —only a few—may walk without pleasure, maimed indeed, but in a straight path, to the end. But he who has nothing, within or without, neither resource nor help, what shall he do, with only his blank, dead life of drudgery, and his fierce human need for a little joy?

It is so simple it breaks one's heart. Such utter wreckage, such ruin and waste and degradation, such lapsing of men into beastliness—and all for lack of a thing like this, a simple human answer to a vital human need!

Sometimes when I think about us—us Southern white folks—I don't know whether to laugh or to cry. We are good people. I've associated with us all my life, and I know that is true. Ideals stir us as nothing else does. If there is anything Southern people will do it is to spend themselves for an idea— once they catch it. We caught the temperance idea years ago—it is really the germ of our late-developing social consciousness

—and we have fought for it as no other section of America has. Somehow, by the blessing of Providence, our preachers got hold of it by its individually religious end, and many of them have not thought of it as "social service" to this day. So they welcomed it to the fold of orthodoxy, and went forth to fight for it with never a Christian to say them nay, or to suggest that social service was no concern of a church dedicated to the preaching of "the pure gospel." As for results, a look at the wet-and-dry map of the United States in this present year of grace will show that the South is the cleanest part of the map. We do things just that way.

But like other grown-ups, we are mightily like children. A child will clean up his playthings in a whirl of enthusiasm over helping his mother; and when she comes in, by invitation, to admire the results, she will find the rubbish not cleaned up, but tucked out of sight, and perhaps ruining some of her most cherished finery in its novel seclusion. Only the obvious middle of the room is in order. We have gone at the drink habit just that way.

The Negro's propensity for drink does trouble us. That is one thing about his condition we are aware of. We even feel the menace to the community which drunken Negroes furnish ; and we deplore a development still so low, after all these years of civilization. Nothing, we say, will eradicate the Negro's love of liquor. (We do not specify what we have tried as an eradicator; but whatever it was, it hasn't worked.)

According to our lights, however, and in all sincerity, we have done our duty. We have passed local-option and prohibition laws. We have made a *fiat* sweep of the whole miserable liquor business, with a view, largely, to removing from the play-hours of our very poor, both white and black, one of their three great resources, which are, for both colours in this poorest class, gambling, immorality and drink. But what we have taken with one hand we have given with the other : not something clean to take the place of the unclean ; but the same uncleanness with the added smirch of lawlessness. In all our cities men, nearly all of whom are white, are allowed to open " near-beer " saloons for the open selling of every known intoxicant, and to make a living from the degradation of our poor, both white and black, with the consent and protection of the authorities. When the poor, who are mostly black, go as the drink drives them, we dive into our pockets for more taxes to build larger court-houses and jails; and the women, whom the prisoners might have supported if they had had a better chance to stay sober, are left to choose between the streets for themselves, or work for themselves and the streets for their children. And so the manufacture of criminals, one of our most stupendous industries, and certainly our most expensive luxury, goes bravely on.

Prohibition is good as far as it goes, even though in our cities it does not go at all. But it will never, by itself, do very much more than just slick life up on the outside. It is a purely negative measure, a gigantic Thou shalt not. It has its place in positive life, as many other negations have: but a negation can never construct anything; its utmost is to clear the ground for construction. And if those who clear the ground construct nothing, somebody else will. Human life, being part of nature, tolerates no vacuum. Temperance measures, to be effective, must be constructive: they must offer something to take the place of what they have driven out. Until the human craving for relaxation, for exaltation of both body and spirit, be cleanly met, it will spend itself on the un-

clean.   And out of uncleanness will come
waste and wreckage, for present and future
generations.

What is there in the South that offers clean
amusement, clean play, to Negroes young or
old ? In a recent investigation made by an
International Y. M. C. A. Secretary, himself a
Southern man, four cities were found having
public parks for Negroes.   Four public parks
for Negroes in fifteen Southern states ! Out of
seventeen cities eight reported having picture
shows for Negroes, and nine none. Of the
picture shows reported half were " very low
and degrading, with the vilest vaudeville
attachments."   In five cities there are theatres
for Negroes—character not specified ; and in
several they are allowed in the peanut gallery
of white theatres ; but the investigator reports
" the better class of Negroes say they will not
go unless for some special attraction, as they
are put with the lowest class of whites."   The
report further declares that the " principal
places of amusement for the male population
[Negro] are the saloons, pool and billiard
rooms."   The saloon people are the quickest
of all whites to recognize the Negro's humanity.   They see that Negroes become
slaves of drink exactly as white men do, and
spend their last nickel for it in the same

manner. In my own city the very large majority of cases in the recorder's court are Negroes, and nearly all their infractions of law are the results of drinking. The city is in a prohibition state. It contains eighty officially licensed near-beer saloons, and seventy-nine of them are run by white men. In practically every city of the South we white people set this object lesson regarding respect for law before the Negroes, and then deplore and despise the innate lawlessness of the black man's nature.

But if diversions other than drinking and lewdness are hard for adult Negroes to come by, what is done for the children? Louisville has two or three playgrounds for them, not very well equipped, but under the direction of the City Park Commissioner, as are the far ampler playgrounds for white children; and New Orleans has recently opened one with semi-official recognition. So far as I can learn these are the only cities in the South which have officially recognized this basal human need as common to white and black. A prominent church and club woman of Nashville gave a playground to Negro children in that city a few years ago; and whites and blacks together have now for two summers provided vacation playgrounds for

Negro children in Augusta, Ga. That completes the list to date.

Laying aside all altruistic motives, turning our backs on Christ's doctrine of human brotherhood, and acting solely from the standpoint of enlightened selfishness, it would pay the South, just in money, to put a three-acre playground next door to every schoolhouse for both whites and blacks, and to add to the teaching force a director of play for each county, under whose supervision the teachers of the various schools could in turn assume charge of the playground after school hours. Folk dances would take the place of games with the older children. We could call them folk games if some of our church people looked askance at the other word. If the universal enjoyment of movement in rhythmical time could be met in this clean and wholesome fashion it would do more to undermine "animal dancing" than any well-deserved philippic that could be hurled against it. The best way to get rid of an unclean thing is to put in its place a clean one which meets the need.

The schoolhouse should be the recreation centre for young and old. For years great corporations have been employing "social engineers" to work among their employees as a matter of sound business policy, to bring up the efficiency of the human end of the machine. A large part of the engineer's duty has lain in providing clean and interesting recreation for folk deadened by drudgery. Lately a city or two has taken the matter up and appointed a city Superintendent of Public Recreation, just as they have a Park Commissioner. There is no sentiment in such an act—no sentimentality, at least. Hard-headed business men have done it, and communities stand to it, and pay the necessary taxes to finance it, because it will pay in human character and happiness, and, in the long run, in dollars as well. So here and yonder, in the most unexpected places, it keeps cropping out in life that what we call Christian doctrines are not doctrines at all. They are laws of human life, and Christ's, not in the sense that He made them up, but in the sense that He understood them and put them into words. When we provide for the human needs of the weakest, we come not upon sacrifice, but on more abundant life for all. For we really are brethren, all of us, and the satisfied need of those who lack is the strength and prosperity of all.

V

HUMAN WRECKAGE

BUT what of the wreckage already achieved? What of that fragment of the world-wide ruin most in evidence to our consciousness—the criminals, young and old, of both races, who fill our Southern jails, and work in all possible publicity of disgrace, chained and striped, upon our streets?

For thousands of years the world has had two theories only about the relation of the state to crime. One is the theory of vengeance, originally the right of the individual, but as civilization progressed a right which became vested in the community. Among Christian nations Moses has been set forth as the champion of this theory; and "an eye for an eye, a tooth for a tooth" is still widely quoted in justification of this outworn delusion, upon which the criminal law of the nations is founded.

It was doubtless a benevolent law in Moses' day which restricted vengeance, not to the limit of the avenger's power, but to that rough justice which measured the penalty by the offense. So far as we can decipher those old records, and those of far later generations, to inject into vengeance an idea of justice was not the least of the great lawgiver's achievements. Many, however, who quote Moses with gusto seem unacquainted with later Biblical literature, in which the exercise of vengeance is distinctly declared to be beyond the province of mankind.

Nevertheless, men cherish it to this day as a sacred and inalienable right. And lest vengeance unadorned should be insufficient, they have embroidered this first theory with the second—that punishments severe and ingenious beyond what vengeance might demand would act as deterrents to criminals *in posse*. On this altar of public benevolence the criminal *in esse* is still offered up, a useless and frightful sacrifice to the blindness and folly of men. It is true the law no longer condemns him to be broken on the wheel, nor burned with faggots of green wood, nor tortured in many of the thousand ways which make the prison history of the past such black reading.

But notwithstanding the rise and spread of a modern penology which is already pro-

foundly influencing criminal procedure in
many countries, the vast bulk of the world's
criminals are still dealt with under a combination of these two theories.   The criminal is
punished because punishment is his desert
and the state's right ; and his degree of punishment must be severe enough to frighten
anybody else from attempting a similar crime.
That severity of sentence does not deter
others from crime is proven by the criminal
history of many centuries, and has long been
openly acknowledged by authorities on crime
in all countries.   It is out of this self-confessed
breakdown of the old system that the rise of
a new one has become possible.

The foundation of the new system is, in the
words of the eminent chairman of the English
Prison Commission, " the accepted axiom of
modern penology that a prisoner has reversionary rights in humanity." It regards a
man convicted of crime not primarily as a
criminal, but as an individual who, " by the
application of influences or discipline, labour,
education, moral and religious, backed up on
discharge by a well-organized system of
[oversight] is capable of reinstatement into
civic life." It flatly denies the Italian theory
of " a criminal type," pronouncing it a superstition, pure and simple.   It offers abundant

evidence that the criminal disposition is produced, largely in individuals physically or mentally weak, by social conditions which have forced their lives along lines of least resistance. It stands for the reformatory, for the indeterminate sentence, release on parole, the permanent separation of prisoners into groups according to type and criminal development, for education, moral, religious and industrial, for labour in outdoor life as far as practicable, for the abolition of prison stripes, and everything calculated to break down self-respect, and for life-detention of all who cannot be restored to society in safety to the community and to themselves.

Twenty-two nations were officially represented in the last International Prison Congress, which met in Washington City three years ago; three additional governments, Spain, the Transvaal, and Egypt, signified their desire to join; and negotiations were opened with the governments of China and Japan which indicate that at the next Congress representatives of those governments will take their place in the body as members, instead of taking part unofficially, as heretofore. The members of this Congress differed, as might be supposed, on many points: but they stood as a body for the principles of the new penology above stated. They also endorsed the principle that payment should be allowed the prisoner by the state for his work over and above the sum necessary for his own support; and that this remainder should be turned over to the prisoner's family if in need.

A point of deepest significance to Americans, North and South, was the unanimous conviction of all the delegates, home and foreign, that American local jails were the worst known to civilization. The United States government placed a special train at the disposal of the foreign delegates, and acted as their host during a tour of investigation which covered most of the country's great reformatories, adult and juvenile, and many local jails. It is said that the Tombs, in New York City, reduced the foreigners to speechlessness. One of the most eminent said afterwards that the only thing to do with it was to tear it down; but the others found words incompatible with the minimum of politeness necessary in the presence of a host. The secretary of the Howard Association of London, when asked, did not hesitate to say that every jail he saw in America " ought to be wiped off the face of the earth," and that "nowhere in Europe do such con-

HOME OF ATLANTA NEGRO WHO WAS HIS OWN ARCHITECT AND BUILDER.

ditions exist." The newly-elected president of the Congress, Sir Evelyn Ruggles-Brise, in extending an invitation for the next meeting to be held in England, begged the Americans " out of their humanity" to consider the case of " the thousands of petty offenders now passing through your city and county jails in such appalling numbers."

The reformatories of a few of the Northern states confessedly lead the world, and the principles of human restoration which they have demonstrated are spreading to the states of the West ; but we of the South lag behind in every phase of reformatory and preventive work. The only point at which we are strictly up with the procession is in the matter of our local jails. They are like those of the rest of America, well adapted to the one specific end of manufacturing criminals out of that vast company of petty offenders not yet beyond the pale of citizenship.

I was talking with a friend not long ago about a certain local jail. A white woman who had once worked for her had been arrested on some charge, and had appealed to her for help. She had gone to the jail with a lawyer, a friend of hers, but had been refused permission to see the prisoner. The lawyer had been passed in at once, but the jailer stopped my friend.

"No, ma'am," he declared with respectful positiveness; "you can't go in there. It ain't no place for a lady to be in, nor to see. It ain't fit."

"And he had a white woman in there!" exclaimed my friend; "a white woman, in a place unfit for a lady even to see! I told him if she could stand staying in it I could stand seeing it, but he wouldn't let me in."

I sympathized with her indignation: but was it any better for a black woman than for a white one? The white woman should have had a little better chance than the other to resist the moral contagion of the place, and should have been less of a menace to the community when she came out. But the Negroes, and many, too, of the whites, if they ever had a chance before the law grips them, lose it in the jail the law provides; lose it before they are even proven guilty of the crime with which they are charged. Men grown old in crime and debauchery are, in nearly all our jails, thrown with first offenders, often with mere boys. The accommodations provided for unconvicted American citizens violate the laws of decency and health in regard to the commonest physical needs.

There is no privacy, no cleanliness. Everything in his surroundings combines to brand on the offender's consciousness the fact that he is no longer regarded as a being with human rights, reversionary or otherwise. His relation to life is purely that of the committer of a crime.

He may be just a boy, his offense a trifle; or, if more serious, the outcome, not of premeditated wickedness, but of a thwarted love of adventure, youth's natural flare of high spirits turned awry. In some of our cities such an offender would get what he needs— separate confinement beforehand, and an investigation, rather than a trial before a specially constituted court. A real effort would be made to understand not what the boy did, but why he did it; and after being dealt with by the judge on that line chiefly, he would be turned over to a probation officer whose duty it would be to watch over him, and assist him to moral convalescence. The law should give the judge, as it does in Denver, certain powers to enforce, if necessary, parental cooperation in helping the boy, and in correcting wrong home conditions. With the right kind of judges and probation officers a vast deal of human wreckage is prevented by these courts.

But we have few of them in the South: and there is little of the kind of care needed given to young Negro delinquents. In what I am told is one of the best-managed juvenile courts of the South the probation officers for the Negro children are Negro women. That is an immense improvement on the old chain-gang way, of course; but adolescent boys, white or black, will not be very profoundly influenced by anything or anybody feminine. They need a man, and a wise one.

In only a few places, however, does the matter of probation come up. For the majority of our lawbreakers, young and old, one sure destination waits—the chain-gang, sometimes more euphemistically known as the convict camp. Here prisoners of all degrees of criminality are thrown promiscuously together, and clothed in stripes to advertise them to all beholders as outlaws from the human family. They wear individual chains in the daytime, which are fastened together at night. And they endure whatever of suffering, degradation, insult and injustice their individual keepers choose to bestow upon them.

A Southern Bishop, living in one of our largest cities, recently had a visit from a white man in a dirty, frowsy, unkempt suit, who announced himself as a convict discharged forty-eight hours before from the coal mines near by, which are worked by convict labour. Being questioned, he admitted that he had eaten but twice since his discharge. A Negro had given him some corn bread the first day, and a barkeeper on the next had given him a sandwich and a drink of whiskey. He refused the food and money the Bishop offered him. He had come, he said, to tell the story of what was done to the prisoners in those mines; he had promised the other convicts before he left that he would carry the story to some Christian, and see if he would take the matter up. If he took anything for himself, he said, it might cast suspicion on his tale.

He was a well-educated man. He said he had been an editor. A wrong had been done to a member of his family; in a blaze of anger he had shot and killed the offender; and he had been sentenced to three years at hard labour, which he had served.

The men were worked in gangs, under convict foremen, and each gang was assessed so many tons per day. If they mined more they were credited with the excess, to be paid for it when they left the camp. All credits, however, were given by the foremen, them-

selves convicts ; and they could, and did, give
the credits, not to those who earned them,
but to those who shared with their overseers,
or bribed them in other ways.   The foremen
carried 'horrible whips ; and they used them
constantly, unmercifully, without warning and
without provocation.   Men were beaten and
kicked and injured until it was not at all an
unknown thing, the convict said, for a man to
put his left hand on the train rail and let the
coal car run over it and crush it off.   Then
he had to be sent to some other camp, being
useless for mining.   It might be just as bad,
of course ; but there was always a chance.
This convict had stuck it out.   He had been
told that he had no overtime pay coming to
him.   He had received the clothes he wore,
taken from some newly-entered convict, instead of the new suit required by law, and
had been turned out, penniless, to go back to
the world in newness of life, and conduct
himself in such an irreproachable manner,
after the lesson he had had, as not to get into
a convict camp again.

The Bishop told his story quietly, as his
habit is, while we sat gasping.

" What did you *do* ? " we demanded.

" I made him take a little money, for one
thing—as a loan.   He wouldn't take much :

but I followed him down the street and begged till he had to take a little. And I talked to some men who have influence. There is a public meeting called for the seventeenth. There will be men from all over the state, and I think the matter will be probed to the bottom. We may get our state laws reformed before we get through."

But one state is not enough. In my own state, which is not the one of the Bishop's convict, the leaders of the Men and Religion Movement in our capital city have published a list of the barbarities of our convict camps which sound like the Middle Ages. Twenty years ago, in the same state, an investigator appointed by the Governor reported exactly the same conditions. And these states are not behind some of the others. Four of our states, however—Kentucky, Missouri, Tennessee and Texas—are in the honour list of twenty-one states which have adopted the indeterminate sentence and the parole law ; yet three of these retain the convict lease or convict labour system. In a few states the Governor has power to restore citizenship to a discharged convict. But in Texas, Kentucky and Tennessee no man convicted of crime remains an outlaw except by his own will. Citizenship is restored by law to every convicted criminal who, after due testing when released on parole, proves worthy of that trust. The last taint of his sin is cast behind him by the law, and he takes his place again, a man among men. "As far as the east is from the west——." Isn't that the normal way, the way that *works* because men are made to respond to it?

I was waiting at a railroad station not long ago when a frightened-looking Negro boy of about eighteen came by in the custody of three big policemen, who stood guard about him till the patrol wagon appeared and swallowed him up. After the crowd dispersed I learned from one of the policemen that the boy had been caught in the act of stealing a box of cigars. The policeman thought he would get fifteen years for it; but seeing my horror, and wishing, evidently, to oblige a lady if possible, he reconsidered the matter and said maybe he would get off with ten years, seeing he was not really grown. I remembered the boy who was sentenced to three years for taking eleven dollars and forty-six cents: but that judge had especially pointed out that the sentence was unusually merciful. This boy's judge might well give him ten years of enforced criminal association for his theft: there was no telling.

I remembered another time, some years ago, when I was waiting for another train, at a junction in the mountains of a Southern state. The county sheriff was waiting also, with two white boys of seventeen or eighteen, moonshiners. The boys were chained together by their wrists and by their necks, with what looked like trace-chains. The sheriff had evidently imbibed their whiskey, probably for safe-keeping. He swaggered about, a coarse, not ill-tempered man, a pistol protruding from either pocket of his coat. He talked loudly, joking the boys about their capture and the becomingness of their present adornments. They tried hard to imitate his manner, and to wear an air of jaunty and amused indifference; but their eyes were frightened and ashamed.

Oh, the folly of it! The blind, stupid, brutal *uselessness* of it, the wicked waste of human lives and souls!

What had any of these boys, white or black, done, in their isolation, their ignorance, their stunted moral growth, unfriended, untaught—what had they done which gave society the right to seize their poor, starved lives and break and poison them in its foul prisons beyond hope of recovery for all time? Even if we had the right, what good does it do ? The veriest madman out of Bedlam would hardly claim that our convict camps benefit the prisoners : but do they deter others from crime?

The census of the United States can answer that question ; and the prison records of all civilized countries will join with the penologists of the world in confirming what the census says. Every year a vast number of arrests are made, and a less vast number of prisoners are discharged. *Less* vast. Each year our prison population receives an added permanent deposit from this great stream of human misery and ignorance and sin, as it washes through those black and awful places where men already injured are permanently deformed. Such measures have never lessened crime : they provoke it always, everywhere, since prisons were. The more cruelly or publicly a crime is punished the more surely it drives suggestion home to some ill-balanced nature, and rouses it to imitation. The punishment seems to add the last irresistible attraction to those on the border of criminality.

So far from stopping crime, our present system, with its public and private humiliations of the offender, propagates crime in both the criminal and the beholder. Whatever beats down a prisoner's remnants of self-respect is a blow not only at his manhood, but at the manhood of the state. Our prisons are great spawning-beds, where the crime of the community is gathered in that the crime of the state may pass over it and fructify it, sending out swarms of new evil influences to squirm and twist and spread in all the ooze and slime of the community, that our criminal supply may never fail.

We need more rational methods in our whole criminal procedure. When one has scarlet fever or diphtheria one is quarantined, not for a specified time, but until one can be safely restored to community life, as shown by one's personal condition. The criminal must also be treated as an individual. Something must be learned of his heredity, his environment, the causes which led to his crime. Only so may one attempt his restoration. To expect to attain it on any other basis than the one of sympathetic understanding is as unreasonable as to expect one course of treatment to cure every form of disease. Even the same disease requires different treatment for different cases; and to fix the term of a man's imprisonment by the crime he has committed is to ignore the dominating factor in the case—his personal-

ity. His personality, not his past offense,
makes him a social menace. He should be
imprisoned as long, and only as long, as his
personality threatens danger to the community.

Dean Kirchwey, of the Faculty of Law
of Columbia University, in a great address on
" Ending the Reign of Terror " said :

" A demonstration of the fact, which we
may well consider indubitable, that criminal
conduct is usually, if not always, the result of
conditions more or less beyond the control
of the delinquent, cannot fail to shake the
theory of moral responsibility upon which the
vindictive idea of punishment is based, as
well as to allay and in time overcome the feeling of resentment which such conduct now
excites. And, on the other hand, a study of
the psychology of the mob, and of the reaction of the existing penal system on the moral
sense of the community will show how far it
is safe to go in mitigating the rigours of the
criminal law in a given jurisdiction .   .   .
[until] such time as may be required to bring
the community to a better appreciation of
the nature of crime, and the conditions which
determine it.   .   .   .

" The doctrine that punishment is inflicted
on the offender as a warning to others has

come to be the orthodox view. . . . There is something touching in the unquestioning faith of the legal profession and of the man in the street in the efficacy of this vicarious suffering for crimes not yet committed. Yet it remains a matter of faith as yet unsupported by evidence. . . .

" The fact that a very large proportion—in some countries more than fifty per cent.—of criminals under confinement have previously undergone prison punishment seems to indicate that as a deterrent punishment by imprisonment leaves something to be desired. . . .

" The principle that punishment may . . . without reformatory influences be a means of moral amendment finds expression in many judicial utterances. It is obviously a well-meant, but mistaken attempt to bring the sanctions of the moral law and of the ecclesiastical dispensation to the aid of the criminal law. . . . This imputes to the law a sanctity which the criminal would be the last to concede to it ; and so quite apart from the vile and degrading conditions under which this work of grace was to be effected, it is not to be wondered at that we find no traces of its efficacy. . . .

" The principle of the reformation of crimi-

nals during imprisonment . . . does not
assume that all criminals are capable of reformation, or even of improvement, nor that
those who are can all be brought up to the
level of good citizenship. It does assume,
however, that most men and women, and all
children, will respond to the steady pressure of
a wholesome, uplifting environment . . .
and it has already proven its faith by its
works. . . . It must have cognizance of
the life history of every individual committed
to prison, with his heredity and environment.
It studies him in prison—his needs, his ca-
pacities, his aspirations, his mental and moral
equipment, his health, his reaction to . . .
prison life. It follows him after his discharge.
. . . It levies on all the sciences that deal
with man—law, medicine, criminology, soci-
ology. . . .

" The next few years will give us new data
of great importance. . . . But there will
be no facts for him who regards the criminal
law as an instrument for venting wrath and
hate on a fallen—and convicted—brother ;
none for him who would keep his fellow man
in subjection to his iron law by terror ; none
for him who would work redemption through
another's suffering. . . . The new moral
atmosphere which has made every man his

brother's keeper will be felt in the law courts
as well as in the home and street. The new
attitude of the state towards children of tender
years will soon mark her attitude towards her
erring children of a larger growth."

Those of us who can find comfort in a fact
so painful may be assured that we of the
South are not alone in the possession of a
prison system outworn and barbarous. Nothing in our awful camps could be worse than
what has been found, in most recent years, in
the state prisons of several of the richest and
most enlightened states of the North and
West ; and if they were all investigated the
present black list would doubtless be longer
than it is. But this fact concerns us only as
it shows that our own conditions are part of
a world-wide horror, which the best thought
of the world has set itself to destroy. The
reformation of our whole prison system is our
part of a world-task.

We need a Southern Prison Commission,
appointed by the governors of the states, not
to revise our prison system, but to study conditions, here and elsewhere, and to formulate
a new system abreast of modern experience,
and founded on bed-rock truth and justice,
instead of on the philosophy of the Middle
Ages. The members of the Commission

should be men of broad humanity and of strong common sense. Such men could, by the authority of their respective governors, make individual and unannounced visits, each to a number of prisons in his own state. Then they could examine the best the world can show them; the Denver juvenile court; the Colorado state farm, where "hardened" criminals are turned into men, without stripes, threats, chains or armed guards; the District of Columbia prison farm; the wonderful work for women at Bedford, N. Y., for men at Great Meadow, and for children at Industry, in the same state; the Kansas City municipal farm, a new idea in local government; the Massachusetts farms for vagrants and inebriates, and many more.

This Commission would find at least three points in the South where Negro lawbreakers are being successfully trained towards good citizenship. In Virginia it is being done at the suggestion, and under the supervision, of a state officer, and with the backing of the legislature. In Georgia and Alabama it is being done by unknown and unlettered Negroes, whose loving hearts have led them into a wisdom not to be attained by any amount of unloving knowledge.

The State Superintendent of Charities and

Correction in Virginia, a large-hearted, broad-minded man, fully abreast of the developments of modern penology, has, in the last three years, taken from the Richmond penitentiary one hundred and fifty convicted Negro "criminals," all under fifteen years of age, and has placed them, under proper supervision, in good Negro homes, as members of the respective families. He tells me one hundred and forty-three of these boys are "making good." They are growing up into self-respecting and wealth-producing citizens, instead of becoming a recurring charge upon the state, which is the usual result of our ordinary methods of dealing with Negro first offenders.

At Ralph, Ala., is the Sam Daily reformatory, still called by his name, though Sam Daily himself has made his humble exit from life with no trumpets to proclaim him a hero, unless the angels sounded them on the other side. He was a full-blooded Negro, with no touch of efficiency as the gift of another race.

A white Alabamian, a city judge, moved with compassion for the young Negro delinquents brought before him, called for some good Negro of like compassion to give the boys a chance. Sam Daily responded, donating himself, his family, and one hundred and twenty-five acres of land to their use. First and last he took about three hundred boys from the Birmingham juvenile court, paid their way to the railroad station nearest his farm, fed them, clothed them, taught them industry, cleanliness and honour. I am told that ninety-five per cent. of his boys " make good."

The most curious thing about this enterprise is the fact that this poor Negro, who was never able to finish paying for his own farm, spent years of his life converting lawbreakers from a public liability to a public asset without receiving any public money to help bear the expenses of the process. Individual white men have helped him, and now help his widow, by making up deficits when they occur ; but there is no regular public appropriation for this great and public service. The Southern Presbyterian Church, however, now pays regularly the salary of a trained Negro assistant at the reformatory. A white man, formerly a large slave-owner, who knows the reformatory well, writes me, in regard to its success with the boys, " I should call this forlorn effort to help the helpless a modern miracle." Only it isn't a miracle : it is natural law given a chance to work.

The third of these demonstrations of the response of Negro delinquents to good influences is made at the Paul Moss Orphanage at Augusta, Ga. Paul Moss is a Negro of rather limited education who gave up an excellent income as a skilled mechanic to devote his life to aiding Negro waifs and juvenile delinquents. He put all his savings into a small farm, where he has supported his charges with a little help from a few whites of the city and one or two Northern visitors. He is able to give the boys not much book education, but teaches them practical religion and a few trades. In the last six years he has sent out one hundred and sixty boys, half of whom were from the city juvenile court, the others being orphans and waifs in process of becoming delinquents. One hundred and fifty of these boys are " making good."

Each of these separate experiments shows that the response made by Negro delinquents to a helpful and sympathetic environment equals that made by the same class of other races—about ninety-five per cent. Would not our Southern Prison Commission consider this method of dealing with lawbreakers economically superior to the one now in general use? Even where we have reformatories for young Negroes under state or county supervision the inmates are treated as prisoners, dressed in some kind of distinctive, branding uniform, kept under lock and key —and eventually landed, very many of them, in our prisons and convict camps. And we think that fact is explained by the Negro's criminal tendencies. The Commission, with all the evidence before it, might decide differently.

The Commission would look into the evils of convict labour as employed in many "model" prisons, so called, where men are driven beyond the limit of health under a contract system as vicious as our own, and turned out after years of alleged industrial training skilled only in some occupation employment in which is impossible outside of prison walls. They would go thoroughly into the question of the state's right, while attempting to restore a man to normal citizenship, to forbid his performance of the primal human duty to contribute to the support of his own family ; and would examine the methods by which innocent women and children are beginning to be saved from this usual and unjust punishment.

They would learn what public services prisoners perform elsewhere, while being at the same time restored to manhood.   We are too much in the habit of looking at the thing done, and ignoring the man who does it. Many of us feel, for instance, that in setting her convicts to work on the public roads—a most beneficent public service—one of our states has taken front rank in the treatment of her criminals.   Yet that state clothes those men in stripes, as we all do, and works them in chains, on the public roads, under armed guards destitute of knowledge or fitness in the fine art of saving human wreckage.

In New Zealand in the last decade the convicts have planted 20,000,000 trees for the state, timbering waste lands, *and reclaiming the men.*   But they do not wear stripes in New Zealand.   The idea there is to deliver them from past degradation, not to sear it in for present and future injury.   Denmark reforests her waste lands with men who, like the land, are in process of restoration. Prussia and Switzerland employ them to care for the great state forests : and they are employed in a number of our own Western states in various works of reclamation, though too often, with us, the uppermost idea is the reclamation, not of men, but of property.

All these things our Southern Prison Commission would consider ; and far above the great and profitable work of reclaiming and enriching the wide waste lands of the South by prison labour, they would set that greater and more profitable work of preventing the wide waste of human life, and reclaiming that already in process of ruin.

A prison system suited to human needs— the needs of prisoners, of their families, of the community at large—could be formulated, and presented to all our states, together with the information necessary, and with the weight of this South-wide Commission behind it.   In principle, if not in all its details, it would be adopted in some states ; and ultimately in all, as the experience of the foremost illuminated the wisdom of its provisions.

We need no revision of what we now have : we need a new penology, based on a conception of human life radically opposed to most that underlies our theory of punishment to-day.

We need to take up the call already being heard throughout the civilized world—a call for *trained* men and women to create the new profession of Healers-of-men-in-prison.   We would not, even in our politics-fuddled cities put fifteenth century " leeches " (if we could get them) in charge of our public hospitals. Yet we count any ignorance competent to take unlimited control of sick souls and abnormal minds. In the recent Prison Congress America and Hungary joined hands to express the conviction of the penologists of the world that this professional training of prison officers—men already fitted by nature for such difficult and important work—was a vital need in the progress of humanity towards a sane and successful treatment of the world-problem of human wreckage.

VI

SERVICE AND COÖPERATION

IF I were asked what the mass of the
Negroes most need that we should give
them, I think only one answer could be
given which would go to the root of the whole
matter. And that deepest need is not at all
a Negro need, but a human one : we ourselves,
as a people, share it profoundly.

They need ideals. The lives of so many
of them seem just a chaos of wants, so that
one stands at first dumb with bewilderment :
so many fundamental needs, so much emptiness where there must be solid foundations if
anything worth while is built up ! But that
which will open a way to fill all these empty
spaces is a vision of something higher in
their own souls ; something higher, yet not
too far or cold to kindle a spark of desire in
their hearts, to quicken them, by vision and
aspiration.

If we will look back over the last fifty years
we will see, perhaps, how little of this foremost essential of human advance we have
furnished for them. Some things we have

done, I know. We have paid millions for their education in the public schools: but have we cared how it was spent? The superintendent of education in one of our states, in a recent report, pronounces the Negro public schools of that commonwealth utterly inefficient.

He charges their wretched failure on the white county superintendents, many of whom, he says, never go near the Negro schools under them, nor concern themselves with the selection of fit teachers, nor with their improvement after they are selected. This story would fit more states than one. We could squander ten times the millions already spent in education like that without creating a single impulse towards better things : there is never any vivifying power in indifference.

Yet our public schools for Negroes have done good—a world of it. Some of this must be credited to those among us who have honestly sought the Negro's good. The rest, I think, is due to the Negroes themselves, and to those once-so-hated " Yankees" who first made possible to Negro teachers a suitable preparation for their work.

Love is the world's lifting-force. It is like the light, which yearly lifts untold tons of cold, dead matter to the tree-tops in the

beauty of green leaves. When we see leaves
we know light has been at work : nothing
else could lift matter up there so that leaves
could be. And wherever we find a trace of
spiritual quickening, a budding of dormant
life, however scant, we know by the same
token that Love has been at work : there is
no other force which produces that effect.
The uplift of the Negroes through the public
schools, small as it is compared with what it
might have been with the same expenditure
of money, has chiefly come, not from our
sometimes grudging provision, but from
ideals kindled in some Negroes' souls by
love and sacrifice other than our own.

The Northerners who came down here to
teach the Negroes were ignorant of our past,
of our conditions, of the underlying causes
of our new antagonism to the Negroes—of
all the circle of white life which looked to
them so inexplicably cruel and wrong. They
were only less ignorant about the Negroes,
their traditions, their stage of race-growth,
their true relation to Southern life. Few
people had learned to be world-dwellers then ;
and these eager Northern folk, who saw a
need and longed to meet it, translated neither
white life nor black into world-terms. They
made blunders, of course ; and a good many

A RESPECTED NEGRO DOCTOR.

PAINE COLLEGE, AUGUSTA, GA.

Negroes acquired some knowledge at the expense of more wisdom. We have all seen white people do the same thing. And certainly the South never tried to help the situation. So far as explanation or assistance went we maintained a silence which was more than felt, while these from another world came and wrestled with our problems in all good faith, and according to their darkness and their light.

But with all the mistakes and friction, the energy wasted or turned to loss, these people brought one thing with them which is never wholly lost. It may be hindered, partly negatived, robbed of its full fruition by many things: but always love bears fruit. They brought with them that principle of life. They kindled a light in darkened hearts; they sent out thousands of Negroes fired with ideals of service to their race. And they have saved the situation, so far as it has been saved, for our Negro public schools.

We gave the Negroes ideals once. The North is dull of understanding at this point, as we are dull at others. It cannot take in the fact that slavery and ideals could exist contemporaneously. Yet once the North itself, and in the most strenuous days of its New England conscience, was unaware of

any incompatibility between the two. It is
the big brother again, forgetting his own so-
recent ignorance, and ready with paste-pot
and label for the younger child.

The existence of slavery we long accepted
much as we did the weather—as a dispensation of providence which it were idle to inquire into. But we had a genuine affection
for the Negroes, and out of it we met this
need for ideals—an even deeper need than
emancipation from physical slavery. Every
Protestant denomination in the South had its
white missionaries among the slaves, and all
together they had nearly half a million slave
members at the outbreak of the war. One
church alone, the Southern Methodist, spent
nearly two million dollars in missions to the
Negroes prior to 1861, and had over three
hundred white missionaries at work among
them when the war broke out. The individual slave-owners, the very great majority of
whom were Christian people, did even more.
Men and women, they taught their slaves the
Bible—not, as has been ignorantly suggested, to enforce the duties of meekness
and obedience, but because the love of God
in their own hearts necessitated their impart-
ing it to those around them. My own
mother was typical of her class, and no one

who came in contact with her could have imagined that her service to the Negroes was caused by anything but the spirit which transfigured her whole life from day to day. Such women held regular Sunday-schools for their slaves, and often the white children of the household sat with the black ones to learn the Law which was over both of them alike. In times of rejoicing or of trouble the white people went to the Negro homes as friends ; and in sickness they cared for them personally, often with their own hands.

Those among us who deny the Negro's capacity to respond to ideals should remember his faithfulness in time of war and temptation, and the beauty of character which even the most prejudiced of us admit belonged to " the old-time Negro." The admission, coupled, as it usually is, with sweeping charges against the character of the Negro of to-day, is the severest arraignment of Southern Christianity which can be brought against it. And we bring it ourselves, unseeing.

But the truth has had its witnesses, all along. There were women all over the South who, like my mother, went serenely on in the path of love, even during reconstruction days, ministering to the sick and the poor about them, regardless of the colour of their skins, and seeing only needs which love must meet. There were, in every state, men like Governor Colquitt, of Georgia, who as slave-owner, impoverished Confederate, and governor of his state, would tuck his Bible under his arm any afternoon in the week, and go to some Negro cabin, where he would read and teach and pray, talking with the family as friend with friends, advising, comforting and inspiring them.

Nor did the next generation utterly fail. Through all the turmoil of reconstruction some passed the spirit of service to their children.   An Alabama woman, for instance, who was widowed by the war, remained on her remote plantation, where she spent her life teaching the Negroes of the neighbourhood free of charge. Her daughters took up her work, and carry it on to this day. I know a brilliant Kentucky woman, daughter of a great slave-owner of that state who was at one time its governor, who has been a helper to Negro church workers, and to any Negro in need, her whole long, beautiful life. Another friend, a woman of wealth and influence, a leader among the women of the South today, taught a Bible class of Negroes for sixteen years, until her strength failed under her accumulating work for the unprivileged.

Space fails for the instances known to even one person. One more must suffice.

Just after the war a South Carolinian, a graduate of Brown University and a devout Baptist, went to a Georgia city and gathered about him a little knot of Negro boys who wanted to become Baptist preachers. He taught them there for years, spending himself to give ideals to the ignorant and the poor, cut off from all other association. For the white people were bitter in those days, and despised him where they did not hate. It was one man's vision against a city's blindness—that world-old story of ignorance, and of light no darkness can quench. He is forgotten to-day by all but a few Negroes, one of whom, a fine, strong man who had felt his touch, told me his story. But the black boys to whom he gave ideals have gone out to give their people light. Their church is strong in Georgia, and these men lead it. One of them is its chief pastor in my own city; and so well has he responded to his teacher's efforts that the white people of the town are all his friends. When he was ill not long ago the daily paper reported his condition, and gave the names of several of the leading business men who went to his home to inquire how he did.

Yet few of the whites who speak of this Negro and of the others who were taught with him, as " the kind all Negroes ought to be " have any idea where the real springs of their lives were found. Some of us, turning away from the South's long tradition of service to the Negro race, knowing only the disjointed years of bitterness, feel only contempt, or at best a puzzled surprise, that any white Southerner should lower himself by stooping to help a Negro, or should persuade himself that they are worth the effort.

Yet we have never offered them ideals out of a living sympathy that they have not responded, for themselves and for their race. No one who knows the better class of Negroes can fail to be impressed with the spirit of sacrifice and service which is shared by nearly all of them. They follow that law of human life under which any race, in common stress of any kind, draws closer the band of brotherhood, and lives for the common good.

And oh, we white people are waking up ! The thrill of the North's awaking, long ago begun, and not yet ended, is with me still ; but these are my very own ! Some of us have worked and waited so long. There have been years when the only warrant for hope was in the long look at the Race of Man, and the Love which leads it on. But that was warrant enough.—And now? Just a few of the signs—a few.

For long our churches have set a standard for us ; and even though they themselves have not lived up to it, the pegs were down, and visible to the careful eye. In 1876 the Southern Presbyterians opened a theological school for Negroes at Tuscaloosa, Ala. For nineteen years the pastor of the white Presbyterian church of the town was also the head of this school, which has had only Southern whites as teachers from the beginning. The yearly income, provided by the denomination, had risen from four hundred dollars the first year to fifteen thousand twenty years later. The theologues pay their board and tuition by working on the school farm under expert teaching. They go out to preach a gospel of love, morality, cleanliness, hard work, and modern methods of farming ; also of friendliness to their white neighbours. I am told, by those who know the section about Tallapoosa, that race relations there are not of the problem kind. There has been response to ideals from both whites and blacks. The present head of the school is the son of a Mississippi slave-owner.

A few years after this school was started the Southern Methodists opened an institution in Augusta, Ga., for the training of Negro preachers, teachers, and other leaders for the race. Its first president was a former slave-owner, who resigned the chair of English in a strong college to take the position at a most problematical salary. It cannot be denied that the school lived "at a poor dying rate" for several years : but the denomination was officially committed to it as a proper work for white Christians to undertake ; Southern white college men and women have officered it from the first ; and for eighteen years the church Board of Education has put its needs before the people, and, in coöperation with its president and faculty, has gradually won for it a better support.

These are, so far as I know, the only schools maintained exclusively by Southern whites for Negroes ; but the Episcopal church has a number of schools for them in which Southern as well as Northern whites teach ; and part of their support, which comes from their General Mission Board, is drawn from the Southern dioceses. The Southern Baptists, who have long made an annual appropriation for the education of Negroes at schools of other churches, are now preparing to open a theological seminary for them.

The first Southern settlement for Negroes is conducted by the son of an Alabama banker and former slaveholder. It is in Louisville, and is of late years jointly financed by the Northern and Southern Presbyterians. This settlement, I am told, is largely responsible for Louisville's Negro playgrounds and probation officers. This city also has a fine public library for Negroes,[1] with a Negro librarian and two assistants, all under the white librarian who is the head of the city system. A children's room is well patronized ; and branches are maintained at some of the public schools. In a private letter the white head of the system declares the Negro library an untold blessing to the race. The use of a room in the building is allowed, free of charge, to clubs and other educational and recreational gatherings. The children, he writes, respond readily to guidance, and are eager for good books. The number of adult patrons grows steadily. The library, which is a beautiful building, was given by Mr. Carnegie, and cost $25,000.00. It is maintained by the city of Louisville. Libraries for

[1] Since this was written a second branch public library for Negroes has been opened in Louisville.

Negroes have also been given by Mr. Carnegie to New Orleans, to Nashville, and to Meridian, Miss., the city authorities guaranteeing ample support.

I can learn of but two other Negro public libraries in the South. One, at Galveston, is the gift of a citizen of that place, whose will made provision for a library for each race. The librarian said that the children were being helped by it to a large extent. The response among adults was less marked. The other public library for Negroes is at Jacksonville, Fla. ; and my last report from it, some time ago, stated that it was not as efficient as it should be, because only a room in a corner of the building for whites was available, so that it was impossible to make efforts to extend the work ; but their present capacity was taxed.

Here is a scarcely-touched opportunity to create ideals for a race. These Carnegie libraries are among the wisest investments in the South. But some of us, like the children in the market-place, are hard to please. If the Negroes care nothing for books we say they are stupid and vicious-minded : if one proposes antidoting this dangerous condition with the best literature, sympathetically applied, we cry out against the

Negro's uppishness, and want him taught to work.

He ought to be taught to work, no doubt. The great majority of Negroes, like the majority of every race, must always work with their hands. There is a deal more of what is called drudgery to be done in the world than of everything else put together; and most of us have our share of it to perform. But no one to whom work is drudgery has ever been rightly taught to work. I believe this lack of proper training is at the bottom of nine-tenths—or maybe eleven-tenths—of all the laziness and shiftlessness of the poor which does not come from sub-normal physical conditions. Drudgery is not work: it is a mental attitude towards work which comes from ignorance or from physical weakness. The narrower the round of a man's life, or a woman's, the more they need outlook and horizon. The world over, the world's poor have been set to do the hardest work in a perfectly detached, unrelated way, without reasons, without background, without a trace of world-connections; and they usually find it a very boring job, and shirk it when they can, naturally.

We are learning rapidly to broaden the white worker's horizon through the industrial

training given in our public and normal
schools, and in our agricultural colleges ;
and in some of our cities part of this training
is given to Negroes, some of it of a high
order. In Richmond County, Georgia, this
industrial work has been extended by the
county itself, with no outside aid, to the
Negro country schools. We have there a
superintendent who looks closely after the
schools of both races ; and the county superintendent of industrial training gives as
efficient oversight and help to the Negro
schools, city and country, as to the white. I
speak of this county because, living in it, I
happen to know about it. That many others
do as well I do not doubt.

But the great impulse towards rational
training, towards an education which really
educates, in the Negro country schools has
come from the Jeanes Fund, given by a
Northern woman, and administered by a
Southern man, the grandson of a great slaveholder, a scholar and educator of distinction. I know of no other one force in
Negro life more beneficent than this. It is
demonstrating in every one of our states the
kind of work needed in their rural schools,
and its quickening influence grows with the
years. Virginia, first of all the South, ap-

pointed a superintendent of Negro rural public schools, a Phi Beta Kappa College graduate and a man for the South to be proud of. Kentucky, Georgia, North Carolina and Alabama have followed the example; and the other states are bound to do likewise or to see themselves out-distanced in the production of wealth in the not-far-distant future. For it is human nature to love work when ideals are put into it, when it has a background and a horizon.

The Y. M. C. A. is doing, through Southern secretaries, a work which can hardly be estimated. Six thousand students have been enrolled in Y. M. C. A. study classes in Southern colleges to study the Negro and the white man's duty to him. Already various forms of settlement and Sunday-school work have grown out of this study. In fifteen years these young men will be the leaders of the South; and even now the attitude of our colleges and universities, faculties and students, is an appreciable factor in the changing public sentiment.

The Y. M. C. A. has also a large coloured organization. Forty-one associations with over sixty thousand members are enrolled. Here again is a great opportunity to help create ideals for a race. In our cities there is no better way to fight intemperance and many other forms of vice among the Negroes, than to provide them with a good Y. M. C. A. building, and to help them get it fully on its feet.

The women of the Southern Methodist church are the only ones in the South as yet carrying on organized work for Negroes. For over twenty-five years they have been the South's women-pioneers along social service lines, first to whites and now to blacks. They opened the first settlement in the South, employed the first visiting nurse, opened the first free clinic, and introduced free kindergartens and industrial training at many points where they were previously unknown.

Twelve years ago they built two industrial cottages for girls at the church's school for Negroes in Augusta, and have since provided for the industrial training there, besides erecting recently a $25,000.00 dormitory. This sum was raised from several sources. Half of it was given by Southern white women, some of them giving as much as a thousand dollars each; five thousand was given by the General Education Board; and the rest was raised by a Negro man from the white Southern Methodist conferences.

In addition to this, these women will

shortly open a farm school for Negro boys in Mississippi, five hundred acres of land having been recently given them by a Southern white man for this purpose.

In 1911 they appointed an Alabama woman, a college graduate, as secretary for Negro work. Her headquarters were located in Augusta, where she has opened the white South's second settlement for Negroes, the one in Louisville being the first.

The Augusta vacation playgrounds, secured by the coöperation of people of both races, are an outcome of this work, which, inadequately housed and provided for as it is, is full of promise and interest. The children, nearly all from the poorest class, are as responsive as—well, as children, the world around : their development, in their various clubs and classes, is as striking as in any children of like class anywhere. The kindergartner is a coloured woman, a graduate of one of the best of the schools established by Northern missionaries after the war, and a power for good among her people.

But however institutions may be built up or multiplied, the South-wide need is a South-wide turning of the hearts of the strong to help the weak both by personal service and by coöperation with capable Negro leaders.

To this need a number of Southern agencies at last begin to address themselves.

The will of the late Miss Caroline Phelps Stokes, a well-known Northern philanthropist, provided for the endowment of fellowships in the state universities of Virginia and Georgia "to enable Southern youth of broad sympathies to make a scientific study of the Negro, and of his adjustment to American civilization." These fellowships were accepted in the spirit of their founder, and in the belief that "any national program looking to the adjustment of relations must be based on a far wider knowledge of actual conditions than we now have." The university of Georgia has just published the results of the investigations made by its first Fellow under this foundation. He is the son of a member of the university faculty, and has spent a year in a close and sympathetic study of the Negroes of Athens, the university town, and of their relations with the whites. His report makes clear the community menace of conditions allowed in the Negro quarters, and calls for the coöperation of the educated whites in upbuilding the homes, churches and schools of the Negroes. Reports like these, coming from a great and beloved university, are sure to leaven the

thought of an entire state. Miss Stokes's
gift, like that of Miss Jeanes, proves the
wisdom of Northern philanthropists who
choose Southerners in sympathy with Negro
betterment to administer their gifts. Such
gifts, so given, draw together the North and
the South, as well as the two races in the
South.

At the recent annual meeting of the
Women's Missionary Council of the Southern Methodist Church the committee on
Social Service brought in the following report, which was unanimously adopted :

" It shall be a duty of the Department of
Social Service to promote the study of conditions and needs among the Negroes, lo-
cally, throughout the South ; also to arouse
the women of our auxiliaries to a sense of
their personal duty as Christian Southerners
to meet the needs and ameliorate the conditions of those of this backward race who
are in our midst by personal service and
sympathy. We recommend the giving of
this sympathy and service in any or all of the
following ways :

"(1) By learning the needs of Negro Sunday-schools, teaching their Bible classes,
training their teachers in modern Sunday-
school methods, helping to grade their schools,

and offering such other assistance as may be needed.

"(2)   By assisting Negro women in forming and directing missionary societies in their churches, giving them information and other help, especially in regard to home mission work among the poorer classes of their own race.

"(3)   By looking into the needs of Negro public schools, requiring of the public authorities that their premises be kept sanitary, helping to secure coloured teachers of a high grade, and favouring the introduction of industrial training.

"(4)   By looking after the recreation, or lack of it, of Negro children and young people ; by endeavouring to interest the Christian women of all denominations in securing for them opportunities for clean play in playgrounds supervised by good Negro women or men ; and by securing coöperation with Negro Young Men's and Young Women's Associations where these exist.

"(5)   By securing from boards of education permission to use Negro schoolhouses as community centres, organizing and assisting the better class of Negroes in each community to take charge of these community centres and supervise them for the pleasure

and instruction of their own race. By interesting white people in the movement, securing white physicians and others to talk on
personal and community hygiene, care of
children, temperance, and other matters.

"(6) By visiting the local jails, by ascer-
taining the measure of justice accorded Negroes in the local courts, and by creating a
sentiment for justice to youthful criminals
whom wise treatment may reform.

"(7) By studying Negro housing conditions and their bearing on sickness, ineffi-
ciency, and crime; by bringing these conditions to the attention of the public; by in-
sisting that the local authorities enforce in
the Negro district the sanitary regulations of
the community; by securing for Negroes a
water supply sufficient for health and decency; by helping the Negroes of the better
class to organize among their people civic
clubs where the young may be trained in
community cleanliness and righteousness.

"(8) By creating in the local white community higher ideals in regard to the relation between the two races; by standing for
full and equal justice in all departments of
life; by endeavouring to secure for the backward race not only the full measure of development of which they are capable, but the

unmolested possession and enjoyment of all legitimate rewards of honest work ; by standing, in short, for the full application to the Negroes and to ourselves of the Mosaic law of justice : 'Thou shalt love thy neighbour as thyself.'"

There are four thousand auxiliaries in this organization ; and even though the work be taken up slowly, it will spread. The authorities at Paine College are urging upon the church the establishment of a training school for Negro missionaries and social workers who may be employed by the whites as well as by coloured churches in all these forms of coöperative effort. The need is so great we can but trust it will be met.

The secretary for the Home Department of the General Board of Missions of this church is working along similar lines. At his instance the Alabama conference has appointed a committee of ministers, laymen and women, to look into the condition of the Negroes within the bounds of the conference at all these points. A consistent plan of conference-wide help and coöperation is expected to result ; and such committees will be asked for in the other conferences until all have taken the matter up.

The deepest significance of all these movements in the various churches lies in the fact that they all look towards coöperation between the better classes of both races for the uplift of the Negro poor. It is impossible to serve the best interests of either race without this personal communication between the two. Where we have had a disposition to help the Negroes the attitude of the whites, both North and South, has been too often suggestive of that of the rich burgher in the play of Rip Van Winkle—"Give him a cold potato, and let him go." We have but given where he and we need that we should share.

There are notable individual exceptions, but many of even the well-educated Negroes are yet unequal to the task of achieving unaided the spiritual emancipation of their people. These need the forming and inspiring touch of educated whites.

In some of our Northern cities more or less money has been contributed for the uplift of the local Negro population through Y. M. C. A. work or otherwise; but often, when the money is given, the Negroes are left quite to their own devices in trying to serve their people; and the result is rarely all that it might be under a system of sympathetic coöperation between both races.

A Northern Y. M. C. A. worker, in speaking of this fact not long ago, said that the Negroes of the North did not desire coöperation, and frequently resented it when offered.

I think some Negroes in the South feel the same way, and are quick to repudiate the suggestion that the Negroes are not entirely competent to take full charge of Negro education and Negro uplift in general. They want white people to furnish the money, and leave them to direct the work.

That some Negroes are entirely equal to such a task cannot be truthfully denied. The logical deduction from this fact is that the race has capabilities of development far beyond the position some of us would permanently assign it. But it is idle to make claims which are not borne out by facts. The finest and strongest Negroes, I believe without a single exception, have come to their high development largely through contact with broad-minded, large-hearted white men and women. For years to come few of them are destined to reach that plane by any other process. I think on this point the real leaders in the South, white and black, are agreed.

There should be some white teachers in every state school for the higher education of Negroes ; but so far Alabama is the only state recognizing, in even a single institution, this statesmanlike and Christian principle. In Mississippi, however, whites have charge of the summer school for Negro teachers; and in my home county of Richmond, in Georgia, the county superintendent supervises in person the yearly institute for Negro teachers, lecturing before them from time to time. This is probably not unusual.

The need for such service is threefold. As the more highly developed race we owe this help to the other race; and unpaid spiritual debts issue, sooner or later, in spiritual bankruptcy. We must render such service for the sake of our own spiritual integrity. The Negroes need to receive all we can give them, that their own power to give, to their race and to the nation, may be enlarged. And beyond these needs is the fundamental necessity for both races to learn, however distinct they must remain racially, to work together in mutual respect, coöperating for the good of their common country, and for the kingdom of God on earth.

The exceptional Negro should be given the most responsible work as a teacher and leader of his people which his ability deserves. But the race would be superhuman if in fifty years of freedom it had become capable of taking its future entirely into its own hands. Some Negroes do not recognize this fact, and are quick to resent white assistance as white interference ; and especially to distrust any measure or method which emphasizes the need for discipline of mind or spirit. Surely we are responsible here. Our long indifference weighs heavily against us ; and our assistance, where offered, is too often tinctured—or impregnated—with condescension. If Christ had come to us that way I think we would be savages still. However fine it may look on the outside, there is no lifting force in any condescending deed. When we set about our task in that entire simplicity and self-unconsciousness which are a necessary part of the spirit of Christian service, we will be oftener surprised by the depth of the response evoked than by a disposition to reject our help. Money alone, though we poured it into institutions for the Negroes like water, cannot settle our debt. The world around, the debt of the privileged involves their personality.

One of the straws which show our new consciousness of this fact blew across my path not long ago as I was returning from a trip to the North. In a travellers' chat with another passenger the subject of women's club-work came up; and my companion, knowing nothing of my own interests, told me of her recent experience as president of the federated clubs of her home town, a thriving city in North Carolina. The club-women had decided on a Clean-up Day, when it occurred to her that in order to make it a real cleaning day the city should be cleaned, and not merely that fraction of it which least needed cleansing. So she proposed to the club-women that for the health of their own households, as well as for other obvious reasons, they should invite the leaders of all the Negro women's societies to a conference, get them interested in the movement, and have a Clean-up Day which would leave the city clean. They expected perhaps a dozen Negro women, and seventy came. The mayor of the city and the president of the Board of Health addressed the gathering, and then the women talked, white and black.

"And you'd have been as astonished as we were if you'd heard those Negroes," she declared. " Some of them knew as much about parliamentary proceedings as we did ; and they were so sensible, they talked so well, they were so glad to do all they could ! —And I tell you," she added with a little laugh, " when it came to cleaning up, we had to hustle to keep up with them.—We don't expect much sickness in town this summer : the place—the whole place—is clean."

And Negroes do not respond to ideals? Let those who give them a chance—a growing group among us—testify.

This North Carolina club is not alone. On the Women's Club page of the *Atlanta Constitution* I read recently, in a single issue, accounts of three Georgia clubs which are co-operating with the Negroes of their respective cities to keep their towns clean and healthful.

The annual meetings of the Virginia State Board of Charities and Correction are open to both races. The Negroes report there their work among their own people ; and the attitude of the Board is one of solicitude and helpfulness towards all dependents and delinquents in the commonwealth, rather than towards those of one race.

It is a Virginia town, too, which is demonstrating the wisdom of another form of co-operation ; a form so simple, so needed, so obviously Christian, that one feels it should only be known to be adopted. I learned of it from a chance acquaintance whose relatives live in the town. The Protestant ministers of

STILLMAN INSTITUTE, TUSCALOOSA, ALA.

the town, he said, both white and black, are members of the Ministers' Alliance. They meet once a month, as brothers of Him who came to serve all races and all classes of men, to pray and talk and plan for the spiritual uplift of the whole community. If Christ came again in the flesh, surely nowhere could He feel more at home than in a meeting-place like that.

It is puzzling that the local churches, of all denominations, all over the South, should fail as they do in leadership in this matter. Every large denomination has officially gone on record, in its highest legislative body, as recognizing the common brotherhood of the races, the common duty of the strong race to serve the weak one. No voice has been publicly lifted, in any denomination, to controvert this doctrine. White ministers have, undoubtedly, the kindliest feelings to Negroes. None of them, I think, would hesitate to accept gladly any invitation to speak or preach to a black audience. In my own denomination, when one speaks to a conference body of ministers about our duty to the Negroes there is, of recent years, a deep, and often moving, response; and the presiding bishop never fails to press the duty home. And we are not double-faced, nor cowards. But I doubt if, in any state, a dozen ministers could be found, in all denominations put together, who make a practice of preaching, even once in two or three years, about race relations, or our duty to our black poor, or the connection between the Negro quarters of our cities and the interests of the kingdom of God. Yet these things enter into the warp and woof of daily life in the South, and help or hinder the growth in Christian character of every member of every church.

It is true the leaders of the South's best thought and action regarding the Negroes are church-members, grown up under Southern preachers; and in at least three great denominations the head of the work for Negroes is a minister, officially backed by his church. Yet the pulpits of the South rarely speak of those problems which press upon us all, and for which there is no solution outside the teachings of Christ. In this as in other things, the country over, the churches have yielded their crown of leadership to members who must do much of their work along lines largely ignored by the rank and file of the ministry.

Yet there are exceptions, each one a shining example of the leadership possible to our pulpits. Not long ago, after an outburst of race antagonism which was being chronicled and condemned in all the papers, I asked a Negro from a neighbouring state if such feeling existed in his section.

"No, ma'am, it don't," he answered emphatically ; "not for a long time."

"Then it used to exist ? "

"Oh, yes'm. We ain't had a thing but trouble till these last few years."

"What stopped it ? "

" A white preacher stopped it. He thought some of the things done weren't right ; and he got all the white preachers in town to agree to preach about Christ's way of treating coloured folks, all on the same day. They all did it again a month later, and once or twice more that year. And as long as he stayed there they all preached about it together that way, a time or two each year ; and there ain't any trouble since. I heard tell two or three white folks got mad about it ; but the preachers stuck it out. And now all the white folks treat us right, and we all are behaving better, and everybody is prospering a heap better than they used to."

Instances like this will multiply as our social conscience quickens. A fresh, clean wind stirs over the South before which old mists of prejudice are lifting. Insufficient

and halting as the work of the churches has
been, it has yet testified to the Christian
duty of service and the Christian doctrine of
brotherhood.   That all the churches must at
some points, perhaps at many, be readjusted
to conditions few who love them will deny: but
in England, and in America, North and South,
it is the churches which have created that
social conscience which some deem all-suffi-
cient without the churches, and at which the
churches themselves sometimes look askance,
as at a rival which would usurp their domin-
ion.   The Southern Sociological Congress is
the first South-wide expression of this nascent
conscience; and no one who attended the
Congress meetings, in Nashville or in Atlanta,
could fail to be impressed with the religious
spirit in which men of many faiths had met
to consider their common duties to the unprivileged of the South.

Out of the first meeting of the section on
Race Relations came the appointment of
a Southern University Commission on the
Negro, with a representative from nearly
every Southern state university.   This commission met for organization in December,
1912.   It reported to the Atlanta Congress a
broad outline of investigation to be undertaken in regard to conditions—religious,

educational, hygienic, economic and civic;
the duty of whites in improving these conditions; and the ideal of race-relations towards
which the South should work.   No one who
has heard these men speak, as several have
already done in public, can doubt that large
hearts and clear brains are at work upon the
whole subject in a spirit of justice and service.

This is not the place to discuss the Congress at large; but it furnished many evidences of a social conscience at last astir on
all community interests.   The sectional meetings on Race Relations were a dream come
true—a dream of a new South, with the old
spirit of sympathy once more in the heart of
the strong, and hands of human brotherhood
held out to the weaker race.   The privileged
South has at last opened its doors of counsel
and invited the unprivileged to enter in and
talk over, men with men, the needs and duties
which confront them both in making the land
a home of justice and opportunity for all.

But that was not the whole story.   With
Southern white and Southern black speaking
from the same platform, and seeing in so
many things eye to eye at last, were men of
that other class so long misunderstood and
misjudged among us—the men of the North
who came long ago to meet a great human

need among those whom we, for the dark time being, had closed our hearts against. North and South and black and white met there, and pledged their common service to a common humanity, a common country, and a common God.

We stood, for those brief days, on one of those mountain tops from which the end is seen, near and beautiful and real. Afterwards, one turns to the rugged path again, and faces the long, long road. But the end is still real and beautiful, and as certain as Love itself. And as for nearness, shall one measure the life of the Race of Man by one's own narrow years; or the world-wide victory that awaits by one's tiny measure of personal failure or success? Though we ourselves pass not over, yet shall our brothers possess the land, and dwell there.

Sometimes a biologist, studying tissues under the microscope, will stain some cells and not others, that he may the better unravel some of life's obscure interactions.

I think God has done that in the South, dyeing our weak ones black, that it may be clear to the most careless what the weak have to suffer from the selfishness of the strong. Once we begin to see, it ought to be easier for us than for others to learn community righteousness, because the effects of evil are made so plain among us.   And those who look on from afar should, rather than criticize us, watch more closely their own community life, where the strong may wrong the weak in less spectacular fashion.

It may be long before it is all stopped. The evil is great everywhere ; and we of the South have been slow to start our part of the fight against it.   But we have started now, at last—not as individuals only, as heretofore ; but as a constantly-growing group of Southern folk who feel the common obligation of those who have to serve those who have not.

And having taken these first steps in recognition of our share of a world-task the main peculiarity of our Southern situation has vanished.   For we have joined hands, we too, at last, with the privileged of earth elsewhere, to set free those without privilege ; to serve our neighbour, not according to the colour of his skin, but according to his need.

VII

THOSE WHO COME AFTER US

BEING parents is the deepest thing in life. It runs away back of humanity, out into the wild, free places, where the bird broods high in air, and the weed pours all its being into its seed, and dies. It is doubtless this blood-kinship stirring in us when we yearn for the woods, and the mountains, and the sea ; some inarticulate inner consciousness knows all these as homes of life, our common heritage, our common trust. With all the weight of suffering of those to whom the highest honours of that trust have been committed, and who have, as yet, failed to be worthy of them, we turn back to these haunts of simpler and more loyal forms of life for rest, and for strength and courage for the long road our feet have yet to go.

Parenthood is a thing to bind all life in one. It is not merely that nothing human is foreign to us afterwards : no life that grows by sacrifice is alien ; and that is all the life there is.

It seems the miracle of the ages that we,

on the summit of life, we humans, should have made this thing unclean: that the power to pass on the torch of life, to call out of nothingness those who shall shape the future of the race—that this, of all things, should be the force to make men beasts again, and to build for multitudes of the women of all races an age-long hell on earth.

At least one good should come of it: it should bind the women of the world in one, Being a woman goes deeper than being of this race or that, or of this or that social station. Red, yellow, or black, or white, we carry the world's sins on our shoulders, its degradation and anguish in our hearts. It all falls on the women, the lust, the degradation, the suffering. And what is a keener agony, a more intolerable shame, it falls on the women's daughters, whom they won in the valley of death. Have we not reason to stand together, we women of the world? A Chinese girl hawked publicly by her owner on the streets of Shanghai, an Indian maid betrayed in the forest, girls of our own race by scores of thousands, Negro girls whom men of no race reverence—where is the difference? They are women, women all; and women bore them: women should stand together for the womanhood of the world

It burns like fire when first we grasp that truth. It is inevitable, in the beginning, when the knowledge of broken lives first flares in our faces, and we reach hands of fellowship to draw some poor outcast back into the circle of human sympathy again, that women's standing together should mean to us their standing against the men. We are quick to hate, when we are young ; and men are an easy mark. Nothing excuses them to us, nothing palliates. An honoured father, a brother whom we trust, a husband well-beloved—these are the accidents of the sex ; creatures in whom, by some great miracle, a touch of their mothers' souls has turned dross to gold : but for men ——. The sharpest trial of faith is no mental question to a woman ; it comes straight from the heart of life, terrible and fierce : Would a good God make women as women are made, and shut them up in the same world with men ?

And then, into such a woman's life, is sent a little son. He shall defy the law of his sex ; he shall be pure, though all men else follow the common path.

She lives her son's life, and so she wins the freedom of his world. It takes imagination, and patience, and sympathy, and time. But when he begins to run with other boys she has his confidence; and so she learns, as we all must, by love, and not by hate.

What chance have they, these little boys, any more than the girls whose lives they poison? Before they know the meaning of words or acts their lives are poisoned, too. We care for everything about them, bodies and minds, except this highest thing, which we call unclean, and hide. It is not a question of a child's being taught or not taught; he learns, as surely as he lives and breathes. It is a question of how he shall be taught: in truth and cleanness, or in lies and filth. And because this power is the highest intrusted to us, because its perversion causes more misery and degradation than everything else put together, the right training of children in matters of sex is a basal necessity for the world's progress in righteousness. Shall we dare to remain prudes when we see what silence costs our children, sons and daughters both? Love takes no account of such childish shrinking, however much love may feel it: love serves the beloved unashamed, and at any cost. And love can find a way.

The future of both races in the South is more deeply concerned in this than in any other one thing. For to the pure all achievement is possible; and for the impure rottenness and decay are certain. There is no reason whatever for believing that any one country or section sins above the rest in this matter. Where two races of different colours dwell side by side, one strong, one weak, the evidences of sin are not to be hidden : yet the sin exists no less, though less visibly, where strong and weak are of one skin. But there is no section of any country which is not implicated in the authorized statement of physicians of world-repute that seventy per cent. of the men of Christendom are, or have been, sufferers from vice-diseases. The meaning of such a statement staggers the mind : the stunted bodies and souls of children, women's long-drawn-out torments, the maiming of mind and flesh, the perverts, the paupers, the insane ! Shall we be ashamed to remove burdens like these from those who shall follow us ? Shall we shrink from sending the children of the South out unhandicapped, strong of body and pure in mind, to build the homes of the future ; homes where white folk dwell, where black folk dwell, each secure from wrong and from fear ?

For it can be so. There is a new day breaking. Old evils, hoary with the centuries until we have accepted them as inseparable from life itself, are being challenged, defied.

The German Government believes the purity of young men not impossible of attainment. It orders the instruction in sex hygiene of every college student in the land. At a recent annual meeting of the American Medical Association one of their leading speakers, in a formal address, called on the churches of America to aid the doctors in their fight against the social evil by the teaching of sex hygiene. The doctors stood long, many of them, for the necessity of " wild oats." As an association they have now endorsed the movement for social purity as a necessity for personal and social health. That great, conservative organization, the Church of England, has undertaken a year's-long campaign against the social evil, with the avowed intention of uprooting it from English life.

Time was when we thought yellow fever was providential. A providence which made yellow fever an integral part of the scheme of things would be benevolent indeed beside a providence which made this loathsome cancer a necessity of human life. We had yellow fever because we had not learned to destroy the breeding-places of the pests which carry it. We have the social evil for exactly the same reason.

Its breeding-places are in the unclean

thoughts of children and young people who were made to think cleanly. There is nothing more wonderful, more sacrificially pure, than the great law of life by which life comes from life, and like from like, strong life from pure, and weak from foul, which runs through all the organisms of earth. When a child begins to question he needs—and she—not lies, but the clean truth. If the mother does not answer somebody else will; and then the poison will be at work.

A child can be taught *unconsciously* to reverence the life-giving power which he holds in trust. When the stress of temptation comes, swift and sharp, he may find himself prepared. He need not battle in the dark, ignorant of himself, of the meaning of life, of its dangers and rewards. A girl can be protected in all purity, that in time of danger she may so remain. Our parents did not know: but for an intelligent parent to send children out to-day defenseless against the contagions of school life is a neglect the child may find it impossible to forgive.

There is a little book by Ellen Torrelle, published by Heath, called "Plant and Animal Children, and How They Grow." One need not be botanist or biologist to make its stories clear to children's minds; and a child who

understands its facts is unconsciously fortified
against uncleanness. There is no room for
impurity concerning the origin of life, not
because it has been inveighed against, but
because its possible place has been filled with
thoughts beautiful and pure. Another book,
which all adults and every adolescent boy
should read, is Lavinia Dock's " Hygiene and
Morality," published by the Putnams. In addition to these, and for many purposes, parents would do well to read Stanley Hall's
" Youth," published by Appleton. There are
many other books, large and small, a list of
which may be had from the National Vigi-
lance Committee, in New York.

The time is not far distant when the teaching of such books as Miss Torrelle's will be
obligatory in the earlier grades of the public
schools ; and when that is secured for those
who shall come after us, the poor man's
home, North, South and West, will be safer—
yes, and the homes of the privileged too.
For this hideous infection can never be confined, while it exists at all, to one economic
class, or to this or that locality. It breeds
misery and degradation for the community,
just so far as it breeds at all.

But education is not the only measure ; nor
need we wait for a new generation to grow

up to introduce wide-spread reform. Health laws should compel all physicians, as they already do those of a few states in other sections, to report not only cases of the lesser contagions, such as scarlet fever, diphtheria and the like ; but also the far more dangerous contagions of the vice-diseases. With this law goes a second, requiring a physician's certificate to the applicant's freedom from contagious disease before a marriage license can be issued. These laws are being widely advocated by physicians of the highest standing, by social workers everywhere, and by many health officers, parents, educators and ministers.

Another law urgently needed in many states, and in no section more than in our own, is one raising the age of consent to at least eighteen years. In some of our Southern states it is ten years. The mere statement of such a fact would come as a shock to any but the most nascent social conscience. What of morality can we hope to evolve in the classes most in need of morality, white and black, when the defenseless childhood of the poor is held so cheap *by law ?*

But beyond all this, what can the privileged mothers do for those unprivileged, the strong to help the weak ? For women should stand

together, for the manhood and the womanhood of the world. Mothers cannot, if they
would, break the tie which binds them to
both sexes, to the whole human race.

Privilege exists for one end only—that it
may become the common servitor of all.
We pray such curious prayers sometimes, in
the pulpit and out of it—prayers which automatically prevent their own fulfillment. We
are so anxious for "especial" care and good,
for "peculiar" blessings, for things which
would mark us as a folk apart, or a family,
or even an individual, sheltered from ordinary trials, lifted above the multitude who
hunger, separated from the common lot,
favoured of heaven beyond other folk!

A god who would answer prayers like
those it should be beneath one's self-respect
to pray to. If he be not equally the God of
all flesh, he is no god for any flesh to petition.
For there is a deep sense in which God Himself must be•thought of in terms of humanity,
so that no one who seeks fullness of life, which
is fullness of love, may dare ask any protection, any mercy, any good for any aspect of our
many-sided life, the giving of which would
imply anything whatever "especial" in the
sense that it is not open, to the limit of his
need, to the least of all flesh who may ask for it.

But more than that. When we get this background of prayer in our minds, this true perspective of our own needs in relation to those of the rest of the world, we see the basis of justice on which the fulfilling of those needs must rest. It is for lack of justice in our petitions that we have so largely been, in all the ages,

"Bafflers of our own prayers, from youth to life's last scenes."

Mothers should understand, because love costs them more, and so they should be wiser in its ways. There can be no safe basis for prayer for one's child except this basis of justice. If we desire protection for our daughters, or purity for our sons, strong bodies for them and trained minds, a place for happy play, freedom and joy in work, a life made rich by love and service, it is strange that we should dare to ask these things of a just God except as we pledge our full strength to effort to secure like good for all the children, the world around, to whom it is denied.

What things that we desire for our children do Negro children lack? I do not mean the luxuries, nor even many of the comforts of life : but those basal necessities to any clean, efficient, hopeful life, however humble and poor: abundant water and fresh air, with a knowledge of their uses; houses where homes are possible; sanitary surroundings; school training which really trains; a chance for clean play; mothers who can approximate a mother's duties; religious instruction related to daily life. Without these things, what kind of people are they foredoomed to be? And whose is the responsibility?

But more than that. Women make the standards for every community in our land. North, South and West, community morals and ideals are exactly what, consciously or unconsciously, the consciences of the privileged women of that community permit. If the morality of the daughters of the very poor is to be safeguarded anywhere, it must be done by the privileged women primarily. And our very poor are black.

We need, in the first place, to see the women of our poor as women first, and black afterwards. We need a new respect for them in our own minds, as children of the one Father, even as we. We need more faith in the possibilities of the poorest life which is born with a capacity, however limited, for divine things. We need to use our imaginations, to put ourselves in the Negro woman's place. We will find the exercise as broadening to our own lives as it will be beneficial to the Negro's. We need to think of Negro womanhood as sacred, as the womanhood of all the world must be. Thinking so, we will begin to honour its possibilities, and try to bring them out. And if we hold up that standard, our men will come to it ; they cannot help themselves. It is women who rule the world—or who can rule it, always, if only they will stand together. It is not merely that we have the men when they are babies. Beyond that tremendous fact men are dependent on women as women are not upon men. When women fix the terms on which men may secure their companionship and their love men must meet the conditions : they have no escape. Only, women must stand together, for womanhood, and for the race.

Let us plan the future of the South we love under a wide sky. Let us plan, not for our children merely, nor for our race, else can the plans never bear full fruit. All that we want for our own let us plan for the children of the South, rich and poor, high and low, black and white : strong bodies, clean minds, hands skilled to labour, hearts just and kind and wise. Children do not grow like that of themselves, any more than roses grow double in the swamps: it is the children's power to respond to cultivation which lays upon us the duty of giving it.

I knew a family once where there were several normal children, and one little child, the youngest, whom epilepsy had reduced almost to idiocy. He was most repulsive to me when I first saw him, before I understood. He seemed that awful thing which some imagine they see in the world's undeveloped races—something in human shape without human capacity.

But his parents loved him so much! Their tenderness never failed for him, their care never abated. They loved the other children dearly, too; but this child needed them so much: they loved him according to his need.

Think of them for a moment—the hordes of the unprivileged of every race; those cut off from joy; the folk whose years are filled only with a great emptiness, with immeasurable ignorance and want; the mass of men and women, really, the vast majority of the human race. And God so loves the world—just so: according to the need.

VIII

THE GREAT ADVENTURE

I CANNOT close this little book without a word concerning those whose childhood is behind them, and who are soon to take their places in that great array of toilers whose hands are moulding the world's life in the present. Life looms before them as the Great Adventure, wherein difficulties and trials may await them, but which, in some unknown, far-off place, shall issue in achievement; in something which shall win them a place and honour which their own effort has secured for them, well-deserved.

We older people, the mass of us at least, look on as the raw recruits pass out, and smile, some of us kindly, some pityingly, some with bitterness, seeing their young enthusiasms, the high resolves and hopes which drive them, the gleam of the half-formed ideals which lure them on. Life will grip these over-confident children, we think, and trim them all to one sober pattern by the time they reach middle age. They will learn fast enough to accept its drudgery and to bow to its yoke. In the valley of old age they will stand much as their fathers stood, moulded by life, not moulding it, their laughter done; strong perhaps, but strong chiefly to accept and to bear the inevitable.

Is that the normal end of youth, the natural outcome of the Great Adventure; or are we so ill-adjusted to our environment that the abnormal is the usual and the normal the uncommon outcome of the quest?

Surely power is never intended for futility, and only ignorance can unmoved see it turned to waste. Yet if we measure in terms of human energy the advance of any one generation, and compare it with the force originally applied to secure advance, with that fund of energy, of hope and joy which we sum up as youth, the waste of power is staggering. It is only the smallest fraction of it which has been utilized: the rest has been absorbed by frictions which have largely wrecked the generators themselves. The energy of youth has gone to the destruction of all that makes youth young and wonderful. The one-time possessors of it stand broken, exhausted, numbed, in the valley of the Shadow; and the world they intended to lift has turned by a hair's breadth, and no more.

Yet some find youth but a gateway into a life which knows no age. Their bodies grow older, but only to reveal to the puzzled looker-on how very little years are concerned with either age or youth. Down to the very last their hearts are young, their fine enthusiasms unspent, their sympathies quick and keen, their joy unbroken, their hope a light no shadow can quench. Out of a long life filled, as we may know, chiefly with drudgeries and trials like our own, they come with young, eager eyes, out of which still looks the spirit of high adventure. Their message to youth is one of courage and hope :

> " Grow old along with me !
> The best is yet to be,
> The last of life, for which the first was made."

Surely that is the normal attitude of age, the natural outcome of youth and endeavour and hope. Wherever we see it, even the dullest of us, it appeals to some deep thing in us which, despite all our pessimism, justifies it, even against our will. It is so beautiful we know it must be true : all age was meant to be like that.

But how shall youth attain it ? What subtle force has turned one life into this flashing diamond, and left another only dull, black coal, though they are both alike compact of a common humanity, and share its common lot? How shall we gear the spirit of youth, how band the individual to life in such manner that he may serve it without being broken by it; that he may drive on towards the fulfillment of his dreams, nor lose his hope, nor despair of the far achievement, but keep even in age

"The rapture of the forward view,"

and the spirit of immortal joy? If life be the Great Adventure how may one achieve it greatly, and know one's self a victor, even in the midnight of defeat?

One must live the normal human life to secure all that. We cannot expect human issues from a life lived on the animal's plane. An animal which is only an animal may come to the best of itself in isolation, an unrelated unit of its race. A young colt, or pig, or calf, left on an island where no other animal life existed, but provided with food and shelter the primal animal needs, would be as perfect an animal as one reared in association with droves of its own kind. But a creature which is an animal and something more never comes to the best of itself when only those needs are met which may be satisfied in isolation. There are several authentic records of wolf-raised human young, and they have all reverted to the animal type. Kipling's Mowgli, fascinating as he is, is inspired by his creator's own imagination ; a real Mowgli could never have taken his place among human beings again, even on the edge of the jungle. Real wolf-children are like the Wild Man of Auvergne, whom a wise-hearted scientist laboured with so patiently over a hundred years ago. Cut off from human association the human in us atrophies beyond recall. For the primal law of human life is that to be truly human it must be shared with its kind.

When we get down to principles of life we are prone, unconsciously, to fall into Biblical phraseology ; the roots of principles seem to run in that direction. It is literally true that no man liveth or dieth to himself : humanity is made that way. Whatever lives and dies some other way is not human, but animal. We live, we draw on the sources of life, we nourish and strengthen it, in exact measure as we share it with the race.

This is the secret of our wasted joy, our lost enthusiasms, our broken hopes : we have failed of the normal human life, the life of race-association, the life of brotherhood.

POOR HOUSING CONDITIONS IN THE SOUTH

The drop of water has lost itself and perished in the desert of individual desire, instead of finding itself in the stream of community life which trickles down through ever-widening associations to the great ocean of the Life of Man.   In a most vital sense, the normal man, full-grown, has nothing to do with sections or boundaries, except as they help him to understand those of his brothers whom they dwarf and bind.   For himself, he is a citizen of the world ; and nothing in human life is foreign to him, past, present, or to come. The sense of race-life in himself, one atom of the mass, of the race-life whose laws govern atom and mass alike, opens all life to him, steadies his courage, heals his wounds, renews his youth, and feeds the flame of hope.

One's individual joy may be clouded so easily, and so soon ; it is such a small, weak thing, taken by itself.   It is part of the law of life that it should be so ; for he who would be man and not animal must be welded into one with his fellows; and love itself is not enough, without pain.

Suffering is so inexplicable, at first ; it sets one apart while life sweeps by.   But one has to be apart to get the perspective of life, to see small and great in their true proportions, to learn the unshakable things, and to get

one's own small personality properly related
to them.   At first, with all of us, it is the old
cry : Was ever sorrow like unto my sorrow,
or difficulty like to mine?—That is the cry
of ignorance, of weakness, of selfishness,
of egotism and provincialism, the world
around.   It has gone up in all ages, and will
go up for ages yet to come.

But if one turns from one's atom-sorrow
for a moment to take the race-wide, age-long
look, one sees that always, everywhere, such
sorrows have been.   They are part of the
race-lot.   And everywhere there are, and
have been, men and women who have borne
them bravely, and lived and died without bitterness or complaint.   Their lives are part of
the race inheritance ; their courage lifts us up.
What man has done we can do ; they fought
their battles not for themselves alone.   The
strength of the race flows into us : we too can
greatly bear ; we too can wear the badge of
courage to hearten those who stumble by the
way.   If the race must advance through suffering we will walk that path.   We would
not be exempt, cut off.   Shall we alone, of all
the multitudes, bear no scars ?

Personal success means something different after that.   The Adventure itself is different ; greater, and more worth while.   The

quest one would achieve is fullness of life; the path to it matters not so much. And fullness of life is never personal, but human. One has cast in one's lot with the race; and in doing that, whatever struggles are yet to come, the visible can no longer master the unseen. One is delivered from that poverty of soul.

The greatest danger of education is that it may be twisted, just like ignorance, to the service of intellectual arrogance, and so may breed spiritual decay. We all need world-association; but especially those need it who are unusually gifted, that they may escape the catastrophe of an emasculating egotism. The man who is the mental superior of all his associates can neutralize that dangerous misfortune only by finding his equals and his superiors wherever, in the race-life, they have blossomed to the light. He must break the shackles of time and place to commune with the mind of the race; and through that communion must learn the humility inevitable to him who measures himself by universal, rather than by provincial standards. Thus disciplined, he may add his atom of force to the race-impetus towards righteousness without pride and without shame.

In such an association the race gains in-

finitesimally : the individual gains the emancipation of his individuality, and walks henceforth at liberty and with joy.   The sting is
gone from the thwarting narrowness of
life ; for the small task, set in its large relations, is at once worth while.   He is lifted
enough above pettiness, his own and that of
others, to know it for what it is, and to be
safe from the hurt of it.   Personal defeat, too,
loses its bitterness.   However his individual
life goes down in ruins, the great powers of
truth and brotherhood to which he has committed himself remain ; that for which he
struggled will triumph yet.   His life, defeated
though it be, is part of the victory of the race.

One's sense of joy is widened.   Indeed, it
has to be, or one could not endure the shar-
ing of the sorrows of mankind.   But the race
is achieving, always.   Each day sees something done which stirs the blood in the long

" World-war of dying flesh against the life."

Each day somewhere the curtains of the
dark are lifted, and new knowledge gives
new light.   Each day men and women of all
races, plain, simple folk like ourselves, are
meeting difficulties with high hearts, unknown
heroes in unguessed fights.   And we are a
part of all of it ; we all work to one end.

Seen from the narrow window of a detached personal experience, life is confusing, baffling, coming no-whence, going no-whither, bound blind to the wheel of chance, and broken as it turns. It is the race-look which reveals the truth. The confusions are temporary, local, born of continued readjustments to higher levels. Whatever its weakness or its ignorance, life tends up. Men die, and races pass ; but Man rises. One is no longer afraid of changes, though to the atom's unrelated consciousness the very foundations seem threatened. There is a Power that guides : and in the end, that which was planned from the beginning shall be.

So it is that the consciousness of race-life forms the rich background of our own small existence, giving depth and colour to our thin personalities, enriching and beautifying the poorest life which may be set against it. It saves us, too, in those times which come to all of us, when a sense of the futility of life descends upon us like a great black frost, shrivelling effort which had promised fruitage, and numbing the sources of energy and hope. It is then that we warm our hearts at the hearthstone of humanity, folded deep in the consciousness of a life which bears our tiny being on its breast, and which moves unerringly, if slowly, through seed-time and harvest, summer and winter, to one sure, high, far-off goal.

But the race-life is not only shelter and solace in days of suffering or defeat: it is also our inspiration and joy.

To him who walks in love among his neighbours in the little happenings of every day, and out into love's wider paths of community service, there comes, sooner or later, a day when every cloud is withdrawn; when he sees back to the low beginnings of life, and on, to its far fulfillment. He sees humanity in its first home, there in the mud and slime of things, pushing feebly forward here and there, driven by sharp necessity, inch by inch, dyeing the path with its own blood, yet slowly accumulating, out of its own sufferings, forces which purify and lift it. It begins to live not by bread alone: each least advance is purchased for it by some sacrificial life. From every rank of the vast savage mass the Givers come, offering up man's life for the Life of Man. Seer and sage and warrior, king and peasant, master and slave, mothers whom no man may number, they pour out life like water, and thereby fructify the barren souls of the multitude, and create ideals for the race.

What else should life be for ?   What trace is left of all the beast-lives lived solitary in the mass, smothered in egotism, cut off by self-ishness—what, but an added weight for these, the Givers, to lift ?

Love is the motive force of life, and it gathers, more and more.   Out of the mass emerge those races whose growing powers endue them with the greatest capacity for sacrifice, for following the ideal at all costs. However the majority of even these foremost races may fall short, however the hard-won earnings of the race are perverted by the many to personal ends, Love does make headway, slowly.   All that the Givers would win for men of liberty, of knowledge, of jus-tice, of joy, filters down unceasingly from class to class, until already some of the most precious things of life grow as common to them all as the air we breathe.

Is not the life of the Givers well-spent ? In all the long, long ages is anything else so well worth while ?   They lost life only to find it ; and being dead, they yet speak to us. Their voices go up

"A cry above the conquered years,"

and the deepest things in us stir in answer. In such an hour we know life for what it really is—the power which comes in all its glorious fullness only to those who hold it in trust for every soul that needs.

Is there room for egotism any more, or pride—those two chief stranglers of human joy? Can one be afraid of "losing caste" by service? One lives in a world so far removed from all that—the world of fullness of life; a world wide with freedom, and rich with love, and bright with victory, however one's own small fortunes may rise or fall. For the soul has come into its own, and found its home, close to the heart of God, in the needs of humankind.

Shall we fail of this wide, free life here in the South because of old prejudice, and black skins over the needs? Shall we, who were once so low, who have risen, not through decades but through centuries, risen by life poured out, reaping our gain from the sacrifice of the ages, heirs in direct spiritual succession of all foregone races of men, shall we, of all mankind, withhold our bread from the hungry, and justice from the oppressed?

We are so ready to use what we have inherited, not for service, but for pride. If humanity be like the earth, we say, we are its mountain-peaks, the Himalayas of the race.—But the seas rolled over the mountains

once ; and seas may roll there again. To
the long look, the true look, the look to which
a thousand years are but a day, mountains
have risen before, and have disappeared.

> " The hills are shadows, and they flow
> From form to form, and nothing stands ;
> They melt like mists, the solid lands,
> Like clouds they shape themselves, and go."

The earth alone abides, mother of all mountains that ever were, or will be.

If life is not to grow dull to us, young or
old, or its glamour fade ; if we are one day
to stand on those heights which belong to
age rather than on the dull, flat barrens at
their base ; if life is to remain the Great
Adventure, full of promise and wonder even
in that last twilight before the eternal dawn,
we must live it normally, through the years,
despising no service that sets another heart
at ease or opens a rift of opportunity to the
poorest and least.

The beginnings of all great things are
small. Indeed, most great things are small
all the way 'through, made up of trifles, and
great only in their accumulated results. Only
the fewest people have great gifts or opportunities ; and often they are not the ones who
achieve the greatest things. A world filled

with ordinary folk and based on justice necessitates a broad path straight from the commonplaces of every day up to the highest heights. And we have just that. The basal necessity is not knowledge, nor power, but love ; and that is the greatest and the most freely attained of all human possessions. Rich or poor or ignorant or learned, the Great Adventure shall be achieved by all who walk in love.

Printed in the United States of America

Religion in America
Series II

An Arno Press Collection

Adler, Felix. **Creed and Deed:** A Series of Discourses. New York, 1877.

Alexander, Archibald. **Evidences of the Authenticity, Inspiration, and Canonical Authority of the Holy Scriptures.** Philadelphia, 1836.

Allen, Joseph Henry. **Our Liberal Movement in Theology:** Chiefly as Shown in Recollections of the History of Unitarianism in New England. 3rd edition. Boston, 1892.

American Temperance Society. **Permanent Temperance Documents of the American Temperance Society.** Boston, 1835.

American Tract Society. **The American Tract Society Documents,** 1824-1925. New York, 1972.

Bacon, Leonard. **The Genesis of the New England Churches.** New York, 1874.

Bartlett, S[amuel] C. **Historical Sketches of the Missions of the American Board.** New York, 1972.

Beecher, Lyman. **Lyman Beecher and the Reform of Society:** Four Sermons, 1804-1828. New York, 1972.

[Bishop, Isabella Lucy Bird.] **The Aspects of Religion in the United States of America.** London, 1859.

Bowden, James. **The History of the Society of Friends in America.** London, 1850, 1854. Two volumes in one.

Briggs, Charles Augustus. **Inaugural Address and Defense,** 1891-1893. New York, 1972.

Colwell, Stephen. **The Position of Christianity in the United States,** in Its Relations with Our Political Institutions, and Specially with Reference to Religious Instruction in the Public Schools. Philadelphia, 1854.

Dalcho, Frederick. **An Historical Account of the Protestant Episcopal Church, in South-Carolina,** from the First Settlement of the Province, to the War of the Revolution. Charleston, 1820.

Elliott, Walter. **The Life of Father Hecker.** New York, 1891.

Gibbons, James Cardinal. **A Retrospect of Fifty Years.** Baltimore, 1916. Two volumes in one.

Hammond, L[ily] H[ardy]. **Race and the South:** Two Studies, 1914-1922. New York, 1972.

Hayden, A[mos] S. **Early History of the Disciples in the Western Reserve, Ohio;** With Biographical Sketches of the Principal Agents in their Religious Movement. Cincinnati, 1875.

Hinke, William J., editor. **Life and Letters of the Rev. John Philip Boehm:** Founder of the Reformed Church in Pennsylvania, 1683-1749. Philadelphia, 1916.

Hopkins, Samuel. **A Treatise on the Millennium.** Boston, 1793.

Kallen, Horace M. **Judaism at Bay:** Essays Toward the Adjustment of Judaism to Modernity. New York, 1932.

Kreider, Harry Julius. **Lutheranism in Colonial New York.** New York, 1942.

Loughborough, J. N. **The Great Second Advent Movement:** Its Rise and Progress. Washington, 1905.

M'Clure, David and Elijah Parish. **Memoirs of the Rev. Eleazar Wheelock, D.D.** Newburyport, 1811.

McKinney, Richard I. **Religion in Higher Education Among Negroes.** New Haven, 1945.

Mayhew, Jonathan. **Observations on the Charter and Conduct of the Society for the Propagation of the Gospel in Foreign Parts;** Designed to Shew Their Non-conformity to Each Other. Boston, 1763.

Mott, John R. **The Evangelization of the World in this Generation.** New York, 1900.

Payne, Bishop Daniel A. **Sermons and Addresses,** 1853-1891. New York, 1972.

Phillips, C[harles] H. **The History of the Colored Methodist Episcopal Church in America:** Comprising Its Organization, Subsequent Development, and Present Status. Jackson, Tenn., 1898.

Reverend Elhanan Winchester: Biography and Letters. New York, 1972.

Riggs, Stephen R. **Tah-Koo Wah-Kan; Or, the Gospel Among the Dakotas.** Boston, 1869.

Rogers, Elder John. **The Biography of Eld. Barton Warren Stone, Written by Himself:** With Additions and Reflections. Cincinnati, 1847.

Booth-Tucker, Frederick. **The Salvation Army in America:** Selected Reports, 1899-1903. New York, 1972.

Satolli, Francis Archbishop. **Loyalty to Church and State.** Baltimore, 1895.

Schaff, Philip. **Church and State in the United States** or the American Idea of Religious Liberty and its Practical Effects with Official Documents. New York and London, 1888. (Reprinted from *Papers of the American Historical Association,* Vol. II, No. 4.)

Smith, Horace Wemyss. **Life and Correspondence of the Rev. William Smith, D.D.** Philadelphia, 1879, 1880. Two volumes in one.

Spalding, M[artin] J. **Sketches of the Early Catholic Missions of Kentucky;** From Their Commencement in 1787 to the Jubilee of 1826-7. Louisville, 1844.

Steiner, Bernard C., editor. **Rev. Thomas Bray:** His Life and Selected Works Relating to Maryland. Baltimore, 1901. (Reprinted from *Maryland Historical Society Fund Publication,* No. 37.)

To Win the West: Missionary Viewpoints, 1814-1815. New York, 1972.

Wayland, Francis and H. L. Wayland. **A Memoir of the Life and Labors of Francis Wayland, D.D., LL.D.** New York, 1867. Two volumes in one.

Willard, Frances E. **Woman and Temperance:** Or, the Work and Workers of the Woman's Christian Temperance Union. Hartford, 1883.